Resurrection of a Sunflower

curated by Catfish McDaris and Marc Pietrzykowski

ISBN-13:978-0-9988476-0-3
ISBN-10: 0998847607

for more books, visit Pski's Porch:
www.pskisporch.com

Printed in U.S.A

Contents

Charles Joseph

Daniel Snethen

Bryn Fortey

Alan Britt

Rona Fitzgerald

Sudeep Adhikari

Kevin Peery

Clint Margrave

Brenton Booth

Ali Znaidi

Wayne F. Burke

George Wallace

Kerry Trautman

Guinotte Wise

Chigger Matthews

Bob Holman

Robert Lee Kendrick

Neil Ellman

Victor Clevenger

Lisa Stice

James Benger

Lylanne Musselman

Ndaba Sibanda

Yoby Henthorn

Tim Staley

Debi Swim

Sheikha A

Maja Trochimczyk

Karen Greenbaum-Maya

Connie Ramsay Bott

FROM NUENEN WITH GRATITUDE

My whole life I've been living in the village of Nuenen c.a., famous in the world because Vincent van Gogh lived and worked here between December 1883 and November 1885, the period which was the most prolific during his career. Not only did Vincent make over a quarter of his total oeuvre in the village in the south of The Netherlands, also his first real masterpiece - *The Potato Eaters* (April 1885) - was painted here.

In July 2016 my family and I moved to a house in the center of Nuenen c.a.. The street is called *Berg*, and it is the same street where Vincent once lived and worked almost 135 years ago. On the other side of the street you will find the vicarage, the former family home of the Van Gogh's. Because I'm addicted to books and nostalgia for over 25 years now (immediately after the move), I have decided to start a physical library, fully dedicated to the life and works of the honorary citizen of my home village. At the moment, the *Vincent van Gogh Library* already contains over 750 Van Gogh related books from all over the globe. Thanks to the Facebook page about my collection, I got in contact with the editors of this stunning anthology: Catfish McDaris and Dr. Marc Pietrzykowski.

It is amazing how quickly he was able to put this work together. My congratulations to all contributors to this great work of art. I think Vincent would be proud of this emotional tribute to one of the greatest artists who has ever lived.

And therefore... how *wrong* our beloved Vincent was back in July 1882 when he wrote to his brother Theo: '*What am I in the eyes of most people - a nonentity, an eccentric, or an unpleasant person - somebody who has no position in society and will never have; in short, the lowest of the low*'

Vincent van Gogh Library
Ralf M.M. Stultiëns

Ralf M.M. Stultiëns
Berg 3
5671 CA Nuenen c.a.
The Netherlands

Theo and the Little Yellow House

Vincent did not want to be a burden
to his brother and his new family.

The apartment in Paris was not big enough
for them all.

In Arles
the Little Yellow House was perfect,
the studio of the south.

Nibbling at turpentine soaked bristles
and painting sunflowers to spruce up the guestroom
as he waited for Gauguin to arrive
from Brittany.

And when the thing went sour,
handing Gauguin that newspaper clipping
that read:
THE MURDERER FLED
before rushing off into the darkness
where both he and brother Theo
would be before too long.

Two Painters

Gauguin tried to get Van Gogh
to paint from the mind
and Van Gogh told him he
could only paint what was there
and after the hours of argument
got them nowhere
they would go out to the brothels
for the evening

and partake in something
they could both

agree
on.

Maybe this is Why Van Gogh Did It?

The kid on the pavement struggled
to move his head
while two older boys held it
firmly in place,
turned to one side
so a third boy
leaning over the screaming child
could hock a loogie,
a long throaty thick one from the depths,
letting it fall closer and closer to the ear
then sucking it back up at the last moment
before it dropped finally into the ear canal
and the older boys ran off
laughing.

Major Depressive Disorder, like Van Gogh

The greatest book ever written
is Roald Dahl's "The Witches".

I had it read to me in grade four
on an orange afternoon carpet
at Steele Street Public School
and hung on every
word.

I saw witches everywhere after that,
ready to snatch up unattended children
and turn them into
soup.

I read it again 25 years later
in a Sudbury nuthouse
and was more convinced
than ever.

The headshrinkers monitored
your reading habits
so I was surprised
when they didn't come back
with: Paranoid.

Along with the Kafka
and the Dostoevsky,
I figured I was a neurotic cloud seeding
shoo-in.

But they gave me:
Major Depressive Disorder,
like Van Gogh.

And many medications to stabilize my mood
so I was impressed with the price

of seedless green grapes
(like the rest)
instead of trolling the internet
each night
looking for Kennedy's real
killer.

Poet's Ear

The woman I am with
says I have a poet's ear.

And I wonder if this is why
Van Gogh cut his off
when he was finally determined
to become a painter
instead.

Van Gogh Yellow

It's not
what you think.

The blow up doll you find under me
is there simply to break
the fall
and the banana in your morning tailpipe
could have been put there
by anyone.

You have enemies;
everyone does,
perhaps it was those wily communists
or hell-bent terrorists
or damn stamp collectors
again?

They even wet the bed
and forgot
to put the toilet seat
down
and slept in
and got fired
after one too many
in a cornfield just outside city limits
full of midnight
ears.

Shucking away the chaff
of Ursa Major
in Van Gogh
yellow
as the belt of Orion
lays into another
screaming child.

Lust for Life

Kirk Douglas
as Van Gogh
is thoroughly
unconvincing.

I guess
it's hard to live
in the Hollywood Hills
and shoot yourself
because you have
nothing.

Filet Mignon
pretends to eat paints
in the south
of France

for
an Oscar.

And I'm left wondering
why Brando
became an actor
when he could have been
a perfectly good
hitman.

Ready, Aim, Fire

Most people seem to think
Tolstoy wrote War and Peace
one afternoon
when he was bored
and ran out of puzzles
to do

or that Van Gogh's penchant
for extremes
could have been managed
by a new car
and profit sharing incentives

and most people certainly
don't understand
why Hemingway blew his head off
when he couldn't
create anymore.

But then again,
most people do not create.

They destroy.

Most people
are part of the world's largest firing squad
and they never tire
of taking aim at,
and destroying,
that which escapes them.

Most people
are little more
than petty hate

personified.

An army of mediocrity
that will never
understand

genius.

Don't forget,
these are the same people
who laughed at Beethoven
banned Joyce
expelled Dali
caged Pound
and kicked Poe in the ass
while he walked the streets.

Christ still got the worst of it
though.

Maybe if he'd ridden into town
in an SUV
to drop his disciples off at soccer practice
instead of on the back
of a mule
to change the world
things would have been
a little different.

But
they never are.

Mediocrity
does not allow

for extremes.

Mozart, Beethoven, Bukowski, Van Gogh

Some have quality
and no lasting
power.

Others
have quantity
and no standard.

Most
have nothing
at all.

And then
there are the few
like milk
from the golden
udder.

Men
that can hardly be born
because they are so damn hard
to lose.

Catfish McDaris

A Grain of Sand in a Van Gogh Seascape

This headline kept him sane,
after she told Vincent, his
hamburgers were weird shaped
and completely unacceptable

Vincent looked at Rosalita
quizzically, she said, "You're
not making tortillas," he rolled a
cigarette and scrutinized the smoke

He got his canvas and easel, paints
and an hourglass and a hammer,
the nude he had almost finished
would now be lying on a beach.

Dreaming of Paris

Intense sheer walls painted
hyacinth and saffron with
brushstrokes of scarlet sulfur

Searching for silver spoon to
make sotol and datura for sun
tea and going on a magic trip

Dangerous peacocks in a raspberry
sky, green sleeping ducks by the
cattail forest and melodic stream

Rainbow cutthroat trout leaping
for the gnat hatch, fat frogs burping,
loons and cranes on stilts hunting

Vincent thought about the dancer
at the Crazy Horse and how she'd
asked him to steal a Van Gogh,
he painted her one instead.

The Blue Throat of Day

Coltrane in the Van Gogh rain,
"Hey Fish, what you working on?"
my boss, Big Joe Cocomo asked
he was from Texas, my black pals

At work loved me being a writer,
I showed my latest to Joe, he said,
"You like Trane?" I nodded yes
"What are your favorite songs he

Plays?" "Lazy Bird and The Night
Has a Thousand Eyes" "You must
have taken beaucoup acid, back in
the day? Who's your sketch of?"

"Vincent Willem van Gogh" "Not
bad kid" we both laughed, since I
was twice his age, back to Gauguin,
he lopped off Vincent's ear with his

Sword during an argument, they
agreed to say it was self-mutilation,
to keep Gauguin out of prison, van
Gogh never recovered his rationality.

Van Gogh Blues

Thinking about Vincent's madness
layering paint on canvas, thick
plaster colors, mountains, valleys.

An earthquake in Italy killed 100's.
A one-year-old baby was hot in
Milwaukee, he tried to climb out

A window and the window slammed
down on his little neck, killing him.
A woman put her baby in the refrigerator

To cool down, she forgot she did it, her
man comes home three hours later, goes
to get a beer and finds their dead daughter.

An eleven-year-old girl was riding her
bike, the driver hit her dragging her for
three blocks and kept on going, drunk.

Vincent, you died at thirty-seven, you
are thought of as a freak that cut off his
ear, I see you in the swirling starry night.

Van Gogh's Spinach

Medical marijuana growing became
legal in New Mexico, an amigo homie
was growing some nitroglycerin weed

He was looking for good names and I
came up with Van Gogh's Spinach,
not only because the potency would

Make a potentate beg and cut off both
ears, back in the day I knew a gymnast
with his last name, she was super fine

One night I was hustling nine ball in
the Copper Penny, she seduced me
and led me to my pickup with a camper

She said drive until the corn fields
surround us, we both stripped and the
sex Olympics began, by morning I
felt like a well ridden pommel horse.

The Day the Sunflowers Died

July 29th, 1890 laid
upon a pool table,
the harbingers of
death called you

The cold steel
against your
stomach soothing

It was finally over,
the unbearable mad-
ness, paint flowed
from your body

It swirled up into
the starry night and
ran thick over the
French cobblestones.

Van Gogh's Ear Is Full of Beer

The sky was drunk, the sun puked lemon
juice, the moon had a toothache, the lady
asked the dope fiend to come to talk to
Jesus, he smelled of absinthe and funk.

Sisyphus and Tantalus

The Little Dipper poured yellow
cream down upon the blue black
mountaintop, he wrote all thoughts
that drifted down his face

Doily sized snowflakes from the north
whipped against red faces, he'd seen a
rabbit and wondered where it slept and
thought time is a strange bedfellow

His poet pal asked him to help name his
chapbook, he came up with A Thousand
Wildfires of the Heart, he heard from Ralf
at the Van Gogh Library in Nuenen in The

Netherlands located on a street where Vincent
once lived and that's how labors of love begin.

The Horseman

He listened to the sun and heard
the moon whisper, while watching
the trees twist in the wind

The beautiful lady shattered his soul,
he became a husk of a man, a shadow,
the sun stared at the him, burning his soul

Vincent bought a white stallion, so
white it was blue, he rode west and
crossed rivers of blood, his heart was
poisoned, his horse and he became one

They became nomads in the desert,
sharks that can't stop moving, specks
of sand in the eternal hour glass.

Foxglove

Magnificent girl
peachwolf browngold
shepherd foxglove an angel

Vincent believes in God
sorrow of men
death of a friend

Each brush stroke
feeding the void

Paint the human
face the inhuman
gold jewels let
lightdrench the
saddest.

Mendes Biondo

It all began with religion

remember to enjoy
when your hands got dirty with things

remember to be brave
do not forget the teachings of masters

remember that also god
enjoyed the creation of universe and animals and plants

remember that he seemed it good
for how they were
for their own being

because he enjoyed and this seemed him good and right

he made also the man with joy
and the same you do
instead of thinking to false masters
and to the mother
and to the father
and to the passed time
and to the teaching you can give

You are a flaming cypress

the leaves must not fear
the stories that came from wind
that came from abroad
because they are read and deciduous

the roots of your trunk
must not fear what comes from east
and smells of spring
and brings words of summer

the roots that lived
too long in the winter cold
become icy and dry
so your luxurious trunk will fall

My working shoes once taught me something

look at that precious stone
that you've just kicked
look how bounces
on the corpse of his brothers
and on cement
and on grass
and on tiny insects

that smooth stone
seems smiling
and it doesn't care
if it hurted his brothers
if the chimeric cement
can suffer
if grass tears
when he passes

that precious stone
only cares to roll
here and there
there and here
as it wants

rolling and smiling
trampling and hurting
these are the only concerns
of precious stones

La casa gialla (The yellow house)

le foglie se ne vanno
spazzate via
dal vento della notte
le strade
pulite
si sporcano
per essere pulite
ancora
sembra senza senso
gli alberi che se ne stanno
a guardare silenziosi
i baci bevuti se ne vanno
dalle labbra amate
di una donna stanca
le labbra
umide
si asciugano
per inumidirsi
ancora
quella foglia che tu eri
quei baci bagnati
se ne sono andati
resta solamente la casa gialla
i nostri corpi abbracciati
queste parole

The yellow house

fallen leaves go
washed away
by night wind

the streets
cleaned
get dirty
to be cleaned
again

it seems meaningless
the trees that stand
looking silently

the drunk kisses go
from the beloved lips
of a tired woman

the lips
wet
get dry
to be wet
again

that leave that you were
those wet kisses
are gone

it rests only the yellow house
our embraced bodies
these words

Il volo dei corvi (The crows flight)

i corvi sentono
che verrà a piovere
lo dicono in silenzio
con il loro volo
la danza dei corvi
va e viene
viene e va
sfiorando i tetti
portando il loro
messaggio bagnato
per tutte le piogge
che cadranno sulla terra
loro sentiranno
loro danzeranno
loro
silenziosamente
diranno

The crows flight

crows feel
it will be raining
they say it in silence
with their flight

crows dance
go and return
return and go
skimming the rooftops
bringing their
wet message

for all the rains
that will fall on the earth
they will feel
they will dance

they
silently
will say

Only painting will save me

in the park under my house
there are dogs running
following the stick
thrown by their owner

their eyes shine
they got fun and they bark
they're right to bark

owners don't care about them
owners don't enjoy it
owners stand

pick up the stick
wait
pick up the stick
wait
pick up the stick
wait
pick up the stick

dogs are fine
for a moment they have
a real goal
in the everyday monotony

the sun falls down the houses
dogs follow their owner on the streets
and everything become meaningless again

The next painting

People will tell you to draw
that every sketch lost
will never come
back   ·

listen what I tell you

lose things
with courage and love
let them come and
go and
come again joyfully

lost sketches will be
the first to search you
in dark and difficult moments
to shine you
to show you the way

give your sketches to wind
give him the immature one
the one that you want to draw

they will come back prodigal
and able to teach you
new mistakes to do

sacrify for them
the best ox
and drink the best wine

those sketches without home
once on your door
will be your walking stick

A letter to Theo

you can have many dreams
projects and desires
exotic pleasure cravings
you can have certainties
solid religious foundations
friends and beloved ones
that will follow you for a life

today
you can have all of this

but hidden behind the dawn
there is a man wrapped
by a dark and deep fog
that will steal you
one by one
dreams
projects
desires
friends
and beloved ones
all this to give you other different ones
as soon as the sun reaches the sky high

so will go things
from dawn to dawn
from sunset to sunset

this man in the fog is
walking with the maneater time

they can't hear your voice
they will change the path
of your streets and other ones
with a pair of dice

and you must await
and you must enjoy intensely
in that particular moment
before the great end

The smile of potato eaters

when the truth
sits near to you
you can see her ribs
the bony legs
the stunted arms
the anorexic body
fragile

she whispers weakly
with a silent stillness
little words without meaning
unheard
unacceptable

that heap of bones and
skin and
words and
breath
you suck

you don't accept her magic presence
till she is not smiling
and you understand to be
a heap of bones
and flesh
and breath
and words
flimsiest of her

Just before cutting the ear

hot lights
from the houses out there
they tease my senses
desires and joys

but

from the houses out there
comes only a silent noise
humming and sterile

it's the snoring of
men with boring lives

Charles Joseph

Head of a Skeleton with a Burning Cigarette

Vincent, I'm sure that this self-portrait
is a much better depiction of you
than you would have cared to admit

so I imagine that that's why
you tried to trick me into believing
that these bones belong to someone else
by smoking a cigarette here instead of a pipe.

But with the layers stripped away
the darkness of your torment
is much more visible to me *here*
than anywhere else

so I'm not fooled, just sad
each time I think about
how vulnerable you truly were.

(*Head of a Skeleton with a Burning Cigarette, 1886*)

Christ of the Coalmine

Like Saint Francis
you saw the glory,
the beauty, and the wisdom
reflected in all creation.

So you tried your hand
at preaching the word of God
only to find that he would
soon have other plans for you.

And Vincent, I'm sure you
must have wondered why
your followers didn't flock to you
by the score while you were alive.

But sadly, devotion, passion, and grace,
are only deemed relevant to mankind
when they can be quickly sold
for a bag full of silver or gold.

(Sketch of a Coking Plant in the Borinage, 1879)

Wheat Field with a Reaper

not even the iron bars of a cell
could keep your eyes from
finding beauty in all things

for you even allowed death
an opportunity to shine
in the heat of the sun.

(Wheat Field with a Reaper, 1889)

A Crab on its Back

Like a crab on its back
fighting to right itself

you wallowed in an ocean of regret
until it consumed what was left of your sanity.

Which to me, Vincent
wasn't just an abominable hex

but it's also proof that one can drown
with their feet firmly planted in field of sunflowers.

(A Crab on its Back, 1887)

The Red Vineyard

Vincent, do you see it?

It's the citizens of Arles
who forced you out of your
yellow house and into an asylum

trapped in a field of fire
toiling away for eternity
as penance for their sins

and you the sun, shining down
from above to remind them
of the man they cast out of paradise.

Vincent, do you see it?

Do you see them?

I do.

(The Red Vineyards near Arles, 1888)

The Sower

With a sure hand and a broken heart
each seed you cast lay dormant for many years
but from what (at times) must have seemed
like a failed crop to you, Vincent—

I assure you, not even death could prevent
the fruits of your labor from taking root
on the walls of hallowed halls.

What a fine farmer you were indeed, Vincent
for all of your seeds grew to be heirlooms
that are studied and admired with veneration
toward the genius of their creator.

(The Sower, 1888)

Sunflowers

As a sign friendship you tried
to extend an olive branch
by painting sunflowers for Paul,

but Vincent, in retrospect,

perhaps a few baskets of bleeding grapes
that have fallen sour and blue from the vine
would have been more appropriate.

(Sunflowers, 1888)

Almond Blossom

Vincent, I see splinters
of Japanese woodcuts
in your almond blossom.

(Almond Blossom, 1890)

Among the Wheat Fields

It was always you and your brother, Vincent

your brother and you,

and although only your bones remain

do not be afraid, Vincent

because it will always be you and your brother, Vincent

your brother and you,

together forever, among the wheat fields

beneath two headstones, covered in earth

where your love for each other lingers on

much deeper than a gravedigger

can hollow out with a spade.

(Wheat Field, 1888)

Tree Roots

Vincent, they say your final words were:
"The sadness will last forever."

And I hope for your sake
you didn't find that to be true.

For what you left behind
millions continue to gaze upon
and what they experience
is a feeling that you longed for—

JOY.

And for that, there must be
a place for someone like you.

A place for those who bring joy
to others but never find it for themselves.

Perhaps, somewhere among the stars
or beneath the roots of a tree you painted
nestled close to the warmth of its heart.

(Tree Roots, 1890)

Daniel Snethen

Octet of Spiders

1.
yellow orb weavers
weave Lakota dream-catchers
cowards tear them down

2.
grayish barn dwellers
intricately decorate
dusty window-panes

3.
slender midnight legs
candy apple red hourglass
ebony widow

4.
rapacious killer
xanthic onyx web weaver
ensnares blue bottles

5.
crab-like arachnids
practice camouflaged ambush
from yellow coneflowers

6.
daddy long-legged
brown double-eyed harvestmen
wield circus-stilt legs

7.
eight legged grey wolves
chase leaping orthopterans
across badlands clay

8.
reclusive hermits
fiddle funeral dirges
as the dying die

Ember

Darkness from a billion
dead and dying stars
engulfed her
barely visible glow
beneath a quagmire of shadow.

She wanted to bring light
to the darkened universe
but the cold darkling void
smothered her
to near extinction.

Each barely visible flare-up
extinguished by frigid blackness.

So little light.
So little energy.

Just a darksome lump of charcoal
harboring a forlorn
hope of survival.

A space-traveler
found her frozen form
on the dark side
of some obscure moon.

Perhaps out of pity
or perhaps out of love
he kindled her faint spark
and fanned it
like a bellows with his breath.

And slowly, she began to smoke
and smolder—and the light
growing slowly at first,

brightened in meteoric fashion,
rising up like
an emblazoned phoenix,
illuminating the world
In her fiery splendor.

And the darkness disappeared forever.

Natural Kill

The cacophonous, invasive
European murmuration
squawked as the warty knot
hopped helter-skelter
upon the sandy beach
while the bale stared
from its floating log.

The drifting sounder
rooted beneath the tree
of the cacophonous, invasive
European murmuration
as a hover hovered
beneath the drifting log
of the balefully eyed bale.

A dabbling spring
paddled and dabbled
the spring-fed pond
in cinnamon-red plumage
while the sound
of the drifting drift
drifted beyond the horizon.

The descent descended
upon the snarled snag
standing next to the tree
with the murmuration
of murmuring cacophony
and drummed its trunk
in discordant harmony.

Then the shadow of a murder
descended upon the trees
surrounding the pond
with the balefully eyed bale

and the hovering hover,
dispersing both descent
and murmuring murmuration.

And the warty skinned knot
hopped from beach to rocks
where the slain naturalist
had walked on the rattling rumba
not hearing its serpentine chorus
above the cacophonous murder
or the winnowing walk in the distance.

Pearl

The little girl
roamed the yellow hills of
China land, carrying a cane stick
to fend off the scavengers
feeding on dead
yellow babies.

The little girl scraped the
rocky hillside soil,
covering up the twisted
yellow bodies.

She reached her hand into the earth,
letting it sift over the tiny corpses.

Later she won the Nobel Prize for Literature.

Huntress

Australian mystique. A tattooed woman.
Indecipherable, un-dragon-like.
Her eyes alive, like a loggerhead shrike's.
Wild, aloof, free willed—enslaved to no man.
Her screeching spirit shrieks: "I am human."
But, she embodies a spirit—shrike-like,
hanging the carcasses of men on spikes—
indecipherable, she is woman.
Neither black nor white but ash ridden grey,
obscuring the tattooed lines of color,
she hangs them drying for another day—
these men of black, white, yellow, red color.
She is a wordsmith, a butcher by day—
at night, an ash-grey killer of color.

Immanuel for Tori

Her eyes are deeper
than Greek philosophy
and her genius is unrecognized,
even by her friends.

Her hair, jet black,
like a panther's,
reflects the depth of her eyes
which spirals deeper and deeper
into the Stygian depths
of her tortured soul.

The darkness therein
illumined only
by the guilt of the guiltless,
 the misunderstanding
of the misinformed
and the unknowing knowing
of her reluctant smile.

Every day I feel her tears
corrode my heart like oxidation
as her silent cries scream
through her red lipstick
scarring my silent lucidity.

Every day I ask if she is okay
and she replies without fail, "No."
And my heart rends and bleeds
and I feel her endless pain
burn like acid poured
over sandpaper scraped skin.

And I wish, I wish I could be
her stigmata, her martyr—
                sacrificially nailed to a tree.

Purple Maggots

Marijuana smoke permeated the air.
The room an amethystine purplish hue.
Serious cerebrial contemplation.

Carnivores consume carrion,
so do scavengers
and maggots
--- but do they kill?
Man does.
Man kills maggots.
Man hates maggots.
Man fears maggots
---when man dies, maggots eat.
Maggots ate Mercutio.

Maggots make man's skin crawl.
---a grim reminder.

I remember a time.
It was during the war.
I marched to the field latrine.
Something smelled like bloat gas.
I peered into the filthy muck.
Maggots wriggled, writhed
feasting, feeding
---metamorphosing.
Not cockroaches but flies.
One lit beneath my eye.
I killed it dead,
rubbed its guts upon my thigh.

Another time,
---in a pig sty,
I rolled over a trough.
Maggots milled by the millions.
One whitish massive motion

synchronized like the pulsating convolutions
of a pallid, hoary brain
mesmerized my mind.

Wiggling, wiggling, always wiggling
wriggling, wiggling maggots.
White and wiggly, white and squiggly
wriggling, wiggling maggots.
Man hates maggots.
Man is mad.
---Maggots do not kill.
Man is stupid.
Man is blind.
---Maggots are man's friend.

Kafka dropped his roach-clip.
He sank down to the floor.
Purple walls and purpled smoke
befuddled Kafka's brain.
Kafka writhing, Kafka changing
Kafka wiggling, Kafka wriggling
maggots writhing, maggots wriggling
maggots wiggling, Kafka changing.
---Purple maggots in my brain.

Murder

straw-stuffed scarecrows scream
murder, murder, at cawing
cacophonous crows

Curiosity

whiskered feline face
peers out green curtained window
watching snowflakes fall

Bryn Fortey

CORNELIA ADRIANA VOS-STRICKER

"Kee" they called her
A mother
Widow
Seven years older than her oddball cousin
And surely more experienced
In the ways of life
In the real world

So maybe she didn't return his love
And had to turn down
His proposal of marriage
But couldn't she have done it
With kindness
Compassion
And a hint of humanity

"Nooit, neen, nimmer"
"No, nay, never"
Cold
Heartless
Ice on iron

She'd enjoyed his company
On their many walks
But Vincent was maybe a diversion
Just an entertainment
While she gave sober consideration
To the realities of her situation
A would-be artist
Unable to support even himself
Let alone a family
Would not cut the mustard
As a long-term possibility

He offered love
A wedding ring
Wanting "She and no other"

"Certainly not him" said Kee
Giving him in return
His first psychotic episode

DOCTOR FELIX REY

A 23 year old intern
At the hospital in Aries
When a new patient arrived
A madman stalked by delusions
Had severed his own ear

Blood loss
Ravings
General ill-health

Some doubted he would survive
And maybe secretly thought
It would be kinder if he didn't
But the young doctor saw only
A troubled man in need

Not only did he cure the flesh
But advised the mind
And offered friendship

Vincent
Grateful
Painted a portrait
As a gift
Which the doctor accepted
So as not to hurt
The artist's fragile feelings
Though he did not really like it

The painting was used for years
To repair his mother's chicken coop
Before being
Got rid of

Felix Rey later became
An expert in tuberculosis

And was awarded a Silver Medal
For his efforts during
A cholera epidemic

He gave Vincent
Both kindness and friendship
A doctor of note
Though maybe not an art lover

CLASINA MARIA HOORNIK

Having accepted that
He had no role to play
In Kee's life
Vincent was on something of a rebound
When he met "Sien" Hoornik

A drunk
Pregnant
Prostitute
With many health issues
He supplied shelter and food
For her and her 5 year old daughter
In payment for modelling

Later he welcomed them
Into his own home
In what would prove to be
The only domestic relationship
Vincent would ever experience

He even considered marriage
At one stage
But the total opposition
From his family
Caused rifts
Which were difficult to overcome

Even brother Theo
Whose support was constant
Throughout their lives
Recommended that he should leave her
And eventually they did split up

Poor Sien
He gave her immortality through his art
She gave him gonorrhoea

THE MAID

Gabrielle
Rachel
Whatever her name
She was the woman
To whom Vincent
Gave his severed ear

Van Gogh and Gauguin
Frequented the brothel
On the rue Bout d'Arles
Part of the local red light district
So he would have known
The unfortunate maid
With the mutilated arm
Bitten by a rabid dog
The wound then cauterised
By a red-hot iron
It would not have been a pretty sight

Why cut off his ear at all?
But
Having done so
Why give it to a brothel maid
For safe keeping?

The bombastic Paul Gauguin
Later claimed that Van Gogh
Had been developing a Jesus complex
Whatever that might mean

The ear itself languished in a jar
On Doctor Rey's desk
Until suddenly disappearing

As for the maid
Her brief walk-on role in the

Van Gogh mythology was over
She faded into the total obscurity
That was her lot.

ELISABETH HUBERTA VAN GOGH

Dear brother
We did not correspond
As you did
Somewhat with Willemina
More mainly with Theo
Yet maybe we should have
Since we seem to have shared
At least two character traits

A need to create
Flowed through our veins
Expressed in painting for you
And words for me
Five volumes of my poetry
Have been published
And a book of my memories of you

The second trait we shared
Was less fortunate
An ability to bring shame on our family
By our actions

Father's sudden death
And the loss of his Pastor's income
Meant I could not complete my studies
And I accepted a domestic position
With a gentleman and his seriously ill wife

You, Vincent
With your track record
Would surely have understood
The vagaries of love, and need, and desire
But at least Mr Du Quesne van Bruchem
Who fathered the illegitimate daughter
Taken from me
Remained true and married me

When his sick wife finally died

Poor brother
Maybe we should have kept in touch

DOCTOR PAUL GACHET

An amateur painter himself
And a collector of note

Previous patients included
Renoir
Manet
Pissarro
Cezanne
Goeneutte
Making Gachet the obvious choice
To oversee Vincent's care
When he left
The clinic at Saint-Remy

Not that the new patient
Was overly impressed at first
Writing to Theo that the doctor
Seemed equally as ill
As Vincent himself

He responded well
Initially at least
Finding the countryside
Healthy and invigorating
But sadness and loneliness
Were constant companions

Drink less
Smoke less
Counselled the doctor
Good advice
But surely more than that
Was called for

Was he friend or foe?
After Vincent's death

Gachet and son were said to have
Plundered what paintings they could
And sought to profit
From having known the artist

WILLEMIEN JACOBA VAN GOGH

Next to Theo
The only other family member
Vincent kept in touch with

An early feminist
With writing ambitions
That remained unfulfilled
"Wil" never married
Working at times as a
Governess
Nurse
Social worker
Teacher (of religion)
She exchanged letters
With her brother
Covering literature, art
And family matters

As time went by
In an unfortunate link with Vincent
She developed psychiatric problems
Spending many years
Committed to an asylum
Refusing to speak
And having to be fed artificially
(Whatever that might have meant)

What a sad end for
The Novel Reader
Which might have been
Vincent's imagined representation
Of his sister "Wil"

RENE SECRETAN

A 16 year old fan of
Wild Bill Cody
Having seen his
Wild West Show in Paris

With cowboy clothes
And a temperamental pistol
That often misfired

Buffalo Bill Jnr.
Looking to break the monotony
Of family summers in Auvers
And the unstable Dutch painter
Was a prime target for mischief

Pepper on the brushes
Of the tramp-like man
They sneeringly called "Toto"
Salt in his tea
A snake in his paint box

Vincent was used to being ridiculed
But these teen antics must have annoyed
And did such behaviour play a part in his death

Did he get hold of the gun
And shoot himself
Even at so unlikely an angle

Did the pistol fire accidentally
During a bullying scuffle

Or did ringleader Rene aim and pull the trigger
In a final wish-fulfilment
Of a would-be cowboy gunslinger

The world will never really know

IRVING STONE

He wrote straight biography
And nonfiction too
But was best known
For his Historical Novels
A genre within which
Facts can be stretched
To fit plot demands
He gave Michelangelo
The treatment as well

Stone's 1934 novel
Was filmed 22 years later
And according to MGM
Lost $2,072,000 at the box office
"He was robbed!" complained
Director Vincente Minnelli
When Yul Brynner got the nod
Over Kirk Douglas at the Oscars

Rene Secretan
Who as a teenager
Had teased and tormented
The painter at Auvers
And maybe more
Did not like the film at all
Claiming *Lust For Life*
Presented a version of Van Gogh
Far removed from the
Lonely and troubled tramp
Who had stalked the countryside
In reality

Stone's book
And the film that followed
Made no claims to be other than
A fictionalised account

Of the painter's life
And can therefore be viewed
Mainly as an entertainment
Though one that helped spread
A worldview of a troubled genius
Who suffered for his art

JOHANNA GEZINA VAN GOGH-BONGER

A true survivor
Strong willed and dedicated
She obviously bought into
Husband Theo's
Love and support
Of his artist brother

Though with health issues
Of his own
Theo had been Vincent's
Truest friend and supporter
All his life
And when the two brothers died
One after the other
Johanna took it upon herself
To honour her late husband
By gaining the recognition
Of Vincent's genius
That Theo had always felt
His brother's talent deserved

She organized exhibitions
Promoting his work
Often in the face of criticism
From *experts* who did not
Share her enthusiasm
And she published
The brother's letters

What a source of satisfaction
It must have been for her
To see the growing acceptance
Of her brother-in-law's
Achievements
An acceptance she never
Stopped working on

At the time of
Her own death
She was translating the letters
Into English

Alan Britt

VAN GOGH

In those paintings about taverns, with the
texture of wavy wooden floors, heavy green-
grey bottles, & partial faces . . . especially the
tavern with the radiating gas chandelier whose
light resembles fragments of straw that swirl
like abstract angels. With those paintings
Vincent actually created poems . . . or else we,
during inspired moments, create Van Goghs.

FLOATING MISTRESS

Far from philosophies,
I travel with my mistress, Imagination.

We spend the night
in a tavern lit by gas chandeliers.

Van Gogh appears
to be sitting across from us,
head supported by one hand.

Women & men in complete freedom
circle the tables.

No police,
no governments.
no ministers.

Manet walks in
followed by a woman with a green hand.

Together we sip absinthe
& chat with Jeanne Duvall
whose careless forearm tilts
as sparks of gaslight glint her golden bangles.

For an hour
that lasts a year
or four seconds.

I rise
on the wings of absinthe,
completely enslaved by her reckless eyes.

CESAR VALLEJO

Volcanic eyes

Aardvark gait

Soul a chrysalis & also
a papoose to tuck his family
into at night

Poems were fists
squeezing
ridicule from his life

Dreams were scorpions
swirling like
Van Gogh's *Starry Night*

PHEROMONE POEM

Bougainvillea pheromones like perfumed gnats
escaping boardrooms.

Smoke detector collects the scent of hotdogs
as pigeon shit splatters the windshields
of commonsense.

Crows carve deer ribs: skull to agates
littering a stubble field, right shoulder intact,
all that's left of this Greenspring Avenue doe.

Van Gogh huffs coffee at the Double T Diner
& proceeds to wash his palette with golds &
Japanese white-cheeked maidens setting tea
& spilling their inky charms into Montana
streams; otherwise, crocodile loafers ⟶ Is that
Teddy, or is she the one bequeathing her
porcelain thighs for the prospect of easy living
plus a congressional retirement to die for?

Teddy taps a shoulder.

America responds.

The clacking of hooves along snowy cobblestones
like wooden tongues searching for sons sheltered
behind one-way mirrors, autopsies pending,
& *everybody's talking*, as Harry said, but nobody's
minding the store.

~~ ∞ ~~

Extract that mischievous quark of DNA
from chimpanzees, the one that implores them

79

to pulverize opponents into a mass of bloody gumbo.

Suck that same quark from humans into a Dyson®
black hole of primordial consciousness,
whore of consciousness. But where would we
be without whores? Nowhere, I grant you.
Nowhere, indeed.

JACQUES, OUR 178-POUND BOUVIER

He has large, translucent, whiskey-colored eyes.

His fur twists like smoke from burning wood.

His ear swivels sideways for one moment
the way a rhino's ear is a periscope for lions.

Outside, dozing on chilly concrete,
his left side flinches like a dreaming pile of fog.

Perhaps he's flying to Belgium
high above a swirling Van Gogh wheat field,
though more likely reliving his first days
back in Port Huron, Michigan.

Actually, he faintly twitches his mud-cracked nose
in the direction of our kitchen door,
just as fried eggs thicken and bacon begins to pop.

ODE TO A RAINBOW

I haven't seen a rainbow like this forever.

Seven Van Gogh illusions smeared
by palette knives made of fish.

Know any good poems about rainbows?

Me, either.

NOT ENOUGH!

One art form alone is not enough. One art form is only one aspect of human potential. Painting does what poetry cannot do. Sculpture what music cannot & poetry what sculpture cannot. Indeed there are other forms of expression less practiced.

Music, for instance, with its first note coaxes the nonlinear soul more easily than poetry can, since words are mainly utilized as tools with which to forge concepts. Though carefully forged concepts are beneficial to human development, our error is reducing words to this utilitarian burden. You see, the *nonlinear* soul soaks it up from all sides. Or rather . . . not from sides at all . . . but as a terrestrial omniscience it experiences vastness, thus abolishing geometry & logical arteries. In this sense, geometry is freed to become a metal bird rocking back & forth in the windy void.

Music fluidly creates nonlinear consciousness. It does so in a manner that delivers great pleasure. In Berlioz we experience nuances to consciousness so struggled for in a Goethe or Yeats poem, though Garcia Lorca & Trakl, perhaps because of their prolific sensual imagery, have an easier time of it. Superficial observation might suggest that with music we experience *pure* emotion. Well . . . all depends upon composer & style, but "pure" emotion is unlikely. Poems harnessed to utilitarian language often struggle hopelessly to achieve visionary intuition. I am completely aware that creating visionary intuition is not always required of our chameleon poems. But, ironically, language that eons ago prodded human expansion nowadays shackles lazy readers who are content to dine on the familiar, the conventional. A bad habit becomes a lifestyle! In art, convention is a distraction providing a crutch for the uninitiated. Too often we view ourselves through the eyes of others, as if somehow others, armed with precious stereotypes & preconceptions, could actually experience our inner lives. Diversity! Variety & growth! Expansion! The cultivation of souls requires diversity!

We cannot shape a flat wing inside a poem the same way we can fashion it with smooth intelligent bronze. We cannot recreate Van Gogh's wild stars precisely with an exalted violin . . . although we can create something new . . . exciting . . . diversified! The human soul requires nourishment from all directions. Once unlocked, it hungers for everything . . . colors, textures, orange-scented oboes. Wisdom & intelligence housed therein is immeasurable but felt & understood instantly!

THE TAVERN OF LOST SOULS

About the color of amber
asleep in a drawer
at a North Dakota fossil lab
an ant descends the crack
of a sidewalk
just below
my approaching Reebok.

I carry the shadow
of Nagasaki
in my walk.

However, my true agenda
is not cruelty.

As a matter of fact,
each morning around 12 PM
the mayor of my village
walks his burro
past the Chamber of Commerce.

Women make important decisions
while our men drive SUV's
to the local reservoir
in search of the Wild Man.

(Fewer capital crimes
are committed this way.)

Adolescents, mute since birth,
stitch fantasy tattoos
across each other's shoulders and lower backs
with the lethal precision of Andre Breton
and Tristan Tzara.

Extended families mingle

the local watering hole.

They cross their shriveled legs
while lighting up a stick
and growl into muddy drinks,
all various shades of amber
asleep in drawers
at a fossil lab
somewhere near North Dakota.

Finally, just around midnight,
a shabby guitarist, with crescent
moon scar and a busted hip, saunters
into the tavern of lost souls.

THE SECRETARIES

1.

Leaning from Brooklyn skyscrapers
secretaries
type hieroglyphs
across the clouds.

The blue afternoon.

The afternoon greets them
as equal lovers.

Stenographers emerge from *mariposa* hibernation.

Lovers in silk Armani suits.

A mythic Uncle with a damaged
liver
stumbles into Mass
at dawn.

His pockets inside out.

The bandoneon
tracing Donne's compass tip
rocks a cradle
woven from straw.

2.

Certain women,
especially those
predisposed
to common amnesia,
resemble the yellow lightning
staining elephant ear plants,
waists attached

to gravity
as their roots roam the darkness.

Tenderness oozes
between the secretaries' exposed hips.

I fall backwards
into a net
of drunken bats
gathered at an after-hours tavern.

My insufferable lover
arrives
with a knife
in her heart.

Crumbling to my knees
I kiss
her suffering hands.

The bandoneon
swirls
the tavern's darkness
around us.

Stars flicker
then vanish
into ashes.

Rona Fitzgerald

Still Life

Walking under a granite sky near Montmartre,
longing for warmth and softness in Provence,
I saw them, alive among weeds, burnt gold.

Later, drinking and laughing with Gauguin,
he chided me, *Why weary greys and browns,*
what about strong colours, and why sunflowers?

Afterwards, I saw things oddly changed
                    ragged edges, distorted shapes
my sunflowers ill at ease.

They speak to me now of decay
                    like putrid wounds.

I need more daring shades
        red earth
                            or blood from a severed ear.

What will they say about my paintings then?

Bedroom

Street lights on dappled autumn leaves
bring me back to Paris on balmy evenings.
Monet's soft avocado and burnt orange.

But Arles suits me, a place to shut
out the voices, to paint and paint,
tasting the salty texture of grey.

Starry Nights

Pinprick stars, washed blue light
whirls of yellow gold dust.
How I love the night sky.

I can feel our planet turn
    and sway. The nausea returns
                  but I must paint.

Almond Blossom

Awakening pink buds
lift my spirits
           give me hope.

My world is not stable
yet, each Spring brings
exquisite delicacy
           echoes of Japan.

I would love to visit
 but journeys are too much
           and, my house worries.

Love

I imagined it as warm
    colours, joyful saffron
        welcoming orange.

But it was blue
    a darker shade
        than the sky.

Yellow House

I look for the right shade
        to craft
           a portrait in light.

Working usually stills
        my fears, my agitation.
I want to make something
        of beauty and belonging.

Self-portrait (with pipe)

I thought a portrait would help
to ground me, to fix my self
                      in time.
I like the pipe, it takes the gaze
                from my wounds

Looking into my own eyes
I see madness, they follow me
                round the room
highlighting
            my perilous grip
                  on reality.

Night Café

My stars are out, sunglow
shades caress Arles streets.

I sip coffee, clean my brush
paint amber and chartreuse swirls.

Dare I ask for red wine
                or absinthe?

Irises

They seem shy
          hesitant
I love merging blue and green
dynamic shades
     they speak of health
               of sanctuary.

'The world's a dream'. Basho said. 'Not because that dream's
A falsehood, but because it's Truer than it seems.'

Future Tense

Bad days always feel like a dream
reality mediated by the chain
mail of doubt, lost images, time.

When my brother admonished me
about money, I knew
                    the end was near.

Even my good days leave only a flimsy
trail like butterfly ash or a footprint
                    on misty grass

Patterns too, feel like a dream
rituals, requirements
                    unless

I'm thinking about the future

All the true things dwell there
sunflowers
            indigo skies
                    tranquillity.

Sudeep Adhikari

The World is a Symbol

The glitter from the wings of dusted ghosts; drapes the city
and my head in a single fold.
the sad joy of never-ending present. The pain and
elation of being a mad passion.

Yes. That Christ of the coal yards in Borniage.

The day is open like a worm-hole on an alien space-time.
you may end up whole, or in pieces falling everywhere on your way home.
You think there is "no" time.

But I see no "time".

Head wages wars. Universes collide and recede,
and I keep hearing sounds; Infra-sonic moans of far-off
stars, trees and some undead voids.

The world is a symbol. It comes at me
 from everywhere, without being understood.

Sometimes you kill the symbol, and sometimes the symbol kills you.

Deconstructing the Language of Soul

You abstract, and extract
a meager figment
from the swirling plasm of becoming
that flares like the solar-wind.
the map is not the territory,
low-key definitions
of Instagrammed Van Goghs.

Ideas and words,
precipitate to a static low
like the calcinated bones
of pre-historic raptors,
as dead as Seattle's Grunge
and Nietzsche's God.

A Madman is Not a Sell-Out

All my life, I haunted
for the single truth
and ended up finding
many whores,
some sleepless rivers that flow
straight from a beer-factory,
few deathless trees that refuse
not to dance for a second
and some coked-out gods
who like to party
wearing a blood-soaked skull for a cap.

I am not a sell-out
but I find no difference either.

[A tribute to "Beer Tankards"]

The Olive Trees

All I have is love and mad reverence, sisters.
The grove of deathless presence
olived ambrosia, drinking life-sap running through
the fractal veins. The rings of time are just numbers,
life, an uncountable sacred integer.
The flower power abides.
or are you a bouquet of wild roses,
Gaia's lovelorn submission to the infinite blue? There is

a bridge, between the celestial and the terrestrial
a portal that connects stars with the underworld
and in-between we stand,
breathing each other in recursion. All I ever wanted,

is to be you, a silent celebration of paradoxes,
Anomalies and relations.
There is infinity in every fraction
a rapture in every ordinary experience. Buddhas are abundant.

[A tribute to all Olive Grove II"]

Mother Gaia

You , the super-soul
are the sleeping infinity
sinning with steller quiet
weaves the cosmic embroidery
of celestial yearn with earthly pain.

Uncountable souls, ghost-like flickers
from eons past. Desirous and thin
how they reach out to kiss you
the prodigal sons of lonesome otherworld
and heartful of turbulent tears.

Unity-agony self- immolates
on the altar of desire-ember.

I fell in love with you before I was born
it was just my body, unborn is my soul;
residing in this naked now
permeates every conceivable
rupture and rapture of time.

I am just an atomic speck
of lilac red, on your fractal-graffiti
painted by Van Goghs from alien underworld.

The Devil is Fine

The night is you. The darkness is your eyes
where is to find the difference, when everything dissolves in one?

It is strange, but the light comes as the great
divide, and I miss getting monolithic with the entire world.

The monochrome of despair and dreams,
it is beautiful. And the black painted by absence and moans.

Turn off the light. Now you can find my pieces falling
everywhere, there are no photons to separate my skin from yours.

Let there be dark, the devil said. And the devil is fine.

[This is dedicated to the painting by Victor Maloney titled " Van Gogh
Painting with the Devil"]

Cold Fires in the Valley of Immigrant Hearts

The canopy of black silence, with few tinges of silvery ice
a river flow midway between the valley of immigrant hearts,
where I will probably never go again.

It is deafening. The sound of void, and soon-to-be-forgotten laughter
I can smell the charred spleen, on an icy landscape by the side
of a broken bridge. It's not only your desires that burn.

Did you ever wonder it is just a matter of few yards between
you and your myths? On a stone-pitched slope, we will all sleep
like a newborn , right at the intersection of ether and sleepless water.

Came out of the void, mothered by the void
gone into the void. To leave behind fairytales and songs of life
on a day, when fire will be as cold as tears.

[The sadness evoked by "Footbridge across a Ditch"]

Sing Me a River

Silver-slimed oysters, afloat careless
await to rest on those simmering dunes
of silt topaz. Longing, longing, longing
like a lonesome night
more longing, ad infinitum.

Now I want to walk, naked and sane
like the first man, who talked
with those ethereal winds
and felt the winter of a shivering rose
without an ounce of thought.

But in all becoming
you are a nomad, a gypsy.
A soul on an experience voyage
rest not on the shore
you slither, you suffer.

[The mystical pain of "Starry Night over the Rhône"]

Shapes of Fire

Everything is a lie
a lowly spoof,
a grotesque caricature
of a paradise lost;
Except the fact
we all are each other
reciprocal dreams.

Matter is no more
than the spirit on meth
and the whole conscious world
we have crafted
out of our head
Is just a madman's dream.

We all are shapes of fire;
A singular super-soul
celebrating psychic entanglements
in God's vineyard.

[The realization that shape of fire is also the shape of a tree to some extent: Mûrier 1889]

Painting the Sorrows

You are beautifully cursed. Sorrow will find you
midst the city of artificial happiness, no matter what.

You can't go mad if you are a robot or a voodoo doll.
only a river can swell to break its bank,
and goes on to realize its self-effacing more.

No microscope to look into the darkest
 depths of our despair. There are no rulers to measure
the emptiness we are actually made of.

Will we be able to see the Sublime, behind the
veil of junk and absurd? Will we be able to swim across
the sea of sufferings, and make a life out of its salt ?

The hopelessness of human's existence, it keeps finding a way
to our soul, and that is ok. But will we able to paint our way out of it?

Kevin Peery

GLIMPSE

Two palette knives
on a watchman's chair

Passerine birds
in the absence of light

Impasto infused suffering
overlooked by the subjective sane

In the Saint Paul Gardens
slash...one forty two

Where olive trees
wave at death...one more time

And irises...oh the irises
reveal everything...in a fleeting glimpse

SKULL TATTOO

Uncle Mike had a Van Gogh print
on the wall of his detached garage in Decatur Illinois
He claimed he stole it from a whorehouse in Mazatlan...
circa 1973

One evenin' after supper...
we got drunk on apricot brandy
and he told me how it all went down

Her name was Alejandra...
she had a skull tattoo on her left ass cheek
the size of a ripe beefsteak tomato

They screwed twice...while listenin' to Howlin' Wolf...
Truth is...she traded the print to Uncle Mike...
for three Quaaludes and a half spent fifth of red seven

RAZOR BURN

As Linda stood in the shower
shaving her long... luscious legs
with a smooth straight razor
in her slathered hand

She was reminded of poor ole Vincent
and how fickle friends can screw you
outside a seedy brothel
just days before Christmas Eve

CYPRESS KNEE

Waving wheat
and a Cypress Knee

Absinthe breath
with hints of pipe smoke
and inner chaos

Blue paint smudges...
on scuffed Wellington boots

Where mercy died years ago...
and nothingness bleeds forever

PALE PINK ROSES

Pale Pink Roses...
Sit silent...in an ancient vase
on a rickety wooden table
Sharing answers to the questions
we're too afraid to ask

Pale Pink Roses...
Reside on the outskirts of Paris
Eclipsing raw emotion...
while healing our hurt
between the refractory periods

ORCHARD SHOES

Southern France
in Eighty Eight

A tattered waistcoat
with the third button missing

Exaggerated yellows...
with thousands of black branches

Worn out heels...
on his Orchard Shoes

Rich brown soil...
with traces of oil and turpentine

Thirstier than weathered leather...
splintered impulses raging loudly

Almost ready...for another drink

VISIONS & VINEYARDS

A black crow sits
with knowing eyes
As Visions & Vineyards
smirk at death

Unraveling madness
while tempting more torture
A lying cow
too stoned to care
suffocates the truth

And with straw hat surrendered
he strolls ever so slowly
into a bastard's oblivion

SORROWS TONGUE

As dark voices echo
from Sorrows Tongue
engulfing unappreciated genius

Artistic Hellraisers
are often cursed by pretenders
and crudely diagnosed by fools

Yet somehow...they survive

Yes...sorrow speaks
despite the suffering...
in a language only few can comprehend

WORMWOOD ROAD

Staggering slow...
down Wormwood Road
With a loaded revolver
and a ripe...juicy plum

Where dust devils form
and the realms intersect
You can almost taste the tears...
on angry faces ya leave behind

LONG SHOT

Pin against primer...
shocking the wheat
A thirty hour wait
in his thirty seventh year

If Vincent could've predicted
it would take so goddamned long...
perhaps he might have used the congealed blood
to paint his final masterpiece

Clint Margrave

Post-Impression

Van Gogh came to my class the other day.
I dug him up, dusted him off,
got him some fresh skin, some organs.

Almost as good as new, I got his
joints working again, his brain rewired,
Franken-Gogh we joked around

before I brought him onto campus.
Unable to grow any hair,
I painted an orange beard on him,

gave him a corn pipe, a straw hat.
I thought the students would be delighted
to learn what the world-famous Van Gogh

had to say about art and life
and the bittersweet throes of posthumous success—
but none of them knew who he was.

The Role of Art

Art is an introvert.

At parties, it sticks to walls
nobody notices.

When it speaks,
it struggles to be heard.

Like all who tell the truth,
Art has few patrons,

is always offending somebody.

Art is solitary,
rebellious,
abstract.

It is not communal.

And when embraced too fully,
has a tendency
to crash things down.

Not wishing to be known,
not wishing to be liked,
not wishing the acclaim of
its more popular cousin,
Cliché,

Art is an outcast,

whose only role
is to protect its value,
by doing everything for its own sake,

and hoping that it matters.

You Are What You Eat

I always thought it was more important
what came out of your mouth than what went in.
But I guess if you have to blame something
for who you are, it might as well be what you eat.
Of course, you are not that pastrami sandwich
or garden burger you had for lunch yesterday,
anymore than you are what shoes you wear,
what you think at certain times of day,
or what you do for a living.

Still, if I could be what I eat,
and if I could eat what I wanted,
I'd eat nothing but the sentences of Ernest Hemingway,
the sculptures of Rodin,
the self-portraits of Van Gogh,
the paintings of Munch and Picasso and Modigliani.
I'd eat all of France and Italy and Portugal and Spain.
I'd eat the UK too, and Japan,
and the entire Mediterranean.
I'd eat the Musée d'Orsay,
and the bars of Long Beach,
the grapes of Sonoma,
the music of The Jam.

If I could really be what I eat,
I'd eat peace and solitude, love and compassion,
all the greatest things about our species,
books of poetry, philosophy,
films and novels,
walls with beautiful murals.
I'd make meals out of symphonies,
snack on sonnets,
devour Melville's every page.

I'd also eat the greatest scientific discoveries,
Newton's gravity, Einstein's relativity,

Darwin's *Origin of Species.*
I'd eat string theory like string cheese,
wormholes like they were made of gummy,
nebulas like nectarines.
I'd eat the sun and all the gas giants
rolled up inside the curvature of space.
I'd eat distant worlds and parallel ones too,
and the texts of every religion,
every god and goddess,
every Job and Judas,
gobble them all up,
until I'm fat and full and bloated
and have to vomit them out,

just to find myself again.

In Our Twenties

Cigarettes were wonderful.
Drinking meant crazy.
Girls felt glorious.
Parents were distant
and hadn't died or fallen ill yet.
Friends seemed plentiful.
Music couldn't be loud enough.
Living with a lover
was like playing house.
Experience was urgent.
Summers meant travel.
Nights seemed infinite.
Hangovers ended quickly.
Work was provisional
until they discovered our talents.
Marriage was a life sentence.
Divorce, parole.
Success was more inevitable than failing.
Suicide seemed romantic.
The world was in love with us.
We were in love with the world.
We swooned inside its magnificent blue form.
We walked with lightness.
We even strutted.
We thought we were invincible.
We thought we were old.

If Lovers Were Books

They wouldn't argue or disagree
or impose on our space
if we didn't want them to.

Their shelf life would be longer,
and we'd always be sure
when we reached the end.

Who knows?

We might even start over,
because they'd always stay the same.
And if we *did* leave, at least
we'd know it was *us* that changed.

We could lay them on their sides,
press our hands against their spines,
and slip between their tattered covers

that we are always free to close.

Sad Women

They come to my door.
I don't know what draws
them to me or me to them,
but we sit together late at night,
smoke cigarettes, drink whiskey,
laugh. This one I know likes to
disguise her sadness in a yellow
cup, she brings with her everywhere,
from which she drinks fear,
self-hatred, suicidal thoughts.
She is my favorite. She is the
saddest of all. We pretend to
like each other, long for things
that can never be, let intimate
moments pass when she allows me
to stroke her hair, run my fingers
down the side of her neck,
caress her sadness. And I don't know
what it is that makes a man open
his door for such sad ones like her,
(my friends say I'm "asking" for it,
that it's all in the choices I make).
But late at night sometimes,
when we're alone together,
I can feel those painful distances
collapse, as if the degrees of
sadness we share have somehow
formed a bridge between us,
the kind from which nobody jumps.

The Math Mortician

Instead of bodies, he sees numbers,
readies them up on time's table,
dresses them in brackets,

uses algorithms over aspirate
to extract each variable,
hypothesizes infinity is but an empty set,

and life an interval between two ends,
whose value isn't absolute,
when death's the only constant.

Why Flowers Exist

What used to baffle scientists most
is why flowers exist at all,
how they dominate the earth,
given the energy it takes
a plant to produce them.

Studies put the first flower somewhere
between 140 & 125 million years ago,
sometime before the first romance,
the first apology, the first affair,
the first heartbreak,
the first unwanted pregnancy,
& eventually,
the first poet.

I once refused to buy a girl
flowers for Valentine's Day
because I was so intent
on not being predictable
just to find a bright & heavy
bouquet already in her bedroom
gifted by another man.

And though I knew it then,
I still stayed three more months,
continued to make meaning
out of our relationship
despite having learned
that all flowers

with their elaborate patterns,
colorful petals,
& sweet smelling fragrances
exist only to ensure
that their species' survive,

& all poets are fools.

Lost

I was ten when my mother left me
at the grocery store.
It must have only been a couple hours.
I didn't take it personally,
spent the time looking for a coin
so I could call her
on the payphone.

Now, thirty years later,
it's she who feels left somewhere,
when she asks me
to pick her up from my sister's house,
where she's lived
the past five years.

"I want to go home," she tells me.

"But you are," I insist,
knowing she means back to that place
before old age and dementia
and the death of her husband.

"I am?" she says. "I thought I lived
somewhere else."

It's not likely she'd remember
ever leaving me at the grocery store,
or how when she finally realized it
she called the manager in a panic,
asking if he'd seen a little lost boy
roaming down the aisles,
wondering where
his mother went.

Sing at Unnatural Hours in the Presence of Artificial Light

There are times I have to remind myself
that a bridge is a way to travel over water
not a diving board for suicides. That airports

aren't just places for departures, but places
for arrivals, and hospitals aren't only
where we go to die, but where we're born.

I'd like to think not a single bomb
was dropped on anyone today, not a single
person was diagnosed with cancer.

Somewhere someone misses you.
A friend remembers something
you once said. Somewhere someone

thinks you're beautiful. A man holds
a guitar in his hands. A couple dances behind
the living room couch mouthing words

they've longed to share with each other.
At this hour only astronomers
and insomniacs find natural,

as the blazing red lights of an ambulance
flicker fear past the window,
I have to remind myself:

it doesn't always mean somebody's
dying in there, sometimes it means
somebody's being saved.

Brenton Booth

REFLECTIONS

The colours too
bright
and stroke too
broad
and never enough
of how all the
others
were doing
it
they wanted history
but what you
gave was
you
all you could give
was you
and that was
more than
enough.

All alone colouring
the darkness around
you;
bright, insane, beautiful:
everything that
reality of course
should be.

Every day a struggle
created by another's
hand
and your hands
forged in the
sunny heavens

to remind us
of the errors
in our ways.

In a golden field
trying to get the
last colours on the
canvas before night
and the darkness
it brings.

THE OUTSIDER

I see you now crying in
your glass at the sombre
ugly dawn
I see you now watching
the beautiful girl with the
ribbons in her hair dancing
so freely outside on the
street
I see you now smiling at
the proud fluttering crows
hanging on strings in the
afternoon sky
I see you now knowing the
names of all the forgotten
peasants working in the
field
I see you now talking to
the enchanting blinding
trees
I see you now looking at
the masterworks and
knowing what went
wrong
I see you now turning the
small walls of your room
into giant rainbows
I see you now frustrated
at all the colours that just
won't come
I see you now running
from the terror and
wondering why no one
else can see it
I see you now mesmerized
by the starry starry night
I see you now in youth

preaching with sincerity
for justice
I see you now laughing at
the dizzy yellow sun
I see you now telling the
other painters they have
it all wrong
I see you now remembering
the touch of her hand
I see you now drunk at midnight
thinking about the bridge you
know you will one day paint
I see you now crushed flat by
rejection not knowing how
many headaches your works
will one day cure
I see you now howling her
name like a wounded charging
bull in an empty forgotten
arena
I see you now looking at the
day and seeing only night
I see you now embracing
your brother in your delicate
trembling arms
I see you now alone again
I see you now awakened by
the glowing sunflowers of
morning
I see you now whipped again
by the vicious sting of
disappointment
I see you now wondering why
she doesn't say your name
I see you now on a mission
to capture all the beauty of
the day
I see you now turning grey

skies into more than gold
I see you now pas de deux
with the whispering autumn
leaves
I see you now sacrifice flesh
for not enough in return
I see you now talking to
faces that could never see
your face
I see you now holding onto
a canvas that would change
your fortunes far too late
I see you now desperate
like a beggar
I see you now hiding humiliated
in your room
I see you now painting a canvas
with more light than a dozen
suns
I see you now the original
outsider
I see you now the guiding light
for the overlooked
I see you now the hope of
the dispossessed
I see you now gun in hand
with wounds more tragic
than fresh melting snow
I see you now
forever now
dying
for
love.

THE ART

He was 38 and
  had just been
  kicked out of
  the bar

  he was quite
  drunk and sat
  on his old sofa
  drinking more

  it was 12:30AM
  and he thought
  about going to
  the brothel

  Emily would be
  there

  he had been
  single for years.
  sometimes the
  loneliness was
  so great he
  wondered why
  he even went
  on with things

  Emily was always
  good to him at
  the brothel but
  never answered
  his phone calls

  and when he'd
  see her next she
  always had a

reasonable
sounding excuse:
to him anyway

he decided he
would have a
couple more
drinks then go
to the brothel

he felt tired and
the whiskey
really burned his
stomach

he hadn't written
a poem for months
and honestly didn't
care: what was the
point really? he
thought

there had been a
time when the
word meant
everything to
him

nothing was more
important than
the next line

and nothing felt
better

he had grown tired
of that though. all
he ever seemed to

get was form rejections
and bad jobs that
took too much time
and energy

he wondered why
he kept going on

he heard a loud crash.
he recognised the sound.
it was the garbage truck.
he must have fallen
asleep. he opened the
blinds. the sun was out,
slightly

his stomach was on
fire and he had no
interest in eating

he splashed some water
on his face and headed
to the park next to
his building

he sat on the same chair
as always. he shook his
head in disgust

he noticed someone
painting. he'd never
seen anyone painting
there before. nice to
see, he thought

he looked closer. he was
momentarily stunned.
the painter looked like

Van Gogh

you really are screwed up!
he thought and looked
at the ground on the
verge of tears

' looks like we are the
only ones here,' he heard
from the next seat and
looked up

it was the painter. ' the
light on that tree is perfect.
I wish I could get it right,'
he said

' you look just like Van
Gogh.'

' I get that a lot. you
paint?'

' no. I used to write.'

' used to?'

' I think I am done
with it.'

' I once knew someone
like that. he was wrong.'

' it's not hard in this
world.'

' you're right there.'

' big night?'

' disappointing night.'

' I hear you.'

' life is so difficult.'

' you got that right.'

' you look so peaceful.'

' I am now.'

' you weren't?'

' for the longest time.
then...'

' what?'

' then I learned to trust
that.'

' what? art.'

' correct. I have to go. so
much to do. it was nice
meeting you.'

' you too. I am Robert.'

' you already know my
name friend.'

Robert heard a loud crash.
it was the garbage truck
again. he was on his sofa.

it was a dream: all just a
dream

he thought about Van Gogh.
he had outlasted him: or
had he?

he stood up. poured a glass
of water and drank it. found
his notepad. opened the
blinds. put on some music.
and got to work.

Ali Znaidi

Sorrow

—*after Vincent van Gogh's drawing "Sorrow"*

You can ponder and ponder
and hold your breath and
ponder some more.
You can drift yourself
into a monu[mental] marathon
of sorrows till your heart skates in hell.
Your naked body is motionless
like a dead rock.
{Apparently, there's no escape}.
Sorrow turns your hair into
an ashtray rife with dust.
Sorrow turns your breasts
saggy and shy.
Never mind, spring flowers are there
to hide your scars!
Never mind,
you store ammunition
inside your breasts!
Never mind,
explosion is yet to come!
{Apparently, there's an escape}.

The Secret Origins of Pain

*—after Vincent van Gogh's painting "Still Life
with a Plate of Onions"*

The angels were circumambulating
(in a disciplined ritual)
around the sturdy wooden table.
Their performance
of gaze was watching over
the plate of onions;
in fact, they were fantasizing about
the opaque truth.
The truth seemed impossible
because it takes many purslane
and fleshy scale leaves
to compose an onion;
miracles to compose a moment
of existence.
He had nothing to do but drink in
the contrasting colours
of yet another candle light;
an acceleration towards divinity.
Once again, the angels were studying
the large, emptied bottle of absinthe;
the abandoned body,
while carving a new expressionist tattoo
in the G-spot of the unknown.
Prophecy and blood were overwhelming him,
while he was studying the shadow
of his ear dancing to the candle light.

Covering Pain with a White Fig Leaf

*—after Vincent van Gogh's painting "Self-Portrait
with Bandaged Ear"*

He was not going to show the severed
ear for a couple of days. If you think
about it, we're always covering pain
with a bandage. If you think about it,
we're always covering pain with a fig
leaf. This time a white fig leaf devoid
of any sin. A white cloth extending
under the chin, towards a crude pastiche
of internal conflicts. Fits of a dream to
evaporate and surrender into the steam
of the mirror. Death will come with a
breeze, with a ray of light, with a capsule
of white paint. He was not going to show
the severed ear. Instead, he was going
to unearth himself, to brush dirt off
the fossilized pain, and to wash the mirror,
preparing himself to an unknown journey
to the apocalypse. After all, each selfie
is a new exercise to death; a new fantasy.

A Piece of Candy

*—after Vincent van Gogh's painting "Crab
on its Back"*

Though we suppose
there is greenery
in spite of drought,
there is also agony.

Most crabs are living
in the blueness of the sea,
breathing salt,
anyhow, spoiled by
depth and largeness.

Blue deep water is better
than greenery. The insides of the sea
do get less rotten. That's why,
it's an ominous thing when
the sea spews out a crab.

It morphs into a fossil;
a piece of candy licked by
the green tongue of a lusty
thick Capitalist ghost.

A Lesson in Struggle

—after Vincent van Gogh's painting "Tree Roots"

He painted tree roots, the sinewy subject
of existence. A double-square canvas
replete with ghosts dancing in the oil
of life. A labyrinth. The impossibility
to identify tree roots and trunks. In fact,
the impossibility to identify reality and
simulacrum. A lesson in struggle.—An
argument which ought to beg the questions:
What is similarity and how can similitude
be perceived? How bisected selves bear
the weight of their own semblances:
The roots grew into a revelation:
The identification identifies nothing
if not itself. Identity, then, is already
made, it is a blurred root redolent of rot
and decay.—A constellation of blue phantoms.

This is not a mere collage

*—after Vincent van Gogh's painting "Wheatfield
with Crows"*

There will be much flashing
of wheat ears and many tales.
Then, the ears would be dismembered.
The sky was always there for the crows
because its blue also loves
slashes of blackness.
Don't go thinking this is a mere collage
of contrasting colours!
Don't go thinking
the crows are mere black kites!
The crows are a chorus singing
and celebrating that central path;
that tempting cleavage leading nowhere.
There will be much flashing
of wheat ears.
The wind was fondling the bare breasts
of the wheat field.
But their milk abounds behind the layers
of the sky,
awaiting just for those who want to suckle
on eternity.

The Lark's Wings

*—after Vincent van Gogh's painting "Wheat Field
with a Lark"*

A lark was taking flight toward
the upper left of a sky patterned
with light clouds. Did you see
the partially harvested field of wheat?
Does partiality come from the sky
or does it come from the unconsummated desire?
(Some kind of desire flies with the feathers
of the lark). The sky became a door
to reflective clouds redolent
of the lark's feathers;
that catalogue of the historical scent.
What is left to say? The Sufism
of each resurrection within each flight.
The sophism of every embrace.
The movement from within the wheat field
and the movement from outside the world.
The true wound in the ear.
The false desire in the light clouds.
The miscarriage of rain in the lark's wings.
But, why is it a crime to love to flight?
Why is it a crime to be drifted into the drunken clouds?
And further, the picture: acres of wheat debris.
Then, angst started to ferment.

A Woman Walking in a Garden

—after Vincent van Gogh's painting "A Woman Walking in a Garden"

Alone, she was walking through a garden.
Each step a dance for survival.
A bit of herself in every walk.
—Every walk a serving to the leaves of grass.
Greenery abounds
and numerous trees were left
in the background like secrets.
Again she found herself alone in the garden,
digging out the guts of worms
in wet grass; the edgy grass
where miniature creatures hide.
She found herself as if swimming
in the grass;
that orgiastic womb where revolutions ferment.
The greenery has swallowed the ground,
swallowed the sky,
swallowed the secrets
and all of this is only a beginning.
The lower part
of her dress was graffitied with red roses;
blood stains still unknown to forensic scientists.
But, the only escape
from this life is a woman walking in a garden.
Her breasts erect enough to start a revolution.

A Few More Puffs

—after Vincent van Gogh's painting "Skull of a Skeleton with Burning Cigarette"

That's passion. A few more puffs.
Inhale with me, to the middle of the void!
We can swallow the world and the darkness
and kick boredom to float with the smoke.
Ignore anatomy and the boring academia!
Don't be too scared to touch the burning
cigarette! We can turn the smoke into
comedy. Imagine the butt a curtain.
You'll shudder with each ecstatic inhalation,
wondering how something so small
can burn you all over,
while leaving you to such a deep euphoria…
A few more puffs. More inhalations
can send the bodies deeper once again
into the bruised eloquence of life,
fighting the fear of cold and death.

The Kitsch of Life

—*after Vincent van Gogh's painting "Landscape with Snow"*

What we see of snow is the white cream
of snow.—A white spell waiting for its
expiry date.—Whiteness that would
wash out details, reducing the world
into an ice field patterned with the colours
of life, although the time is eerie, cold,
and misty.—But a libidinal desire for details
grows between the puddles and slush
left by the melting snow. The brown dog
never stops barking, just echoing the kitsch
of life. The brown barking dog still walking
behind the man in the road cutting across
the plain. Seasons come and go. Soon
the snow will perish. Soon we'll begin
to hallucinate. Soon the privacy of
the snowy leaves will unfold
in the intimacy of death.

Wayne F. Burke

POTATO EATERS, PREACHERS, AND PAINTERS

SETTING

The mother, Anna Carbentus, marries at 30 and has six surviving children—the last born when she is 47. A stillborn named Vincent—Vincent #1-- dies one year previous to Vincent #2's birth in 1853. #2, unlike his siblings, is a healthy independent-minded and obstreperous child. At age 11 he is sent to a boarding school 13 miles distant from the family home. Two years later he is sent to an even more distant, and cheaper, school. He quits school before he is 15 and at 16 goes to The Hague to work for Goupil & Cie, art & print sellers, a company co-owned by Uncle Cent van Gogh, the mother's brother. (Vincent's younger brother Theo will also go to work for the company when he turns 16.) Vincent is an unenthusiastic employee and has difficulty getting along in the mercantile world. In a kind of banishment—instead of his being terminated—Vincent is sent to work at the London branch of the firm. In London Vincent becomes disillusioned, perhaps depressed, and withdraws from all the family except Theo. Soon after, Vincent is transferred to the company's Paris branch where Theo also works. Meanwhile, Vincent has found religion and what he believes to be his true calling. He uses the book "Imitation of Christ" by Thomas a Kempis, for instruction on how to live righteously. In Paris he manages to further alienate himself in the work place and is dismissed by Guptil. He returns to England and to an unpaid post as teacher in a boy's school in London. Tries to initiate a romance with his landlady's daughter, but she rejects his overtures. Decides to become a missionary, of some sort—a "preacher" perhaps—and returns to Holland for Christmas. Accepts job in another Uncle's book store then quits after 5 months to pursue the "preacher" idea while he lives at home. His rich uncle's agree to finance some of Vincent's study for a ministry, and Vincent moves to Amsterdam to live at his Uncle Jan's house (Jan a retired Admiral). After the first year of a 7 year course of study Vincent quits and returns home. Home is an unhappy environment for him and he goes to live in Brussels to become a "lay preacher" but shortly after arrival leaves and resettles in a poor mining district, the Borinage where he becomes a minister of sorts, ex officio, only too excessive and out-of-touch with his "congregation" to last long; he returns home (beating a dizzying path, like that of the young Rimbaud), after having been away for a year. Home is still intolerable to him and he returns to the Borinage then back home again, aged 27 now, and a cross for the family to bear. The family can bear no more and decide to have Vincent committed to an asylum (the mother is the leading advocate for the asylum idea). Getting wind of the plan, Vincent decamps to Brussels again, and after a suggestion by Theo, decides to dedicate himself to art. No longer an evangelist but now an apostle of art... Theo begins monthly payments to his brother (relieving the parents of their burden). In the summer Vincent returns home and sets out to master art with his usual fanaticism for work. He also, at this time, convinces himself he is love with his cousin Kee Vos and pursues her with such zealousness as to frighten the girl and her parents and further alienate himself from the family circle. After being thrown-out of the house by his parents he goes to Anton Mauve, a 2nd cousin, and well-paid artist, to learn about painting. Vincent's art-knowledge grows under the tutelage but he soon alienates Mauve who cuts Vincent cold. With use of Theo's money, Vincent takes up with a prostitute, Sien Hoorick, and starts a "family." Sien has one child and another on the way; Vincent has the clap and serious dental problems...Vincent moves out of The Hague and to Drenthe in the Netherland's northeast. Leaves his "family" behind. Painting now with compulsive earnestness, he once again returns home after a two month stay in Drenthe. At home, a neighbor, 43 year old widowed Margot Bergemann, 12 years Vincent's senior, falls in love with him. The Bergemann family vociferously disapprove of the relationship as do Vincent's parents. Forbidden to continue with Vincent, Margot takes poison but survives and is subsequently sent "away." Theodorous van Gogh Senior dies after a stroke at age 63. Vincent's sister Anna tells him that he "killed" his father. The father who offered only kindness and tolerance to Vincent (though on his, the father's, terms)--Vincent wanted understanding too but this the old man could not provide. The sister leads the effort to kick Vincent out of the house. He goes to live in an nearby apartment which he converts to a studio and paints his first masterpiece "The Potato Eaters." Leaving Nuenen, he goes to Antwerp. Contracts syphilis. Enrolls at the Art Academy but comes in conflict with teachers and students and ends his attendance. Has a third of his teeth pulled. After a two month stay he leaves for Paris, and Theo. In Paris Vincent attends a prestigious art atelier but quits after 3 months to go his own way. After Theo proposes to his girl, Johanna Bonger, Vincent threatens to "do away" with himself. Meanwhile, Gupil & Cie has changed hands and Theo given charge of introducing the "new" art of Impressionism to the public, via the company gallery. Theo is turned down by his girlfriend. Vincent abruptly leaves town, remarking that he is leaving so that he will not "kill" Theo as he, Vincent, "killed" his father (ha ha). Vincent travels to Arles, a 16 hour journey by train. In Arles he sets himself up in "The Yellow House." The painter Paul Gauguin is invited to join Vincent in The Yellow House and Gauguin accepts the offer. After Gauguin's arrival a friendly interlude between the two painters follows but complications ensue and they have a falling-out... Vincent cuts his own ear off and is afterward involuntarily committed to an asylum. Later, he volunteers for a stay at a different asylum. A year after this voluntary commitment he leaves the asylum and goes to Paris to see Theo, Theo's wife, and their baby boy (Vincent #3). Meanwhile, a favorable—laudatory even—article on Vincent's work, by the critic by G.-Albert Aurier, has been published in a prestigious art magazine, Mercure De France...Theo sells Vincent's painting "Red Vineyard" for 300 francs. Vincent leaves Paris after a three day visit and settles in nearby Auvers where he makes contact with a Dr. Gachet who has made arrangements with Theo to look after Vincent, perhaps even "treat" him...Seven weeks, and eighty paintings later, Vincent shoots himself in the stomach and dies.

THE STORY

Vincent van Gogh did not come out of a working class environment but from one of bourgeois respectability. His father, the parson, was not paid a large salary but was given a house to live in plus there were other perks to the job. The family lived comfortably. Vincent never lacked for anything except possibly a mother's love. The mother, Anna van Gogh nee Carbentus, maintained a distance between herself and eldest son, a distance the son was never to breach.. The mother's emotional coldness is thought to be due to the death of Vincent #1 the stillborn baby one year before Vincent #2's birth. The thought is that she was still grieving the death and was emotionally unavailable to her new born who, reportedly, was a handful from the get-go. An obstreperous child who became irascible when thwarted; he may have fit somewhere on the Asperger's disordercontinuum considering his reported indifference to others and the degree of his self-involvement, spending long intervals alone with his collections (bugs, bird nests) and in roaming the heath of his native Brabant.

Vincent never held a so-called "regular" job except for the ones his Uncle's gave him, minding the store in The Hague and London and Paris where he was fired after pissing-off everyone concerned with the outfit. His other "jobs" as lay minister and teacher were likewise disasters...The boots in his "shoe pictures,"side by side in pairs or triplicate and painted with utmost fidelity-- and having aspects of muddied and wearied person-ages--were not his boots but ones he bought at flea markets and battered for aesthetic purposes. For most of his life Vincent dressed like a gentle-man, which he was, though of a rough exterior with a oftentimes gauche-ness that went with his idiosyncratic character.

During his evangelical career he goes to work as a sort of ex officio minister to the poor miners in the area know as the Borinage and sleeps on the floor instead of his bed to identify further with his "congregation." The Borins must have despised the "do-gooderism" of the bourgeois fop in their midst for converting his masochism into martyrdom for people who did not ask him to be their Christ. A rookie evangelist who coated his face with coal dust and wore rags...The Borin's called him "God's Mad-man." All his life Vincent seemed to seek punishment, and if not receiving any, gave himself some.

Theo begins his regular payments to Vincent in 1881 after suggesting, to a distraught Vincent (complaining of feeling "useless") that he become a painter. Also, in '81, Vincent meets a fellow artist, Anton van Rappard, a man about town financially backed by a well-to-do family. The two artists work side by side. Vincent respects his new colleague's work. Van Rappard recognizes Vincent's "eccentric originality" and comments on Vincent's "fanatical soberness." Vincent set to work drawing with the idea that, one day, he would be able to sell illustrations to magazines like The Graphic and Illustrated London News and other publications he had become famil-iar with while living in England. He was yet to speak of his art as transcen-dental, and not for magazines, but for the ages—the people of the future.

Back in Nuenen and the homestead in '84, the 30 year old Vincent, a drifter of questionable sanity in the eyes of his parents, uses his anger and paranoia against his father in acts of physical intimidation and against Theo in accusatory and venomous letters. He also worked with a will at his art, producing the great series of exquisite pen drawings—Winter Garden, Pond in the Vicarage garden, etc.--works equal to the British literary-artists he admired (Broughton, Mallais) and "surpassing them in poetic intensity."

In '85 the father falls, dead, a stroke. Vincent paints 'The Potato Eaters' which he considers his first masterpiece. A dark picture though lustrous with green and gold tints. Somewhat chilling with a cold aura: mud creatures in a mud hut drinking black mud and preparing to eat what look like lumps of flesh...The creatures have insect-like segmented faces and hands—only the lustrous sorrowful eyes of the two figures at far right identify these creatures as human. An etymological view of the peasantry. A study done, not in identification with the peasantry, as Vincent claimed, but with the detachment of a scientist—an anthropological view of a sub-species of underground dwellers remote as the pygmies of the rain forest were in the 19th century. Van Rappard criticized the work for it's "cavalier disregard of gestural and spatial plausibility," a frosty academic-sounding critique that Vincent rejected (and that ended their friendship)...Vincent maintained a whirlwind of activity, painting a series of 50 heads and another of 100 figures. No doubt this was a time for Vincent of pleasantness in work—joyousness—but it soon ended when one of his models—the girl who posed for The Potato Eaters—became pregnant and Vincent was named prime suspect. A local priest issued Vincent some kind of stern warning and afterward Vincent discovered that the peasants would no longer pose for him nor would his landlord renew the lease on the studio. The hostility made it imperative Vincent decamp...Fate had intervened and henceforth Vincent would be an adventurer rather than homebody. He would never return to his homeland.

After a stay in Antwerp, 25 miles distant Nuenen, Vincent moved to Paris and surprised his brother. In Paris Vincent painted the first of his many self-portraits—as if, now that he was an adventurer, he needed to discover what he looked like, to himself and others. The Paris stay, in his brother's apartment, lasted two years and must have been an exciting time for Vincent though he later disparaged the city as an environment unsuitable for him. At Cormon's Studio the rustic outsider was thrown in with a group of notable painters and personalities, Henri de Toulouse-Lau-trec, Louis Anquetin, and Emile Bernard among them--a kind of fraternity. It was or must have been a head-y time for Vincent and for the newest so-called Impressionists and future post-Impressionist painters vying to unseat the older schools of academic-painters...Vincent threw himself into the mix with his usual fanaticism. The fraternity with his brother deteriorated at the same time. Theo found Vincent's more outre antics intolerable and in a letter to their sister, Wil, cited the two sides of Vin-cent's character: one "dignified, fine, and delicate," the other "selfish and heartless."

During his two years in Paris Vincent painted over two hundred works. In '88 he left for Arles with the idea of working in the southern light and of starting a sort of painter's colony, or School of the South. With this idea in mind he invited Paul Gauguin to come south.

Gauguin should have taken the self-portrait that Vincent did for him as forewarning. The painting shows Vincent with his head nearly shaved and not, as he wrote, looking like a "simple bonze worshiping the Eter-nal Buddha," but like a dangerous criminal; not a saint but sinner or mad monk wearing brown tonsure of a coat...the snake-like head with strange-ly upraised eyebrows is tinted green and sunk into a vertiginous green background. No sympathy exists for subject or viewer. A stark disturbing work that should have tipped Gauguin off as to the unhealthy state of Vin-cent's mind. Gauguin, far from sainthood himself, sent in reply an equally dark self-portrait looking somewhat wary and hostilely inquisitive, like a police inspector. Gauguin did not share Vincent's hopes for a Studio of the South. His trip to Arles was almost strictly a business dead. He would be paid by Theo (acted as Gauguin's agent) to spend time with Vincent. While in Arles, which Gauguin considered a backwater town unworthy his interest, he might, perhaps, produce some salable work which Theo, who had previously bought a Gauguin, might purchase outright. And if not, he would be no worse off than in his present penurious condition...

The results of the Van Gogh/Gauguin collaboration are too well-known to bother repeating here. A question one might ask though, is why the ear? Why not nose? Or finger? Was the ear attacked as source of the aw-ful news of Gauguin's decision to leave? Gauguin, like Theo, had found Vincent's company uncongenial; found his love "tyrannical"--a love that "allowed for no interruption, no change." Rather than asocial Vincent was "hypersocial" extending to his few intimates—Theo, Gauguin, Barnard—a loving assault that overwhelmed and left reeling the recipient. Gauguin's decision to leave precipitated the crises that deranged Vincent. Gauguin's decision meant, to Vincent, that his dream of a Studio of the South was over, and also that he would be alone again, which terrified him as he hated being alone (had set-up house with a pregnant alcoholic prostitute in The Hague so as not to have to live alone—or so it seems...). The source of Vincent's derangement has been much debated. Did he have temporal lobe epilepsy and did he hear a voice telling him to kill Gauguin? Did he go after Gauguin with the razor he also used to cut off his ear? Gauguin is the only teller of that tale, and he told it long after the fact. Supposing it were so, did Vincent cut his ear because it was the source of the voice directing him to act against his own interests? It seems plausible—as plausible as all other theories...After cutting himself, it is known that he took the ear to a brothel and, reportedly, gave it to a prostitute named "Rachel." A book by Bernadette Murphy, VAN GOGH'S EAR, 2016, disputes this version of the story, claiming that "Rachel" was not a prostitute or even a "Rachel" but a "Gabrielle" and a cleaning woman at the establishment who had been disfigured from the bite of a rabid dog earlier in her life, and thus Vincent, a connoisseur of damaged women, presented his ear in "a noble act"--a gift of part of his body to replace Gabrielle's damaged flesh. In his mania, or whatever you care to call it, Vincent thought himself a Christ who could heal scars...An interesting story. Murphy also rescues the bad reputation the town of Arles acquired for it's seeming cruelty and indifference to Vincent after his "attack." One of the crueler acts being circulation of a petition by the citizens of Arles to have Vincent incarcerated as a "public menace." The petition, said to be signed by 100 Arlesians, is signed, according to Murphy, with 30 signatories and of those signatures most are either associates or family members of a certain merchant—the house agent, who wanted van Gogh out of The Yellow House in order to rent the place and to make capital on improvements Vincent had made while living there.

In what seems a cruel act of a God both deaf and dumb Vincent was struck down at the height of his power as an artist. From whack-job he went to lunatic. A danger to himself and others. Almost as if the gods decided that Vincent had come too close to their domain—had scalded paradisaical heights and had to be brought down, rendered merely human again...A cruel fate. Like that of H. L. Mencken, the American writer, who, after a stroke, was rendered aphasic and could no longer read or write; and Mary Cassat, the American-born Impressionist painter, who spent the last ten years of her life totally blind; and Sherwood Anderson, the American writer, who died of peritonitis after swallowing a toothpick..Such is fate, which is out of our control—leaving only destiny to us.

The cause of Vincent's derangement? (Or"disease," as he called it.) Temporal lobe epilepsy? Lead poisoning? Manic-depression? Tinnitus? Alcohol toxicity from drinking absinth? Probably at least one of the above if not more (let's add inferiority complex, since he seemed not to care about his physical health plus thought himself "ugly." He had a strange notions about health care, counseling his sister Wil, in a letter, that the best cure for depression and all other diseases was to treat them with contempt).

See "Ward in the Hospital in Arles," painted in '89. The inmates of the asylum sit around a pot-bellied stove while nurse/nuns go about their business. Look just beyond the left hand corner—see it? Gauguin's chair! And with a burnt-out candle on the seat. Did Vincent consciously place Gauguin, in spirit, in the asylum? If not for spiritual succor, then because he, Vincent, believed Gauguin belonged there? Or is inclusion of the chair punishment for Gauguin for leaving The Yellow House?

During the last year of his life Vincent attempted a rapprochement with his mother. A conciliatory gesture of a portrait, painted from a photograph, was sent to her. The picture shows a ghoulishly green-faced woman possibly in early stages of dementia—a wax-like image belonging in Madame Trousseau's museum. An act of unconscious vengeance by Vincent against the mother who thought his art "ridiculous" and never accepted or even tried to understand him (what the mother thought of the gift is unknown).

Did Van Gogh work himself to death? Work is what he lived for, he said; gave his life to painting, art, though as late as '87 he is thinking out loud, to Theo, that he, Vincent, could become a male nurse or take some other job than making art...He threw himself into his work to divert his mind, he claimed, from dwelling on his inner torments; it was also a part of his character and heritage to work hard though one wonders if some of it was done to show others, like Ma & Pa, that he was no slacker or loafer but worked for his daily bread (though Theo could sell none of the art Vincent sent). Vincent's letters to his brother record a tortuous struggle of a man wrestling with art and life. The art, he triumphed over. That is Van Gogh's legacy—the man who bent art to his will. The life, he never could figure out and went from one disaster to the next like a drunk reeling down a city street. He was miserable much of the time,due, it seems, to his inability to live as well as he worked. In the work however is where he knew joy in the act of creation; where he must have known an abundance of joyousness...Why did he not address the inner torments? The complexities that drove him and oftentimes made him unhappy? Too bad there was no practicing psychoanalyst around. Or a twelve-step program, though it is doubtful that anyone could have deflected Vincent from his chosen path..."My pictures cost me a great deal," he wrote, "at times even my blood and my brain" (letter, 571). He was always willing to pay the costs.

Like many others—though to a degree greater than most others--van Gogh had some sort of emotional disturbance, the nature of which defies easy explanation. Many of his problems have their root in his childhood and upbringing; much of his difficulty he brought upon himself by his indignant and irascible character that made it almost impossible for anyone to get along with him for long. It was not so much what happened that stultified his growth as a person but his reaction to what happened. He demanded understanding instead of trying to understand himself and others. When he did not get it in amounts sufficient enough for him he sulked and turned against the world at large. The world became a weight that crushed his spirit. "Screw the world," one hopes to read in the letters, but never does. Van Gogh carried on in the spirit of "duty." Physical and mental illness added to his burden. He was a great artist as well as a certifiable lunatic. Before becoming great artist, and lunatic, he was a whack-job, a borderline personality who often lived on the sufferance of others—tolerated rather than liked. He was the family toothache for many years and never felt that he belonged anywhere, not to a family or a country. He was a stranger on earth, who, in his strangeness, or because of it, brought beauty to the world in the form of incomparable masterworks of art. He walked on clouds and worked, not only for himself, but for posterity; worked with "transcendent" ambition," and faith in his art and the artistic life...Maybe he was, as the song claims, too "beautiful" to live.

George Wallace

A FATAL MARRIAGE WITH THE SEA

It is plain as the bump on your nose and will remain so until apples
jump back into apple trees that the north sea holds no love for men,
only reckoning, dead reckoning, and the surf yellow as split pea wants
nothing more than to swallow someone up, the innocent or
the damned,

but like the north sea and my mother before me I am moody too,
'churned by constant winds and inhabited by monsters,' and would as
soon stand like Tacitus under black clouds than with my easel and the
white wind blowing,

let the big dunes hurl fists of sand into my eyes, one with the shellfish
gatherers in their bodices of serge, holding on for dear life, one with
the seabirds flying and the little white horse whinnying by
the woodencart,

one with the fisherman's flag lashing this way and that –

and the ship's hull coming to, cresting in the surf, clumsy as
a circus bear

NOTES: *View of the Sea at Scheveningen, 1882*; Henri Alphonse Esquiros' Scheveningen prose passage
copied by Van Gogh prob May '77 (*Even Tacitus pictured it as being churned up by constant winds and
inhabited by monsters, in the foreground it is a scummy yellow, Their dress, especially the women's,
is distinctive. In the winter, they wear a bodice of serge or calico, the whinnying of the waves that run,
without a bit and foaming at the mouth, about the boat's keel*)

LANDSCAPE WITH DECAYING OAK TRUNKS

In Drenthe, transfiguration is in the peat,
   Just like Ruysdael, just like Jules Dupré,
I think I have found my little kingdom of
   Melancholy, a lonely place with a little white
Path running alongside, this bog with muddy
   Boots, reach toward heaven, oak stump
Buried for a century or more, what do you
   Offer but sheer decay, some black, some
Bleached white, ghost mongrels, relics of
   The great gothic shore, Race of Titans all laid
Bare and grasping toward stranger gods
   Than Heaven, a peasant is walking past, black
Against the peasant gloom, the white sky,
   Shovel to shoulder, and yes windmills are
On the horizon but in disrepair or quite nearly
   Ruined, the gloom, the gloom, two old women
In white peasant caps on the heath, cutting
   Peat, all the variations, same sterile landscape,
Charcoal metamorphosis, new life from the pool of
   Death itself, a sweet Melancholy, a Holier light

NOTES: Landscape with Bog Oak Trunks, 1883; To Theo, Drenthe, 6-7 Oct '83 (Just like Ruysdael, Just like Jules Dupre; a little white path ran past it all; buried for a century; black figures against the white sky; I think I may have found my little kingdom); To Theo, Paris, 9 Sep 75 (Pa wrote to me recently, 'melancholy does not hurt, but makes us see things with a holier eye')

CAFÉ TERRACE AT NIGHT

White horse coming up the
alleyway an hour ago it was
hired carriages drawn from
light to light across cobblestones flowergirls and the
muffled sound of Brahms or
was that my imagination the
tobacconist's lamp across the
way is definitely fading, one
by one the shutters overhead
are being snapped shut, gables
and rooftops of Arles are fading
from violet to blue to black whatever it was we thought was sacred
in this town has dematerialized --
this café is emptying out, I count
twelve drinkers who are not ready
to go home yet they are drowning in
yellow lantern light -- how long can this go
on across the café carpet the waiter's
feet are beginning to make an old
and very familiar dragging sound

NOTES: _Café terrace at night, 1888_; To Willemian Van Gogh, Arles, 14 Sep '88 (On the terrace, there
are little figures of people drinking. A huge yellow lantern lights the terrace, the façade, the pavement,
and even projects light over the cobblestones of the street, which takes on a violet-pink tinge. The gables
of the houses on a street that leads away under the blue sky studded with stars are dark blue or violet,
with a green tree.)

ROULIN THE POSTMAN

Instead of painting the dull wall of a mean room, I paint the infinite

it is a shame the people in Paris have no taste for the rough things, weather beaten things, oxherds in straw hats, men with hoes and heavy shoulders, *le vieux paysan* cloving through darkness, rugged dialect, feral gaze,

Curmudgeons in old slacks living on a piece of bread, their faces set in furrows like hard potatoes,

A pity there is not in Paris more taste for rough men in wooden clogs, plowmen in the furnace of their work, terrific men blazing like hot tin, drinking and smoking, ruby cheeked men in russet sunset, or Roulin the postman, old cleftbeard with his cap on tight,

Bluesuited Roulin, the raw dignity of his pitchfork gaze, broad forehead, broad nose, the shape of his beard, my only friend and drinking companion in all of Arles, sitting in a straight back chair before green floral wallpaper, singing the Marseillaise

NOTES: *Patience Escalier, 1888*; *Portrait of the Postman Joseph Roulin, 1889*; To Theo, Arles, 18 Aug '88 (what a mistake that Parisians haven't acquired sufficient taste for rough thing; in the furnace of harvest time; oranges, blazing like red-hot iron; instead of painting the dull wall of the mean room, I paint the infinite; one day I saw him singing the Marseillaise); Rosenberg, K, New York Times,1 Nov '12 (the subject's feral gaze)

A SYNTHESIS OF ARLESIENNES

I get the feeling we are all a little dazed

To feel deeply
to feel subtly
this is my
ambition
a nobody
an oddity
this need to
paint Madame
Ginoux Ginoux
Madame Ginoux
a synthesis of
Arlesiennes
eyes calm
flesh green
heart like a
carved olive
elbow to table
book unread
how to form
a green whole
among olive trees
colored with the solemn
tones of nature:
Madame Ginoux and
2 young girls, climbing
a stepladder among
cypresses -- how
to know
heaven
in the
gleaners'
hand

this rage to paint orchards
won't last forever

NOTES: _L'Arlesiennes (7 variations) 1888; Women Picking Olives (1889)_; To Paul Gauguin, Aubers-sur-Oise, 10 Jun '90 (It's a synthesis of an Arlésienne if you like, as syntheses of Arlésiennes are rare);To Theo and Jo van Gogh-Bonger, Auvers-sur-Oise, 7 Jul '90, ripped up and never sent (My impression is that as we're all a little dazed); To Theo, Arles, 6 Nov '88 (I have an Arlésienne at last, a figure (size 30 Canvas) slashed on in an hour, background pale lemon, the face grey, the clothes black, deep black, with unmixed Prussian blue. She is leaning on a green table and seated in an armchair of orange wood); To Theo, Arles, 9 Apr '88 (This rage to paint orchards won't last forever); To Theo, St Remy, 3 Jan '90 (coloured with more solemn tones from nature)

RED HERRINGS

They think I'm mad 'cause I drink like them and dance
with their wives until late at night but I am not I am
just a stranger in their town up all night and out at
break of day a stranger who walks out at dawn into
the fields with easel and brush, pipe clenched tight
in his mouth and his eyes on eternity -- well people
are idiots, Theo, the things they find to meddle with
and petition against, no business of mine, venomous
layabouts to a man -- well let them call the gendarmes
and have me hauled in like a fish -- let them lock me in
the asylum and lock me out of the little yellow cottage
by the railroad station I've called mine -- never mind I
squarely accept my profession among them, madman!
-- because you see I have a friend with a bad reputation
-- Signac, the pointillist --who comes to visit -- Signac the
violent, simple and plain, who is not afraid of my work
and will smash the lock and get me in
　　　and o *I am tied to earth*
　　　　　by more than earthly bonds
including gratitude for the friendship of a man like Signac
and access to my work in the little yellow cottage -- and so
I have given to Signac the pointillist a picture i have made –
　　　still life with red herrings

NOTES: _Still life with herrings, 1886;_ To Theo, Arles, 24 Mar '89 (Signac was very nice and very straight
and very simple when the difficulty arose of whether or not to force open the door closed by the police,
who had demolished the lock... As a keepsake I gave him a still life which had exasperated the good gendarmes of the town of Arles because it depicted two smoked herrings, which are called gendarmes, as
you know; Do you know that expression by a Dutch poet I am tied to the earth/With more than earthly
bonds. That's what I experienced in many moments of anguish – above all – in my so-called
mental illness.)

A COMMUNE IN THE BOUCHE DE RHONE

Sometimes in life they hand you a deck of cards no matter
how many times you shuffle them each hand's worse than
the last -- a loser a loser a loser – something's got to give
something's got to suffer but something's got to offer itself
eventually too, to a man of talent, to a man of patience so
Vincent confined to an asylum in St Remy fabricates two
peasant women out of thin air

And yes Millet's Gleaners and a memory of the north

Two peasant women eternally bent over, double down in their
white peak caps, digging a grave in a field of snow and for what?
At least Millet's Gleaners have something to dig for – a stalk
of wheat a wee bit of loose grain, life itself

How long have these two been at it, holding this preposterous pose for
a crackpot

Patience my dear we are confectionaries
as Flaubert phrases it *talent is long patience*
he's completely daft he's besotted he has vision
see how his brush flies now

It is 1890 it is a commune in the Bouche de Rhone Vincent's muse
lies buried in asylum sheets and pillowcases -- death is root crop,
Vincent Van Gogh is digging through dead snow himself -- mad
potatoes! So cruel so unspectacular what shall we make of this
thing, asylum mates?

Even the sun squatting fat and yellow on the horizon between
the rooftops and snowmad clouds cannot explain

NOTES: *Two Peasant Women Digging in a Snow-Covered Field at Sunset 1890;* To Theo, Arles, 22 Mar
'88 (what Flaubert's phrase might have meant, 'talent is long patience' — and originality an effort of will
and intense observation)

ILLUMINATION AND FIREWORKS POSTPONED FOR STORMY WEATHER

the fishermen know that the sea is dangerous and the storm fearsome

A field of wheat under troubled sky, a wheatfield called mankind, what do we name this field of man, ruined corn, what do we call this loaf of bread, tumbling clouds -- and all men fall to the sickle or the storm some day

The prospect goes dark, limbs get lost and orchards flood in stormy weather, but too much calm isn't good for a man, and i live and work by the day, do not condemn me, beyond the wall there are new hills rising where old hills fall

Do you remember no fireworks at the municipal baths and the Bengal Light postponed 3 times, well the Bengal Light went off eventually, nothing can stop the municipal authorities from having their way –

And the people of Arles hate me now and the gendarmes have come to put me away

But whether the people at the inn smile or take my money, whether they turn or look the other way, it's all just billiards and beer, whether the sun glows green over almond trees at dusk or if, at dawn, the light of the world goes dim, i must continue my work

I am trying not to lose my skill after all, it is difficult to acquire a certain facility for production, i will continue my work til the last brush falls from my hands

Look at my hands, this is Holland
Look at my hands, surrounded by
sea -- this is Holland, fair weather
or foul –

The herring fishermen do not remain long
on the shore, or soon put up their oars

NOTES: _Chestnut Tree In Blossom, 1890;_ To Theo, The Hague, 29 Sep '72 (Illuminations postponed due to bad weather, Bengal Lights); To Theo, The Hague, 16 May '82 (the fishermen know that the sea is dangerous and the storm fearsome; To Anna Van Gogh-Carbentus, Auver-sur-Oise, 14 Jul '90 (I'm wholly absorbed in the vast expanse of wheatfields against the hills, large as a sea, delicate yellow, delicate pale green, ... I'm wholly in a mood of almost too much calm); To Theo and Jo Van Gogh-Bonger, Auvers-sure-Oise, 24 May '90 (it's difficult to acquire a certain facility of production, and by ceasing to work I would lose it much more quickly, more easily than it cost me in troubles to acquire it)

TERRIBLY ALONE, FOREVER YOUNG

There is in most men a poet who dies young, while the man lives on'

But Sainte-Beuve was talking about Millevoye the
poet, Millevoye who loved to write about death,
not life -- elegies to the young, glamorously written,
romantic and doomed, 'woods that I love, farewell!'

Whereas Vincent, just 22, had fifteen more glorious years
of poetry paint and hell ahead of him, possessed of Sainte-
Beuve's fine flower of feeling and desire, aka madness,
not one for whom life's primal dream was likely to vanish

Into humdrum
work or the business of life

37 or a hundred, a man in whom the poet will not die
is young forever

Not even a revolver shot to the heart can kill the poet
inside a man like that – the man dies, the poet lives on –
27 July 1890, nearly dusk in the village of Auvers-sur-Oise,
northern France, Vincent Van Gogh, absorbed in an
immense plain with wheat fields,

Up as far as the hills, boundless as the ocean, delicate yellow,
delicate soft green, left his easel against a haystack, went
behind the wall of a nearby château and fired a bullet into his chest –

Mad dying young and alone
terribly alone, forever youn

NOTES: <u>Wheat Field With Crows,</u> 1890; To Theo, Paris, 15 Jul '75 (St Beuve said 'There is in most men
a poet who dies young, while the man lives on') Saint Beuve, '37 (there exists or there has existed some
fine flower of feelings, of desires, some primal dream, which soon vanishes into humdrum works and ex-
pires in the course of life's business); The Fall of the Leaves, Millevoye, 1796 (Woods that I love, farewell);
To Anna Van Gogh-Carbentus, Auver-sur-Oise, 14 Jul '90 (I myself am quite absorbed in that immense
plain with wheat fields up as far as the hills, boundless as the ocean)Emile Bernard to Albert Aurier, 2 Aug
'90 (On Sunday evening he went out into the countryside near Auvers, placed his easel against a haystack
and went behind the chateau and fired a revolver shot at himself)

MISSING PORTRAIT

East of coffins, in the manner of all eyes which cannot quite read the sky, uncertain eyes set in a bold fabric of arabesques, landscapes printed with cornflowers and forget me nots, eyes like coiled rope, oilrags piled in a corner of the room, painting what you are told not to paint, with your hands, with your eyes, with your mouth and your beard,

The sun stands still in wheatfields, almond trees are blossoming again,

The noisy beast and storm within in your head won't quit and where is that calmness you said was going to return to the world, where the smooth as sea glass, where the old currency, your hair is wax candles, Fou Rou, your dead ear dumb as a ditch canal, your beard is pewter, eyebrows locked in mock ruin, your eyes blazing like two tabs of acid or butter in a frying pan,

No one is safe from you, Vincent, your gaze is crooked

Crooked as a summer pavilion for mad women to do their dancing in

NOTES: _Dance Hall With Dancing Women 1885;_ To Theo, Arles, 22 Jul '88 (if the storm within gets too loud, I take a glass too much to stun myself)

Kerry Trautman

Sunflowers (Vincent van Gogh, oil on canvas, 1888)

Their gold-ness is less so—
as they
dry and die
over weeks—
is less so than the gold wall glow
behind
clay vase and table below.

They've no fight left inside
as they die—
slow drying—
no will to compete for
gold-ness,

as they die.
Their old companion sun
is no matter—
snipped, shut—
tilted as when they last
faced him,
absorbed what little light's
now crusting
drooped and muting.

Gold no matter
when they die.

Cutting off Ears

We watched this thing on TV
about a painter
who slowly went mad, and
about his wife
who stayed with him,
in love.

I slid my hand on his belly
and said, "will you still love me

when I'm a crazy artist?"

I smiled and so did he,
but only a little.

"Will you be..." he said,
pressing my hand,
and his belly grumbled,
"Will you be a crazy artist?

A crazy writer?"

And somehow,
I took it as a dare.

Irises (Vincent van Gogh 1889)

There is growth here
among the mad,

there is a lengthening
toward sky

a deepening and
spread of rhizomes
below red earth.

There is a lush
cacophony of purple
dimming the minute
orange marigolds
like less-loved children.

Among the madness, still,
there are these ever widening
grins drinking in
dew, sun,
bees.

Self-Portrait with Bandaged Ear (Vincent van Gogh 1889)

His stare says
it doesn't matter why
he did it.
If he did it or
someone else did.

His stiffened back says
he'd do it again.

It's not much
longer now, after all.

Not much more burning
of brushstrokes into brainstem.
Swirl of lead and absinthe,
bake of sun.

His hat and cloak say,
of course, he's cold.
He's out of money.
His brother's out of money,
out of patience.

Not much
longer now.

The bandage says,
we endure these voices
longer than we should.

Jeanne Calment of France

Did she know who he was—
van Gogh—
when as a girl she sold him paints,

noting his eyes glazed
like halved oysters in their liquor,

his verdigris skin
like centuries-old copper
or birches rough with lichens?

On her death
age 122, did she still
think of him as back then—

"ugly as sin and
smelling of booze,"

tainting her shop like a burnt thing,
producing art like hydrangeas—
brilliant blue in acidic soil.

Irises in Vase (oil on canvas, 1890)

Did he watch those
leftward leaning purple stems
awaiting falling
and what murky water they'd
slosh to the green tabletop?

In the gardens
knife in hand
there is a scattering of ladybeetles
as the sliced stems snap
and bleed clear
to early summer soil.
There is
a thieving of
bearded perfection.

He had to realize, now—
pitcher after vase after
jar after bowl—
had to know he must work quickly,
that with each blink
the tabletop beauty
cries out.

To the Iris

I had not anticipated how
you would dissolve yourselves—
your upward standard petals
collapsing and congealing,
dripping violet ooze to the bureau top.
Such dramatic gore,
unlike other flowers' demure
beige wilting—
their slow fade until one day
I realize what I have displayed
in a tall glass vase now
is death, is yesterday, is
what-used-to-be
atop woody spindle stems.
But not you,
liquifying yourselves
to a resentful purple glop,
perhaps seeking my apologies for
clipping your succulent high stems
when your falls were at their zenith,
were spread to spring's spare sun,
beckoning bees to
your bearded, veined convolutions.
You will not go gently.

Wheat Stacks with Reaper (Vincent van Gogh, oil on canvas, 1890)

Voices don't dare follow
from dank wood room
out

to stark sky
dotted with
cawing flocks, with
whipped-free leaves.

There is this yolk
of easel hefted
midfield
mid void.

Voices shushed by sheaves and
raven feathers.

There is canvas unrolled
revealing brushes and
crushed oiled pigments
to a sunrise
that shames them.

Odors and their
associated poisons
dissipate.

There is voice
within heaps of cloud, within
fields of
un-reaped seed.

Abstract

Because he'd painted it for her—
stretching the canvas, sized for hanging
over her sofa, away from direct sun—
because he'd avoided reds, knowing
she gets anxious around red and all its
unseemly, private connotations,
she tried. She tried for days to like it.

She tried to force order into its random
brushstrokes, tried to imagine why
this turquoise streak here and not there,
this ochre there, not here.

Like a Rorschach, the gold and olive smear
in the corner became the steel-roofed shed
behind her parents' house, where
a neighbor-boy taught her to tongue kiss.
The deep green near the center—
a broken-necked tropical bird.
Each element became anything,
anything other than pieces of him, of them,
abstractions and nothing more.

She wondered how the man she knew
could have left the straight-lined,
marine blue splotch in one corner,
a splotch where he, working on a flat surface,
had obviously dropped his brush,
it's dirtied handle stamping its impression.
The man she remembered would have growled,
thrown the ruins to the corner.

Instead, after months without their speaking,
he'd driven the painting to her back door,
left it exposed for her to find,

still bloodied though without red.
And now she searched it for why—
after months without a brush, without
coming home with new tubes clenched in
his fists, eager to spread them,
without pouring her wine, lighting her,
grabbing her by her upper arms to pull her
to his mouth—why now? why this?

Houses in Auvers (Vincent van Gogh, oil on canvas, 1890)

Sunrise burns off overnight rain,
dripping still audible down roof tiles,
from leaves to tulips to grass.

Some hours later a boy will
rustle through greenness, pantlegs
swishing loose the last drops.

Katydids will flee from June heat
and boys to cool shadows.

Some years later, these chimneys will
collapse in a windstorm, masonry
clunking onto the woodstoves or stools or
tables below set with yellow
cloths and a bowls of beets.

A boy sits on the low stone wall,
dampening the seat of his pants,
cold, rocking back and forth
where he knows the capstones are loose.

Some years later, he knows,
things will give way.

Epiphany

Rodney Brooks' colleagues at MIT
assumed robots had to be stable
but he watched a film of insects
tripping, colliding, dropping food—
making mistakes
so he built Gangus, an android
that behaved like an ant
scrambling, falling – rectifying errors

Tarantino too noticed something of this
reading Elmore Leonard's novels—
cops chase criminal, criminal hijacks car
car's a stickshift—
criminal can't drive stick
he said this ruined the genre-moment
a truth he always strove for

if you can recoup you can survive
(by either intellect or luck)
for the I-Ching says
that in moments of danger
the important thing is moving forward
but chance is indiscriminate
and genetic software in the long run
always trumps
the roulette wheel of fate

so Brooks began programming robots
with sequenced feedback loops
building complexity upon simpler forms
because evolution really only tinkers
developing cleverly
on that which came before

rarely producing the best design

the vertebrate eye being so flawed
that the retinal neurons face backward
as if we're looking into our brains
light toils through a confusion
of light-degrading capillaries
before it's even detected
then redirected through layers of retina
to the optic nerve where it's then sent back
and processed for inversion and blindspots—
a pinball machine of misengineering

in Pirsig's analogy of this evolution
with that of societies
neither is seamless
they advance in ratchetlike steps
lent from punctuated equilibrium
and these dynamic advances
need shielding static patterns—
vulnerable DNA, to survive and evolve
needs a protective shell of protein—
as an idea, to advance, needs a skull
or a book with a cover
sheltered by a library
defended by a weapons-bearing
organized society
analogous to the symbiotic relationship
between conservative and liberal
vital to the survival of any culture
for without dynamic quality
an organism or society will not grow
and without static quality
an organism or society cannot last

two pinecones spinning in tandem
is what a millwright saw in his mind
as he ground coffee one morning

so he carved his idea into cone-shaped bits
carried them into a Shreveport bar
and happened upon Howard Hughes Sr.
other riggers scoffed at the model
Hughes bought it – perfected it
and tore into oil deemed invulnerable
mutating the industrial age
lacta alea est
for genius – like evolution
really only trifles too
ever building upon prior forms, ideas
in science as well as art

when Hughes Jr. watched the first film
to win a Best Picture Oscar
he felt he could do better
and spent part of his father's fortune
making Hell's Angels
a film that would influence Kubrick
just as Lucas's cinematography
was conceived of Kubrick's work
but like crudely carved models of rotary-bits
a work of brilliance is rarely deemed such
upon its conception—
and when Lucas's friends screened *Star Wars*
everyone was speechless
aghast at how bad it was
except for Spielberg
who said it would triumph
(no one believed him)
too when Cézanne unveiled his paintings
people laughed
impressionism, rococo, baroque
all derogatory terms
like Indian names: Navajo, Apache, Sioux
names from the outside – derisory, insulting
but genius recognizes talent
and Hemingway said he wanted to write

like Cézanne painted
said a person could do this
if they lived right with their eyes
he wanted readers to live what he wrote
and some did
further tangling the cobwebs
of art and history
for in *For Whom the Bell Tolls*
Robert Jordon thought a single bridge
the point at which humanity might turn
and so too perhaps a book
for Engels deciphered the French economy
by reading Balzac's novels
and after Castro read Engels
he studied *For Whom the Bell Tolls*
and used what he'd learned
to fight Batista's troops in the Sierra Maestra—
and though its author called such civil war
the best war for writers
he also said Napoleon
taught Stendhal to write
Napoleon whose nephew
helped distend the walls of the Salon
allowing impressionism to prosper

dynamic ideas precede sudden change
(mutations for good or ill)
for an odd mistress is genius
bestowing her gifts
on angels and demons alike
but civilization and knowledge
make little progress outside conflict
and those who advance science, art, society
are, at the start, deemed criminal—
threats to the status quo
brilliance rendered too often extinct
(rather red queens or court jesters)
throughout history hung, burned, crucified

and so prone to self-destruction
brilliance sung in a fanatical key
the heartbreak of a suicidal Van Gogh
(hopeful monsters fighting in his soul)
and these fates of the brilliant
are analogous to the most able societies
where jevons effect and the diderot effect
bore south adjacent
in a deadly anthropogenic grinding
in vis est exordium quod terminus
cultures enacting the story of Cain
(Quinn said written from outside)
and when Cain confronts Abel
only transmutation or death result
as when the Tuppan Basse mutated
after Peter Carder washed ashore
a Tycho Monolith fallen from heaven—
invited to help them attack the Tapwees
he taught them to fashion battleshields
the result was a slaughter
changing the nature of Brazilian warfare
a single sprout from the seed of Europe
planted by Columbus
and during the festival of the god Lono—
James Cook sailed into Kealakekua Bay
and seeing the *Resolution*'s white sails
slapping across her spars
the astonished natives
enclosed the ship in adulation
thinking it Lono himself
come to bestow his blessings
(they were wrong)
and when Nicolas Roosevelt was a boy
fishing on Minetta Brook
he watched a millwheel churn the water
and wondered if it could push a boat—
decades later he steered the *New Orleans*
down the Mississippi

the Indians thought it a god to destroy them
(they were correct)
as with the fate of the Tuppan Basse
the leftover smears on Van Gogh's pipe
blue, green, and yellow
for Malthus said most seedlings
were not to grow to trees—
by the time Darwin arrived on the *Beagle*
the Spanish were exterminating them
and he thought to himself
that when races met
they acted like specie of animals
fighting, cannibalizing, trading diseases
but then came the more lethal struggle—
which ethnicity was better organized

then he voyaged to a place called Eden
islas encantadas 'the enchanted islands'
that in Spanish means not beautiful
but bewitched—
where an English governor
used tortoiseshells for flowerpots
and told him which island they'd come from
by looking at the edge of their shells—
a seed of knowledge to beget revolution

two such epiphanies I had
one, sitting on my grandfather's bed
looking out the window at birds
as he explained their songs as not music
but a series of warnings and threats—
I felt for days
that someone had kicked me
then – long after his death
I'd come home from work
and unlocking the door to that same room
I heard a thud and looked down—
a squirrel had fallen

it lay in the grass stunned, motionless
white belly toward the sky
then it shook, looked this way and that
flipped to its feet
and darted up the same tree—
I'd not known such mistakes to happen
but we don't learn so much
from those things we do correctly
so perhaps it's best we see poorly
through our misconstructed eyes—
for El Greco's work was astigmatic
and Van Gogh said he saw better squinting
seeing stars and sunflowers different
seeing wheatfields askew

Beyond the Dark River

there is family, near all of my father's
driving to watch him graduate basic
when hit by a semi
his mother and brother and sisters
a cousin and her daughter
and all the Viet Cong he took it out on
during two consecutive tours
but he didn't get the ones
who killed an uncle I was named after
shot down in an OH-58
and there was a cousin on either side
both men, both shotgun-suicides
one to the heart and one to the gut
and so many friends
cars, pills, ropes, needles, cancer
cyber-stalking former jobs
I Googled my old live-aboard
just to find I'd lost a divemaster
on Que Brada in Belize—
we dove that wall a hundred times
they never found the body
Scott shot his girl and was incinerated
after he'd hung himself in jail
and of cremation, there was that time
working refractory
when my foreman, who may too be gone
as when the rest of us wore respirators
he would sit on scaffolding
Marlboro dangling from his lips
as he jackhammered asbestos
and sucked in lungfuls of thick dust
and cigarette smoke—
crawled, trowel and mortar in hand
into an oven, as I leaned in
to hand him firebrick
over a grinning cadaver

the lips and nose having burnt away
before the wall collapsed—
and of crematoriums
there was that old lady I worked with
at the nursing home
maybe ninety, weighed as many pounds
as I had to lift her onto the toilet—
and I would roll-up her sleeve
as she jabbered in Yiddish or Polish
(I know not which)
and turn her thin arm, soft loose flesh
and stare at the blurred numbers
verdigris with age
Birkenau? Majdanek?
(again, I know not which)
found cold among her dolls—
so close she was
to being among the number-dead
sixteen million in WW I
sixty million in WW II
number-dead unlike history book dead
as history book dead have faces
like Jeremy Bentham's
(present but not voting)
at University College London
but I don't think the head he's fit to
is authentic
the original having outlined utilitarianism
broadened by John Stuart Mill
who talked of approaching happiness
sideways, like a crab
reminding me of my favorite Van Gogh
as I've so often felt like that crab
Van Gogh did too
so many artists do
and writers and writers and writers—
I once read more Americans
died in the Civil War

than in near all our other wars combined
and that more writers kill themselves
than in all the other arts combined
victims of a Faustian bargain—
Hemingway and Hunter Thompson
a gunshot to the head
being the last chopper out of Saigon—
Ross Lockridge Jr.
asphyxiating himself in his car
(over Hamilton Basso's review)
and now David Foster Wallace
hanging himself on his patio—
but Fors Fortuna doesn't always smile
and nature's author is chance, verba volant
scripta manent

Adrian Manning

Sunset At Montjamour

years spent in the
darkness
of a Norwegian attic
wrapped in sackcloth
the sunset at
Montmajour
abandoned to an
eternal night

the garrigue in
familiar strokes
the colour of life
and living
unconscious
agony

the ruins of the
abbey
see it there
a dark, dying tomb
clawing at the light

aloof and desperate
in the distance
wanting, waiting
to be whole
and needed
again

waiting to be found
and exposed
urgently
dreaming

of warmth
and salvation

dreaming
of days
of new
suns
of new
light

Cafe Terrace At Night

to dream

to be bathing
in illuminated
life

I'd count the angles
of the stars
the shape
of the banality
of the passing
endeavours

night lacking
blackness
green hues
and shadows
dancing

I'd sip
at the glass
of silence
and drink
down
experience

store it
for
times
ahead

When Van Gogh Went Mad

Gauguin saw
the flash of silver
before his eyes
the blade in
place of the brush
new strokes
on canvas air

but he didn't hear
the voices in his head
or feel the tearing
of flesh

or acknowledge the
gift of a package
to a prostitute
carefully wrapped

no, Gauguin
left, fled to Paris
with the sanity
of one
who didn't
want to offer
a second chance
to be saved
or destroyed

The Night Cafe

drunks and derelicts
grace the cafe
in the frozen
moment
prostitutes
file their nails
sipping on gin
behind the partly
drawn curtain
I think of
Bukowski
fifty years later
he would have
loved this place
as long as the
waiter brought
the damned drinks
and someone
roused long enough
for a fist fight
in the back alley

Dear Theo

"don't bother
with the money anymore
I think I've finally
done the thing
you remember the blade
the one I waved at Gauguin?
that only took a part of me
and the paint?
tasted bad but didn't do
the job
well I finally got hold
of a gun
put it at my chest and
pulled
a sharp pain and now
dull agony as I linger
but I think this is it
the end
so keep the money
buy yourself a drink
or a loose woman
I don't need it
anymore
yrs Vincent"

Vincent the First

Imagine the brother
had lived, not been
still born

the one they called
Vincent

would there have been
a painter
a crazed genius
a drinker
a wild man
on a suicide trip
so many works
left behind

or another minister
or art dealer
or dreamer of
dreams
that never lived
just like him

The Potato Eaters

a darkness of the heart
ugly crones and
peasant habits
small light
and flickering hope
something to eat
at least
to stave off the famine
of the blackened soul
there's no joy
in living
in starved dread
a darkness of the heart
a darkness in the soul
there's no joy
none at all

The Postman

caught off guard
it appears you disturbed
his thoughts
the eyes widening
awoken from thought
rudely it seems
there's drink in those eyes
or the madness
of the over trodden path
maybe its age
tired, weary legs
the long fingers
that have carried
the utterances of
others
with no knowledge
of the damage
done

Sunflowers

we could talk of
sunflowers
but enough has been
said
and sunflowers speak
volumes for
themselves
so all we could
say
would serve
no purpose
at all
than to highlight
our ignorance
of the
truth

Resting In The Hay

to rest
to sleep
to dream
under the blue of those skies
in the yellow of that
hay
the best blue
and yellow there is
to pull your hat
over your eyes
to bask in the warmth
of simple labour
and ignore the world
and it's madness
to rest, sleep, dream
such beauty
and peace
and to smell the hay
feel it on your skin
natural is all
all is as it should
be

Eve Brackenbury

A STUDY IN RETROSPECT

   Van Gogh had already been dead one-hundred years when I married a man who wooed me with stolen poetry. He'd done cartwheels at work after getting down my pants, and five months later, cried at the altar. I try to look at those four years with the insight of an art critic, seeking fellow-ship with the bright influence of avant-garde drinking buddies. I fail to see anything at all. I would rather have had his tattered ear as payment for services rendered. I didn't realize his poetry was stolen until years after I had taken up the habit. A curse of misery and poverty and unrequited lovers.

COMING TO BALTIMORE (with a nod to Van Gogh's *Starry Skies*)

Well you know I went to Baltimore
So confident and wise
And as I breathed she breathed no more
And she did surely die.
    ~Lyle Lovett "Baltimore"

The night was clear, the stars staring, and the moon yellow. I wondered why yellow and not white or orange? It was an ominous sign, telling me not to drink again tonight. Consequences had nothing to do with tonight. Tonight was just for feeling all those things that I hadn't felt in so long. Except for last night and every night since coming to Baltimore.

A NIGHT WITHOUT BLACK
(Inspired by Van Gogh's *Café Terrace at Night*)

Wandering through a foreign city, watching pigeons play hopscotch on cobblestone streets, I am embarrassed by the filth I wear. I walk slowly past a sidewalk café where a fastidious, aproned native shoos me from open tables. I want to join the birds and dance for a cup of black coffee. I want to chatter and coo for a hunk of white bread and tumbler of red wine. I want to alight upon this scene at night and peck at his eyes and soil his towel. I don't want to stand in some dreary line with my hand out or explain my misfortunes and swear I will do no harm.

IMMOTET: THE IMMORTAL FLOWER

My sisters flaunt their beauty, praying only
to be pollinated and then beheaded.
They prefer such a violent end.
to die, tired and forgotten, is a horrible fate.

I agree.

But, once I stop depending on the sun
and earth for sustenance, I realize I don't
have to die.

I can submit my soul to luminaries and poets
and let painters plunder my beauty.
I shall let them bury me in books,
pressed between pages.

My lovers will never forget me.

FINDING BEAUTIFUL

"Though we travel the world over to find the beautiful, we must carry it with us or we find it not." ~Ralph Waldo Emerson

I look and look
and look again
and still can't find beautiful.

You give me a beginner's paint set
and set me to coloring,
warning me to stay
in the lines or suffer
the consequences.

I slip and get a little
green in your eyes
and a little silver
in your hair.
I am inspired
and color me blue
and the night
dirty yellow.
You just laugh
and touch up
the stars
With turquoise.

DID ABSINTHE MAKE VAN GOGH'S MIND WANDER?

Woman, with her resolute rightness,
cannot bear to hear me sigh.
I pour another round of compliance.
Small measures of defiance.
Cheap shots, man.
Them and silence.

NO USE IN STAGING A PEASANT REVOLT

(inspired by Van Gogh's *Potato Eaters*)

"I prefer the fellowship of potato eaters," I said. And it was finally over. All her garish accessories and lipstick posturing. She was determined to be an art critic, and I suppose me, her prostitute. She wouldn't know a stiff dram of absinth from a frozen stick of cool-aid if she made it herself. I liked the dark side of Vincent, although I would never tell her. His light was her god, and my God was dead. So be it.

STILL LIFE

(inspired by Van Gogh's *Gypsy Encampment* and *Starry Skies*)

Walking through gallery corridors,
I notice the eyes of the dead
waiting to be forgotten.

You point to a gypsy encampment
and ask if the little boy in blue
ever gets tired of standing still.

Even the stars, long dead,
are tired of our gazing.
God, how I miss you.

IT WASN'T JUST A PLATE OF ONIONS

(inspired by Van Gogh's *Still Life With a Plate of Onions*)

A full pot of tea.
A good book and a pipe.
A post card from an old lover, post-dated a lifetime ago.
An empty bottle.

DUST TO DUST

My eyes are the color of my grandfather's
depression-era shot glass. My skin is as
white as his mother's might have been,
had she not been colored by sun and wind and dust.
My nails are a chipped devilish color, like the brandy
I sip from my grandmother's ruby red goblet.
My mascara runs, leaving behind incriminating residue,
as did the gunpowder on her father's hands.
My bosom nestles my fingers while I ponder,
just as did hers, when she told me not to wander.

Richard Wink

The Crows

(inspired by Wheatfield with Crows,1890)

Gluttonous, looming in the sky like lazy bats.
They are Europe's vultures,
only far more beautiful and sophisticated.
They land with an expectant hunger.

A dead Muntjac deer.
Bulldozed by a speeding lorry.
Its innards expelled.
The road is quiet and the Crows appear.

One pecks at the gore.
The others linger, no bird song, no communication.
They all know what to do,
yet none of them follow.

Roots

(inspired by Tree Roots, 1890)

Erupting from the soil, crooked gnarled roots.
The stumble causer
sending dog walkers
face planting into a mass of fallen leaves.

Moss covered, left for decades.
Vines weave over and above.
The shy fox eye's
a gathering of rotund woodpigeons and bland grey doves

Curry Night

(inspired by Bedroom in Arles, 1888)

Sitting on a sofa that's falling to pieces, listening to a podcast.
The podcasters talk about how they cleaned their tenant's brains off the wall.
He'd shot himself in the head after his significant other died of Lupus.
The curry sauce spits from the pan and hits the kitchen tiles.

My bedroom is my living room, bedsit misery.
I can't believe a couple of months ago that I had a woman back here
and when we screwed on the floor she asked –
"when was the last time that you cleaned your carpet?"

It's curry night and I've made enough basmati rice for a family of four.
The strong scent of tantalizing spices cause my nostrils to flare.
I sing to myself and mangle the lyrics.
Rejoice, rejoice it's curry night!
The delicious song of decimation and procrastination,
I open my mouth and sample temptation.

Glorious Crab'n

(inspired by Two Crabs 1889)

I always remember the car park that seemed to be 100 feet high, over-
looking
the water.
We'd drop orange lines down below to the scuttling crabs.
The bait would be looped. The claws would latch on.
Then we'd pull them up and chuck them in a plastic bucket.

Nightmares would shake me and lather me in sweat about that car park.
I'd imagine that I was trapped in a Volkswagen Golf,
handbrake off.
The car would roll and drop 100 feet down,
and sink.

I'd smash my small fists against the windscreen.
Salt water would spill in.
Drowning. Dead.
The crabs would pick at me.

Carcass

(Inspired by Lying Cow, 1883)

Caught in the field, three acres of stubble and rough.
A cow on the ground.
Father used to say this was a sign of rain.

Approach the beast,
see the steam rise from its nostrils.
It's alive, but why is it here and alone?

Scope the horizon, see no sign of cattle, no trail of its brethren.
Worry about its health.
Its eyes are close. It seems endangered.

Blue Joanna Bar & Kitchen

(inspired by Café Terrace at Night, 1888)

Sat outside, blonde fringe and Steve Zissou impersonator.
Hand rolled cigarettes filled with top quality baccy.
The couple look through me as I stand by the window
and take in the haunting glow of candlelight.
I hear the faint sound of bongos
and it takes us back to Marrakech.
You were there, I wasn't.
You are here. I'm not.
You're alive. I exist.
You're in the moment. I'm not present.

"Who's that guy over there?" says fringe.
Zissou looks.
I'm gone.

The Inventors House

(inspired by A Pair of Shoes, 1888)

We walk along the plank, which crosses a ditch.
Darkness makes me wonder how deep the fall is.
Once inside we dump our sleeping bags and rucksacks and shut the
door behind us.
Something's unusual about the place,
nobody's home, but a pair of shoes.
Brown brogues. a touch of understated class.
Inside there's a pipe on the table by the sofa.
Papers strewn on the table. Hastily drawn sketches.
This is a dead man's house,
yet there' still life, unmade bed, food in the fridge
and that pipe,
a smoky scent lingers around us.

I felt sorry

(inspired by Sorrow, 1882)

I brought along her watch. She left it behind a couple of days ago.
That night we screwed until empty.
Now we sit in an arty café forcing conversation.
There is something that isn't being said.
I can't interrogate her.
Instead we talk about chocolate brownies.

In the rain she tugs at my sleeve.
She tells me that her lips touched Jim's again.
My lips soured before trying to blow sympathy.
I whistled instead, turned on my heels
and walked off in the opposite direction.

Feet up on the table

(inspired by Crab on its Back, 1888)

They leave the room and I always wonder
where they retreat to.
The receptionist comes through and passes me a note.
The t's look like j's and I just about decipher the scrawl.
The message informs me she is sick and can't make it in.
I lie back and put my feet on the table.
There's an edginess, an hour to kill.

I pull on my coat and walk to the beach.
I pick up crab shells and seaweed.
I skim stones through the waves.
There is nobody around to hold my hand
as I communicate with Canute.

These evenings when I think about my death

(inspired by At Eternity's Gate, 1890)

Cherished by the mirror. A tear forms a lurid bead in the corner of his eye.
Heaven would be a soft hand on his shoulder.
The shove is in his head.
A spade lifts then drops the sand which dries his throat.
Mistakes are forged in spikes and plastic tokens.
His thoughts corrupt and melt away
 rationality.
The months ahead are cavernous.
The years are fantasy.

Remember to be sad.
Accept that in a fight, two might get battered and bruised,
one will go on to better things.
The other will get defeated by themselves.

Guinotte Wise

They're Still Stealing Van Goghs

While researching Nazi art thefts for a novel, *L.A. Hardscape*, I was brought up short by the audacity and sheer scope of the crime. I had seen *Monuments Men*, but that had seemed like an entertainment, an embellished tale based on fact, and it didn't really dilate my cortex like the tons of print that you can dig up on the thefts and I just scratched the surface. Hermann Goering's "collection" alone, amounted to almost 2,000 works of art when you count sculpture and tapestries along with the 1,400 paintings. And, like a true obsessive bureaucrat, he and his minions catalogued every single one. Including who they stole it from. These guys were nothing if not methodical. And it should be mentioned here that the entire amount of stolen art and artifacts is much greater than what adorned the walls of Carinhall, Goering's chalet. The Third Reich 's amassment of looted objects was in the hundreds of thousands and storage in salt mines, caves, warehouses and tunnels from 1933 to the end of the war are legend. A lifetime could be spent researching the thefts. Goering's collection alone has taken researchers years to trace. Efforts are ongoing.

I found myself looking up painting after painting and, being an artist myself, sighing over each and every one. This guy surrounded himself with beauty and splendor, the best of the best--I don't know what the metaphor is here; this truly evil ratbastard of sewer/vomit heart and mind making his grand chateau outside Berlin, Carinhall, the depository of the world's art genius. There is no metaphor so I won't struggle for one. Hitler's number two man was one hell of a collector, emphasis on hell.

I was wasting a lot of time looking at great paintings (Can that be time wasted? If you're trying to get a novel done, I suppose it could be.) many of which I'd glimpsed in art history courses in art school. My eyes were glazing over. Just one of these paintings could set me up in fast cars and tall cotton for the rest of my life.

At this point I was eyeing Van Gogh's *Bridge at Langlois in Arles*. And that's when I made the decision to follow the Nazi trail of theft through one artist, thus paring down the time spent and making the task less gargantuan. I looked up this painting and found that the bridge at Arles was the subject of four Van Gogh oil paintings, some watercolors and a series of drawings. All of these are just superb, as you would think. He was about thirty-five when he produced them in 1888 in Arles, France, where he lived at the time and where he enjoyed the height of his career and productivity. In less than fifteen months he produced more than 200 paintings.

The bridge reminded him of his homeland, the Netherlands, and he sent a framed version of it to an art dealer there. One of the 1888 versions was taken by Goering and it was one of his favorites. He stole Van Gogh's *Portrait of Doctor Gachet* as well, but ended up selling it in 1937. But not the bridge. That stayed at Carinhall. But where is it now? I lost the trail at Carinhall, though a book might provide some clues.

A 518 page book, "Beyond the Dreams of Avarice: The Hermann Goering Collection," published in 2009, could possibly shed some light on which bridge painting was in that collection, and also provide a trail of provenance, which in many cases is labyrinthine. The only information I could find on Van Gogh's *Portrait of Doctor Gachet* was that it had reportedly been sold. To whom, was not divulged. But another, third, *Portrait of Doctor Gachet*, of which only two were known, showed up in Greece in the inheritance of a struggling author, Doreta Peppas. It had been "liberated" by her late father in a Resistance attack on a Nazi train. They'd been after ammunition, but Peppas' father also made off with a crate of paintings. One of the paintings was the Van Gogh and other items included a notebook of his drawings. Nazi stamps on the backs of the items were validated as official, and the items themselves appear to be indisputably authentic. Why isn't Doreta rich? No one will touch the art, possibly because it may cast doubt on the authenticity of other Van Gogh paintings now hanging in galleries and private collections. It's a byzantine story but suffice to say she may be the richest poor struggling author in the history of literature, and by way of the Nazis, the art world. She remains penniless, and the art is in a temperature controlled vault which further drains her meager income.

The art trove is hers, having been traced as far back as possible, and no one has come forward to claim the pieces. Not the family from which they were stolen, or anyone else. It's quite possible the previous owners were the last of a family line and met their end at the hands of the Nazis. The crateful never reached its intended destination, where it would no doubt have been catalogued.

The notebook alone is probably worth $3.5 million and a respected authority said he believes it to be Van Gogh's student workbook from the Royal Academy of Art in Brussels. The age and the paper have been confirmed in separate tests. Other tests and samplings have further cor-roborated the pieces as genuine. The Van Gogh Museum offered to au-thenticate the Gachet painting but a contract they sent stated they would keep it forever. For free. Meanwhile Ms. Peppas has lost her home due to search, storage and authentication costs. The Nazis, it appears, have left their mark, and curse, on Van Gogh and the world's fine art market once again.

The total estimated worth of her crate of stolen Nazi art, which includes a Cezanne nude, is over $100 million. Conspiracy theorists are blaming a bullying art cartel for refusing to legitimize the find until they can get their hands on it some other way. I don't know who is to blame in such a bizarre situation, but it does irk me that the art isn't shared with the world. Isn't that the point of great art? It's almost a sure thing that the art is real--none of the tests would seem to indicate otherwise. Begs the question WTF?

Anyway, the trail ran cold on Nazi looted Van Goghs. But mysteries abound and who doesn't love those? Especially mystery writers. (litera-ture seems to be intertwined in this stolen art business) Bestseller Lynne Kennedy (*The Triangle Murders, Time Exposure, Pure Lies*) came upon just such a mystery while researching *Deadly Provenance*, a novel of deception involving a Nazi looted Van Gogh oil titled *Still Life: Vase with Oleanders*. Who better to pursue it? The Brooklyn-born author worked with the San Diego Sheriff's Department and SDPD Crime Lab in forming forensic studies for teachers and students. In adding authenticity to her books she worked with museum and historical experts as well as crime-solving officials at a time when the CSI tv shows were becoming popular. Great credentials for investigating a lost Van Gogh. While she solved the case in her novel, the painting remains missing in real life, and Kennedy herself is still on the case. If anyone has any leads they are encouraged to con-tact her; a good start is her website, lynnekennedymysteries.com There, you'll find fascinating links to interviews and progress notes.

The painting, also known as *Vase on Yellow Background*, was one of thirty or so that had been at the Bernheim-Jeune gallery in Paris. Suspect-ing an imminent Nazi raid in 1940 the owners packed them off to Cha-teau de Rastignac near Bordeaux. In 1941 the Nazis tracked them there, looted as much as they could, and burned the chateau to the ground. The paintings, including the Van Gogh, have not been seen since. And Lynne Kennedy has unearthed some very interesting information in her search, having contacted people and museums who are close to the source.

Nazis weren't the only thieves interested in Van Gogh paintings. Two of his paintings were stolen in 2002 from the Van Gogh Museum in Amsterdam, a seascape and a painting of a church in Neunen where his father had been pastor. The burglars climbed to the roof using a ladder, broke through a window and exited out the side of the building using a rope. The theft seems like the stuff of movies. During an investigation of the Camorra Mafia family in Italy, the oils were recovered in 2016.

At the time of the crime, the paintings were worth about $4.5 million. Works by Van Gogh have sold for up to $82.5 million at auction, but the stolen works were from his Hague period, and of a style that sell for a good deal less.

Another vase-and-flowers Van Gogh oil *Poppy Flowers*, was stolen in 2010 from Mohammed Mahmoud Khalil Museum in Cairo. Its value is around $50 million and one can imagine a white-suited, red-fezzed Sydney Greenstreet bargaining with Humphrey Bogart for its return. Egyptian officials believed they had caught the perps of the painting pilferage, arresting two Italian suspects attempting to board a plane at Cairo International Airport. No deal. It's still among the missing Van Goghs. It had been stolen previously in 1977 from the same museum and recovered ten years later in Kuwait. If you see a small painting of a bunch of yellow flowers and a couple of red ones in a vase, give the museum a call.

If you have a Van Gogh or two, you might want to beef up your ADT alarm system with some of those impenetrable lazer-lined security mazes that only George Clooney could negotiate. Or was that Cary Grant? In one of my books, *Ruined Days*, a New Orleans art gallery uses holograpic images for its most expensive sculptures. A Degas ballerina revolves under a light, for all intents and purposes a solid bronze figurine, until someone reaches for it and touches only air. As the gallery owner explains to the main character in the story, "Some collectors prefer to have the original in a vault somewhere. We make these up for them so they can appreciate the piece with no reservations about it being damaged or stolen."

Perhaps in the future, Van Goghs, Titians, Klimts and Caravaggios will be exquisitely projected images. Once the lights go out in the museum or gallery, so do the paintings. You're still in the presence of genius, once removed. And you're not supposed to touch the works anyway. Sort of like zoos of the future; holographic images, and if your kid jumps into the gorilla cage they won't have to shoot anything. That, to me, is preferable to jailed animals. But hey, that's me.

Back to Van Gogh, Nazi loot, and paintings of questionable authenticity that continue to surface. This one, signed Vincent, was purchased for a few hundred guilders in the Dutch city of Breda around the time WWII began. A still life featuring an open bible, clay pipe, and some other items such as a bottle, and a drape of some kind behind, is primarily monochromatic yellow ochres and greens. The owners, Catherine and Malcolm Head from Guildford, believe it to have been painted at the parsonage in Neunen, where Van Gogh lived between 1883 and 1885. They've spent a great deal of money on age testing and other samplings which do corroborate the time, if not the artist. But the Van Gogh Museum dismisses the painting as a fake, citing stylistic differences.

They stated that it is more likely the oil was by the lesser-known female Dutch artist, Willemina Vincent. Hence the signing "Vincent" in the lower corner. Although, to me, it looks like Van Gogh's signature style, but it is slanted uphill. As art restorer Robert Mitchell says, "It could well be a genuine painting by Vincent Van Gogh but everyone in the art world will say no before they say yes." That one's been around since 1997 and shows no sign of conclusion.

In the "You just never know" department, Van Gogh's *Portrait of Doctor Rey*, which now hangs in the Pushkin Museum of Fine Arts, Russia, has an interesting backstory. It was once used to plug a hole in a chicken coop. Dr. Rey worked on Van Gogh after the legendary ear incident, and to show his gratitude, Van Gogh painted his portrait. Rey never liked it much, as evidenced by its disposition as chicken house insulation. I wonder if whoever found that painting had any problem making people believe it was genuine. "I was tearing down an old chicken coop and there was a Van Gogh on the wall inside. Yeah, I think it's real, don't you?"

By the way, that ear thing? Nobody cuts off their own ear, even if severely depressed. Or, as some have said, suffering from the tormenting tintinnabulation of tinnitus. There are much easier forms of self mutilation. A new German book, *Pakt des Schweigens (Pact of Silence)* contends that he made up the story to protect his friend Gaugin, who, perhaps unintentionally, whacked off the ear with his sword during a contentious argument in the dark. Gauguin was a fencer, and he could have been protecting himself. The authors, Hans Kaufmann and Rita Wildegans, believe that the two artists had a hellacious fight because Van Gogh was upset that Paul was leaving, going back to Paris. It was common knowledge that Van Gogh was infatuated with him. At any rate once the shit hit the fan and the ear hit the floor, the two made a hasty pact to keep mum, Gaugin, to avoid jail time, and Van Gogh, to keep the friendship from disintegrating further. The incident took place near a brothel, and Van Gogh wrapped the ear in cloth, presenting it to a prostitute, who passed out when she realized what it was. Van Gogh went home and passed out as well. He would probably have bled to death had not the prostitute alerted police, who found him in his blood-soaked bed. They took him to a nearby hospital where he asked to see his pal, Gaugin. But Gaugin refused to visit him, left that day, and they never set eyes or ears on one another again.

Van Gogh wrote to Gaugin saying, "I will keep quiet about this and so will you." Some years later Gaugin wrote to another friend that Van Gogh was "A man with sealed lips. I cannot complain about him." Van Gogh's brother Theo also had some knowledge of the night that hints at circumstances other than self harm.

It all took place in Arles in 1888, no doubt interrupting Van Gogh's supremely prolific period during which the bridge paintings and drawings and hundreds of other works had been produced. The Nazi highjacking of *Bridge at Langlois in Arles* took place years later, and its whereabouts are still somewhat clouded. No one has heard anything about the ear, though it was supposed to have been kept in a jar of preservative. One hopes Dr. Rey didn't dispose of it in the chickenyard. What was it with that guy, anyway?

It wasn't long after the hearing loss that Van Gogh died in the arms of his brother, July 29, 1890. He was only 37. And even his death has an ear, I mean air, of mystery about it. Anyone with his roller coaster ups and downs would have been diagnosed as manic-depressive or possibly bipolar these days, and medicine might have smoothed it out some, extending his years of incredible creative genius.

His death: no suicide note, but days before, an ebullient letter to Theo. And he had just ordered supplies and paints. Mood wise, he was on an upswing, if anything. And the fact he'd been shot in the stomach is another question mark. Grossly evident powder burns from the sooty gunpowder of the day were missing indicating the weapon was fired from a distance. The position of the wound would have been extremely difficult for Van Gogh to accomplish, especially with his right hand--and he was right handed. Plus he had been receiving accolades and painting busily, even after the loss of his ear.

It should come as no great surprise that a bioengineered replica of Van Gogh's ear enjoyed a New York debut in 2015. Titled *Sugarbabe*, the auditory oddity actually contains natural DNA from Van Gogh and a direct male descendant. It was displayed at Ronald Feldman Fine Arts. The genetic donor was Liewe van Gogh, Theo's great-great grandson. Created ("It's alive. And it hears...") by Diemut Striebe, it employs a computer processor which stimulates nerve pulses allegedly allowing it to hear. One wonders if it was embarrassed at the opening. Some gallerista having imbibed too much free wine can be imagined to say "Ears to you, Vincent." or "Anybody got a Q-Tip?" or maybe whispering sexual innuendos into it.

Some words of advice: if it needs cleaning don't stick anything sharp in it. Or around it. And guard it carefully. If they're out there plotting to steal Van Gogh paintings, they'd sure as hell want his ear. Or a close relative.

While the Van Gogh Museum may not be interested in *Sugarbabe*, and often declines to accept surfacing paintings as authentic, they do, through diligent research, welcome the ones they deem worthy. *Sunset at Montmajour* is such a painting and it's not even signed. Inventoried in the collection of Theo van Gogh it was sold in 1901.

No record of it existed until a Norwegian industrialist bought it and displayed it in his home. Advised that it was not a Van Gogh, he stored it in the attic. In the 1990s the Van Gogh Museum dismissed it because it was unsigned. "Hey, not so fast," someone said. In 2011 they started a two-year investigation. Exhaustive tests and a letter of provenance from Vincent to Theo resulted in a 2013 unveiling and hanging of the oil in the museum.

Meanwhile they're still plotting thefts out there. And fakery abounds. But I just saw one on eBay. "Vincent Van Gogh Painting. Bearing "VINCENT" Signature at bottom left. This piece appears to be in decent good condition and will be sold 'as is.'". Hmm, where's the phone number of the Van Gogh Museum? This might be the break I've been looking for.

Chigger Matthews

Holier than thou

In Borinage
After giving his baker-street blessing to the poor,
Vincent slept on straw-mats following
Christ's advice to the rich man.

"Vinny," said the church:
"Don't you know it's just a metaphor?
We're going to have to let you go:
You are too damn good
And you make us look bad."

So Vincent walked to Brussels,
Holier than the shoes
That kicked him out;
Holier than the shoes
On his feet;
Touched in his mind
By God.

The Kee to Van Gogh's Heart

How could anyone be surprised when
He said, "I love you!" And
"Let's make a life together-
Marry me!"

Nooit.
Neen.
Nimmer.

Could it have been more apparent
Or cruel? For the man of actual romance
No dramatic gesture is sweeping enough:
"Let me see her for as long as I can!"
Said he of the Kee to his heart.

This passion
Nearly burned a hole in his hand.

Vincent Reborn

Nowadays Vincent Van Gogh moonlights
As a prison guard, the captain no less.

He writes poetry about all the women
He ever loved (and some of those he didn't);
How the bathroom mirror reflects
On an unlovely honesty: liquor,
Cigarettes, and loneliness
In still life.

Nowadays Vincent Van Gogh loves
God in the starry night of his children's eyes and
When he brings pie to us potato-eaters who
Love him not because he's created
Beautiful works of art
But because he is himself
A beautiful work of art.

The Ear-thing

Why is everyone always on about
The Ear-thing?

If they don't think I can hear them
Whispering about me,
Kindly inform them
I can.

Oil and Water-color

Vincent caught gonorrhea
From street-walkers he hired
As models for his art.

The elites
Looked down on
The pedestrian and,
As Vincent was
Well-known for walking,
He suffered that stigma too.

Around this time
He switched from water-colors
To oil paints.

Years later,
The world is glad
He took the high road.

My Brother's Keeper

Dear Vincent:

You are my brother,
A fact of which I must constantly remind myself.
You test my patience as if
It had no end.
How have I failed you?
You are a burden I will love
Until the end of my days.
I know you are unlikely to heed my
Advice, but please consider it:
Be good to yourself.

Theo

Lunatic

Fear, sadness, and confusion:
The unholy trinity of a godless sanatorium and
"Why can't I sell my paintings?"

Like the self-effacing moon,
My lunacy,
Sometimes shining brightly,
Waxing, or
Else, waning,
Not at all.

It is a cycle that my brush
Cannot encompass.

Vindication, or Sunflowers

$39,900,000 (U.S.)
Now the world appreciates your mad genius
But first
You had to die.

The Cafe

The Cafe is a place
Where anything can happen:
Coffee,
Wine,
Or maybe just some
People drinking
Sex and violence.

This, That, and the Gauguin

You don't know a thing,
Gauguin.

The sun gives its life to the world
And the world with everything in it
Gives this life back. That is the
Beating heart of earthly art. Don't you
Know this is God?

Bob Holman

Van Gogh's Violin

GOOD

Good morning, Vincent
It is early December, 1889
Time to get up and paint
"Wheat Field with Rising Sun"
Hurry before the firmament
Starts to fall apart again
Right now it's all singing
"Good morning, Vincent!"

YES YET

This remarkable day
Goes between
Because I paint it
With me in it

PERFECTLY GREAT

It would be great
To eat an apple
But there in the tree
It is perfect

PARTICLE BEARD

Flesh covers face
Wheat covers field

CLOSE-UP

My nose sticks out
  A doorknob

As my poor ear grows
Like a worm back to my head

A crack, that is my brow
And yesterday is my lips
And my teeth are rocks
   I walk on

MISANTHROPE, OR...

Shy of people
Friend to star in sky
Where am I?
In a park watching children
Play without thinking

PAINT TONGUE

I cannot stop
To think

DETAIL

Black bites deeper
Spitting red beside the bed
Struggling through deep forest
Limb line limn time
It's all detail! Everything!

HEIGHTENED WITH WHITE CHALK

Running chalk over my lips
Ecstasy directly transmitted
To grass blade after blade

INTERRUPT DREAM

All joy of LIFE flashes
Blinding revelation green

Simply morning, all the
Racket, all the LANGUAGE
Broken dream pours in
Nothing holds blue
Corners of REALITY
As I reach out, brush
One more tree in the garden
Under the masterful sun

IT'S IMPORTANT

To put up with everything
As you get it down on canvas

LAST PASS

Plow down the sun
Second wind, Old Bay
Last pass on this acre
Go home, go home
Wait -- gold. More gold!

POTATO IN SKY

The back of the shed
Needs painting
What next!

PLYING MY TRADE

If I sit here long enough
Maybe I'll figure out what it is

SHEAVES OF WHEAT

There is no stopping now
What I want is everything
And everything is arriving
At once to me

LIFE

Blend foreground
     in background
Temperance in the midst
     of ecstasy
Ha. Lalala. Fill up
Holes with death

VIOLIN

Write everything down
Throw everything away

SUNSET

This morning I raised my eye
And saw the stars
Had not moved
Sweet Death, my Love,
I will never lose you again

IMPRESSIONS

Deep in paper a line:
Push me over, artist
Clamber aboard train
Of Thought and Nonthought
Just look at it! He squealed
A ton of cake and on the walls
"Gentle Persuasion" for all
To see giving the Impression that

AN ARTIST

As he stands there
Looking at me
I think about him
Looking at me
Until I Stop

He does not
He paints on
I think on
Clearing my throat I ask
How is it going
He does not respond

I read his hands
The sounds they make
Red yellow blue green
My face my face

VAN GOGH'S HARMONY

In a boat
We take a bath
A trail of clouds
In trousers

THE BAR

The mirror is
More like it

THE BALL

We are having one

APRIL MOON

Only it is 2:29PM
In August
And all is well

WELL AMONG DUNES

Don't whatever
You do look down!
You will see
Me looking up

Pail hits head ouch
Sand trickles from
Your squeezing instep
Only you and water
Makes two
Me and you

WHAT SKY?

Look! Look!
The sky gets in here
Keep looking!
Or it will stop. Look!

SIGNATURE GESTURE

Old Van Gogh signed his name
Quel horreur gesticulated
A bank clerk madly twirling
His pencil balance on his nose
The elbow is a lump of shape!

BEFORE THE MIRROR

Behind his back
There is no me
Wrapped in gold brocade

UPHILL

Death what else
Whatever else
Inconveniently located
Cemetery bottom of hill

REREADING

That water, in your painting,
From the well, on top of the hill

VAN GOGH IN VENICE

Blue pants unbuckled
Pour toi, ma Canale Grande!
Thwack thwack
The sound of the brush
On the rolling gondola

THEY ARE OFF

How fast can you see how fast
He painted the speed of the horse
Gallop on, my Love
A hoof on the brush in your eye

MOSS ROSE

Hand-worked fluff
Into the table gray
Death's pink face
Mirror today

AS I WAS SAYING

Vincent was painting
Vivid wind

NOT INDICATE

Flying flow floats free
Paint not anything only
Canvas night Saint-Paul-de-Mausole

FLEET

Easel down
Canvas up
Paint on

Take pee
While stroking
Sun onto beach
Drink beer
Blue umbrella
Salami white chair
Home done
Almost a black line

IT'S A BIG MOUNTAIN

A little village
A swell bay
A dirt road
Flowers trees

OCCASIONAL SPONATEITY

Like now

B HORIZON

Swam near Arles
Today and went deep
Into what I thought
Was the sea
It was when
I looked up
You were looking
Down at me
Framed perfectly
By the sun

WAVER

Stop me!
Trees are not red!
It is a cry for help

HER PIPE

She'd smoke it
When no one watched

IMPOSSIBLE CATCH

Clasina Maria Hoornik sits by the jetty
Nothing else does
Nothing else abandons gesture
She does

CRAZY HOLLYHOCKS

They go insane!
And jump in
The painting
Is water too

HANGING THE LAUNDRY OUT TO DRY

Waiting for rain

ROOSTER

Egg balance
On my head

WOULDN'T YOU KNOW

Pissarro got lost
Painted his way out
Where are you

BYROAD

Met you by the byroad
Have a word or three

Keep walking orange
Keep riding blue

VINCENT OR THE BATH

Lean over a little further
Vincent or I'll get splashed

AT HOME WITH VINCENT

Your song swells
Makes trees lift off
Dancing roots tickle
My skin and the wind

OUT OF SHOES

Into bed

JUST THINK

A crab on its back
Can teach you to fly

Robert Lee Kendrick

Cateechee Blue Yodel 1

the devil took me out into a wheat field
said god told him I should be a priest
said salvation waits for you in blue and gold and green
but first you'll have to take a walk with me

the devil took me up into a windmill
said blessed be my children of the soil
they'll dig until their hands are split and kill for the cold crop
you'll taste their salt hearts if you walk with me

the devil took me deep inside a coal mine
said breathe my earth's black kiss into your chest
you'll spite your dark dust skin and curse your birth with every step
for bread and bed you'll take that walk with me

the devil took me to a brothel by a river
said here you'll meet a woman with my eyes
you'll be the bastard at her breast your soiled seed will stop her breath
your canker heart will burn now walk with me

the devil took me to a mirrored garden
said introduce me to each gentleman you see
the bearded gutter diplomat the beggar in the black felt hat
the bandaged one will walk closest to me

the devil took me out into the moonlight
spun each star like a bullet in a gun
said you'll find the one to light your rest and take its fire into your chest
you'll bleed that nightglow if you walk with me

the devil took me up upon a mountain
said look over the valley and the sea
your eye will have its empire and your name its blue demesne
if that's worth what I ask of you then walk with me

Cateechee Blue Yodel Number 3

Wet with moon glisten, Night
pulls a wrench from her hip pocket,

checks for daylight sneaking
over her shoulder, ready

to knock it back east.
Her pit bull wind raises his hackles,

shoves snout to ground, trench knife
tongue whetted for meat. The creek

wraps its moon gash in moss,
slips between stones to die in the lake.

Seven times seven years back,
I was born on a blood star,

damn near killed my mother.
Daughters I never fathered

dance around logs, cast possum
bones into fire pits, keep the omens

to themselves. With razor and hook
I come to pull spawn from stream belly.

When I strew carp gut runes through mud,
the creek suckles on my curses and spells.

It will take anything to its lips.

Cateechee Blue Yodel Number 5

White whips hang from tree limbs,
snap collapsed veins. Too many hits

to the mainline, needle fine
splinters strewn over ice.

Dusk spits hooks from its mouth.
My pig bone necklace clinks

over my heart, slaughterhouse
shape notes of nothing foretold.

Seven times seven times
spit on my grave that hasn't been dug,

I swore on goat blood
and the King James Bible

I stole from my mother
that I'd gut the moon

for taking the panther eye
face mask I see through in sleep.

He can run to the other side
of the world, but he can't hide

from me. The creek covers
her children under her skirt.

Coyote howls *best not let
the boys in*. He knows this snow

will glow like fresh coals tonight.

Cateechee Blue Yodel Number 7

after Catfish McDaris

she rode down from the Blue Ridge on a panther
dipped ditch weed laced with glue and gasoline

kicked in the door at Bob's Road Kill Grill
Coyote Zeppelin howling on the stage

she snarled for double shot of brimstone
copperhead chaser and a line of salt

barkeep swung a King James Bible like a hatchet
said "In the names of God and Moses I rebuke thee

get thee to the flaming bottom
of thine subterranean lake"

she threw her panther on the bar
the cat whipped out his knife and Colt

she said "he doesn't like the way you speak"
"bring me nectar of the rattlesnake

with black-tooth lightning of the bear
or I don't know what sweets my friend will take of thee"

I was easing to the door when her red eye fell on me
she let her panther dance behind the bar

she caught me with a bull whip round the ankles
rolled me in a choke hold out the door

I kicked and bit and clawed and spit
she wrapped her big legs round my hips

I yanked her black hair in my fists
she stabbed and stroked her cold tongue on my neck

we threw each other in a smoking river
we scared the moon and stars out of the sky

the eagle tore his crown and crest
the oaks and beeches ripped their breasts

the mountains clenched their teeth
and our beast took its first breath

Cateechee Blue Yodel Number 9

moon tries to gnaw itself free with its rusty hacksaw teeth
river boulders crawl for cover on the bank
dirt hides its face with vines and howls a blue note through the trees
red eye woman's coming down the hill for me

she wears a bear tongue necklace and a boar tusk in her cheek
she wrote my name in snake bites on her leg
she took one of my ribs and washed the wound with kerosene
red eye woman's coming down the hill for me

I offered her a headless blacksnake on an oak stump by the creek
I burned her sign with lightning on my chest
I laid out a barbed wire bed and hung a hog skull canopy
red eye woman's coming down the hill for me

seven times seven times she hooked her big legs round my spine
we chained each other to a flaming sea
seven times seven times I've drunk cold ashes since that night
red eye woman come on down the hill for me
red eye woman come on down the hill for me

Cateechee Blue Yodel Number 11

got two brimstone bloodhounds
howling thunder on my trail
blackjack paws shaking mountain earth and sky

got a fist full of moonlight
got a possum skull and spine
to whip slits in the wind where I can hide

red eye woman left me bleeding
in the dry creek bed
my bones still rattle from her shotgun kiss

her napalm falcon
slashes gashes through the valley
molten serpents rise behind me in the mist

she calls trees to bar the forest
she calls hills to rise from creeks
she calls seas of crows to drown the light

seven chupacabra angels
seven dead skin walking priests
swear they'll guide me through this iron night

deep in a sunless hollow
there's a roofless cinder shack
poppy blanket and creek stone for my head

thirteen jawbone heralds
guard the front door
thirteen spear-tongued king snakes guard my bed

dawn stabs rose-tipped daggers
through the crow tide
cuts a razor halo path to the shack

I slash my feet on brambles
I score my skin on rocks
red eye woman's hounds are at my back

if I get out of her forest
if I get off of her ridge
if I can shake her hell hounds at the stream

I'll scatter bone dust at my door
I'll carve hoodoos on my legs
I'll roll and tumble when she tastes my veins in dreams

Cateechee Blue Yodel Number 13

Over my shack's missing roof, arthritic branches
stroke blue dark. Morning stars bore exit holes,

yellow snakes in a hurry to eat their own tails
before rose starts a creeping barrage.

On the next hill, a silent steeple, top heavy
with its sliced tongue bell. On the church step,

the pastor slumps with his head in his hands,
as he has all night. The wind's blue yodel

through the valley. When the sun sows
shards over the river, red-eye woman will know

undertows again. When the moon pierces
water with its teeth, she will leave the deep channel,

call me from the woods, as she does each night.
Dawn fingers my cinder block walls.

No bread or cigarettes.
No money, but I will go down to the village.

Where girls in yellow dresses turn sunflowers,
show me their backs. Where widows shut their windows.

Where butchers sharpen knifes in time with my steps.
Where the brothel madam shows me her missing tooth,

fine bones under her skin. Where a mother's
arms flush as she gathers her children.

Where dogs refuse alms.
Where the thief knows

I am a useful distraction.
Where a father's curse finds a wooden bowl.

Where the alcoholic sleeps behind tavern,
wraps his great coat over rats as he sleeps.

Where the sheriff shows me his revolver by the gate.
Where the doctor waits to make the long walk to my shack,

say there's nothing he can do,
clear his throat and turn straight back.

Neil Ellman

The Potato Eaters

(oil, 1885)

We who eat potatoes
know the taste of the earth
as it stains our faces
and our tongues
as if we were grown together
from a common root
dependent on each other
for sustenance and life
ploughman and plowed
tiller and tilled
with dirt on our souls
till death do us part.

Bedroom in Arles

(oil, 1885)

There are no visitors
to this simple room
with yellow chairs and bed
where I can hide
beneath the sheets
undiscovered and alone
like a child
hiding from the stars outside
and demons from within.

It is where I go
to be apart from the easel
and the brush
and to contemplate
the beauty in the weave
and rush of paint.

Self-Portrait with Bandaged Ear

(oil, 1888)

When the deed was done
I could no longer hear my art
the sound of oils
moving like rivers across
a barren land
of paint drying
under an obdurate sun--
the price I paid
and must endure
to live in the silence
of my art
with little left
but my visions in a dream.

Entrance to a Quarry

(oil, 1889)

How many others
have walked the path
(overgrown, seemingly
impassable)
between reality
and the hollows
of a nether world
of quarried stone?

I am not the first,
perhaps, nor last
but I am drawn
to darkness
like a bat
in an infernal cave
as a brother of the night.

The Starry Night

(oil, 1889)

The stars are at war.

They explode like artillery shells
in a battle for the night
and the reality I seek.

When the sun goes down
and the clouds have cleared
it happens again and again
in a never-ending fight
for inches of mind and sky
above a village
of people I barely know
waiting for the peace
that will come
again and again
with the rising sun.

Irises

(oil, 1889)

It is how children play
with the wind
in their ears
telling secrets to the sky
and the sky repeating
its answer
as blue fleur-de-lis
that cover the fields
in spring with new life.

The Church at Auvers

(oil, 1890)

What is it about the old church
on the edge of day
that beckons me
to another time—
its windows like my mother's
suffocating eyes
its steeple rising
like my father's arms
in brutal indifference
to my soul?

There against a cobalt sky
I learned of piety
but here in the hallowed fields
I learned of passion and of art
here where I
was truly born.

The Langlois Bridge at Arles

(oil, 1888)

To the travelers, farmers
and artisans
who cross the bridge at Arles
from their world to another
speaking a different tongue
from another point of view
it must feel as if they are lost
without a nation to call their own
with little purpose
other than to cross alone on feet
that touch the wooden boards
that sound the uncertainty
of their lives.

Sunflowers

(oil, 1887)

I

To paint a bowl
of sunflowers
is to capture the sun
like a firefly
in a transparent jar
and watch it live and die.

II

Moonflowers listen
for direction
in the darkness
of their night;
sunflowers speak
with the eloquence
of a star.

III

The sun gives back
the praise we give
the prayers we make
as flowers in a bowl
reaching for the sky.

Self Portrait with Pipe and Straw Hat

(oil, 1888)

I have portrayed myself so many times
I cannot choose the one I am
or wish I were

a simple peasant on a farm
lit by the noon-day sun
a farmer in a field of straw

with a hat composed of light
who smokes a corn-cob pipe
to pacify my inner demons

and become the man I wish to be
an artist of myself
who knows the likeness of my soul.

Victor Clevenger

Love

is a wildflower
growing mad

all over the hillsides
of every man's soul.

Sorrow

"have you ever wanted to kill yourself, kill yourself because of a girl?"

"sure, i have considered suicide before. hell, homicides before too; at my age a man has been around long enough to have seen, or read several instances of both. it in a way gives a man many options, so many options that he becomes indecisive, unless of course, he is just impulsively crazy in his head, or crazy in his heart."

A Noose of Fingertips

close to meeting death last night,
tobacco pipe pressed against lips,
as he tried to strangle himself
repeatedly with his own two hands

a few times, he had a pretty good grip
on himself & he squeezed hard
until he started to see streaks of colors
jumping through his eyelids

when the colors jumped, he would try
to squeeze even harder, but each time
he squeezed harder his ears would pop
& he would fall down to the floor.

he gave up on trying & cried tears
that were thicker & harder than rock salt;
when he woke the next morning,
he had a headache, & he asked god
to give him strength.

he swears that god laughed out loud.

Van Gogh Pie

"what did you expect, vincent?"

"i expected to die."

"to die? but you're still young, vincent, your guts are still pie filling."

"pie filling?"

"yes, pie filling, & your skin & bones are sugar & flour."

"sir, my brain?"

"your brain is the hot oven that will complete the treat that the world will devour. tomorrow, after coffee, let's paint the ships that spread the ocean's legs."

"forget tomorrow, sir, let's paint them today."

Days In The Hague

"does romance last?" she asked.

"i allowed romance to splatter my brains
like a bug on the wall, it was wonderful,
the colors smudged black like a coal miners
fingerprints on the back of his poor lover after
an embrace."

"you've gone mad, my sir vincent."

"no sien, i haven't, not yet anyway."

Absinthe O' Blue

the sky is a glum color
of battered reality.

dreams, oh beautiful dreams
turn to nightmares,

as the prostitute puts on her shoes
& returns to the streets
you could never pave in gold
for her.

Bonded

"i don't feel well this morning, my love,
i fear that the sickness has taken my blood
hostage; it feels much like the prick of a needle
to a finger missing a thimble.

"oh, vincent, it is okay, i have a sickness too,
together, it will be like a loving bond
between us."

"yes, yes, i guess so, how late will you be
working tonight, sien?"

"the butcher has asked that i sew some
fabric into a new dress for his wife, so
it will be after night falls, but he has offered
some stew meat as payment."

"that's fine, but remember that you have
promised to let me sketch you, & i want to
capture your pure flesh, & all the marks
you may bear. it will also be a loving bond
between us, just slightly less painful."

Turpentine

you need no ears to hear what is
being spoken inside your own head,

something isn't right though,
the straight lines are stale & fatty

sticks & stems must have bends
to dance in the hospital garden,

bristles & lips are now soaked,
& dr. rey looks on from a distance

knowing that there is pure brilliance
within the man who wears the bloody
bandages.

Admittance

"go to the end of this hallway & then turn right, once you turn right,the waiting room is three doors down. good luck, sir," she said. following her guidance, he ended up walking into a small room that was filled with several wooden chairs which looked as if they had been built for small sized children; there were five people already sitting in the room & all their butt cheeks hung over the edges of the chairs— he picked a chair that sat in the west corner of the room, his butt cheeks drooped sorely for thirty minutes as he sat there waiting, watching people enter & exit the room. "i'm here to see my son, ten years ago, i was a patient for two weeks in this very facility," said one of the men who was sitting in the room, "i tried to kill my father with arsenic & when he didn't die, i minced my wrists up with an old straight-edged screwdriver. my father slapped me in the ear for trying to kill him & my mother admitted me here for help." "i tried to kill my father too, & i'm here to see my mother," said a woman; the man & the woman started their own conversation while everyone else sat quiet. a woman walked into the room, but she didn't sit down, she walked around for a moment & then said, "vincent?"

"yes, ma'am," he replied.

Fame Is A Hat He Never Wore

it took the death of a newborn
& a year for vincent to appear,

thirty-seven years, a bullet,
& two days to make him a ghost

that now walks tall through each
& every stroke he has ever cast.

Lisa Stice

The Yellow House

where I slept—
restless in a starry night

where I sat—
at the window
one shutter closed
to hide while I watch
the coming and going

where I ate—
meals in solitary
or did not eat
and let the food
grow cold as
the people outside

Wheatfield with Crows

the birds are hungry
steal from golden fields
gold before the reaping

and here am I, hungry
with an ache that burns
like fields on fire

Girl in White

her face seems sad
or maybe her downcast
gaze only meets the ground
to watch for unevenness
of footing among the flowers

she is far away, but
I paint her close, welcome
her into my home
and tell her I do not have
much time left for sorrow

The Potato Eaters

share a plate
under dim light
in a dingy room
together

The Red Vineyard

grapes are ripe for the picking
thick clusters bleed, stain hands

the pigment which stains my hands
is a mere imitation of life

tonight I will drink my wine
and sleep well with my dreams

Night Café

silent as night should be

heads bowed
some resting
on folded arms

I am on the other side
of the room
alone in a corner

Irises

deep purple of hope
the bruise of faith
when hope is my company

I cultivate a garden
and wish you a promise
of love of friendship

but oh how sorrow
stabs when those
petals unfurl

At Eternity's Gate

how else could I paint this—
the knowing of an end
how darkness creeps
and shadows blend into night

the hunch of shoulders
a rounded back, tired
the weight of it all
cradled in two hands

and everything is now
behind and old and
does not matter any longer

.

Tree Roots

a tangle
a secure anchor

because
isn't that where life begins
anyway

in the ground
buried where no one
sees or hears

Wheat Field with a Lark

it is morning
and I hear your song
sweet friend

as you fly solitary
wings unmoving
on the breeze

and the wheat sways
golden waves
to accompany you

will you be there
with your holy hymn
when I reach the gates

James Benger

Bother

Then there was that
particularly unproductive night,
when after a few too many drinks,
I asked him point-blank,
"So why do you bother?"

He took another sip,
considering the question,
ran a free hand
through his orange beard.

Finally, he looked up from his wine,
leveled his gaze on mine, and told me,
"Because to not would be death."

I asked him if perhaps
he was being a bit dramatic,
but he seemed
unfazed.

When news came of his death,
I went back to that night,
and couldn't help but
be absolutely certain that
the moment of his last breath
was completely void of struggle.

From the Dark

Sometimes it's hard to see the sun
when the clouds keep coming.
It's hard to imagine those burning days
outside with the kickball or the dog leash,
the shovel or the tennis racket,
or maybe just a good book and a cold drink,
when the days are nearly as dark as the night.

You can find yourself wondering
if all that was some strange, beautiful dream.
Like you've finally waken from a coma,
only to covet your past sleeping self.

And when the clouds finally part
only to deluge the world with a cold,
unforgiving rain, the kind of rain that has
nothing to do with cleansing, nurturing or rebirth,
the kind that only sows the seeds of black ice,
and elderly broken limbs on winter sidewalks,
it makes those golden days of sun seem all
the more like some staggeringly lucid fever dream.

But here from the cold, from the dark, from the wet,
I can tell you, those days were real, and will be
back again. I have seen it.

Hope

I've seen him before;
he does this a lot.
Pacing the block,
hand on the door,
then backs away,
almost comically,
practically making a
cross with his fingers.

He spent every night
here for so long,
I was sure he'd be stuck.

But he's trying,
trying.
Some nights he wins.
Few and far,
but some nights he does.
I suppose that's what
keeps him going,
keeps him hoping.

The streetlights blink
into life, and his palm
is on the door.
I hold my breath until
he walks away for
another lap,
talking himself up
to talk himself out.
I hope he wins.
He's working at it
hard enough,
he deserves to get out.

Into Tomorrow

On this rooftop
we dream of tomorrow's
lights as we stare up at
countless yesterdays.

The past is mapped out
in a tapestry of pinpoints
and milky swirls, but

the future is found in
the crackle and charge
between out fingers.

As the sun sneaks from
the ground and erases what
came before for another day,
we guide ourselves
into tomorrow.

Potential

(after The Café Terrace, Ales at Night*)*

Under the awning, cigarettes glowing,
the patrons convene with only the
percussive music of the midnight rain.

Boozy scents swept free by the autumn breeze,
couples in arms, acquaintances in deep discussion,
life on a somewhat corrected keel.

Windows behind backs rattle from within,
streetlamps flicker with no promise of dawn,
yawns hidden behind callused, overworked palms.

Outside reminds us of what life could be.

reproduce

sinking substance
sliding sanity
flowing fields
of one

one last line
one final flourish
one stopping stroke
to the floor

a fury of impressions
stockpiled to nothing

hopelessness wears
a new face every day
the pain is always
a shock

bleeding through the brush
ousting specters

they always reproduce

Seen

Follow your swirls,
your blues,
and your madness.

Find the truth,
the line,
the cohesion.

Run with the brush
to the distant night,
the stars,
the river
will illuminate your face.

A soul within the torment,
under the weights,
beneath the body.

Let your pigment show,
you will be seen.

spiral

falling down,
down,
falling.

embrace
the descent,

embrace
the tumble,

embrace
the madness.

in the end,
nothing will matter
but the art.

Stepping Into Night

(after Café Terrace on Place du Forum*)*

On a café terrace
we whiled away hours,
coffee turning to tea,
tea melting to wine,
wine back into tea,
and a good whiskey
as the stars illuminated
the sky a vibrant cobalt.

Beneath our golden awning
the waiter diminished our needs,
our conversation grew freer,
our experience entwined.

As the evening progressed,
the passersby slowly shifted
from families on a day out,
haggard but happy parents
toting sugar-laced children,
to young couples,
fingers and eyes,
groundless steps,
to young men on the prowl,
liquor breath and hungry eyes,
staggering gates,
superficial fulfillment.

We sat across from one another.
We were,
would be,
had been
all of those who flowed about.

We stepped into our own night.

Vincent's Ghost

Vincent's ghost
walks head down
through lonely, wet streets,
dark cobblestones
reflecting shards of
white moonlight.

Vincent's ghost
solemnly passes
the girl under the trees,
orange smears of leaves
against a white dress,
and a lonely dead man.

Vincent's ghost
clandestinely joins
the potato eaters,
a single candle
illuminating joyless
strong, dark tea.

Vincent's ghost
surveys the rooftops of Paris,
stubby chimneys
never matching
the ascent of the scant birds
elevated to the morning skies.

Vincent's ghost
sits alone in the corner
of the Night Café,
waiting for the man in white
to take up the game,
all other heads down.

Vincent's ghost
returns to his small room,
rips his paintings from the wall,
extinguishes the candle,
and falls into his cold bed,
wishing we don't repeat his mistakes.

Lylanne Musselman

The Art of Seeing Value

I went to see Vincent
van Gogh's painting
on loan from Paris,
Bedroom in Arles,
in Detroit, a place
so bankrupt, city
officials are looking in-
to assets the Detroit Institute
of Arts owns. Yes,

Michigan politicians
and many citizens
could prostitute
irreplaceable art. It exhibits
how some would
sell their souls, aid
the American idea
　　　money saves
at all costs. In Detroit,
citizens comment:

　　　Sell the DIA and open
　　　a money making business
　　　like a casino; Art is
　　　just a perception, it might
　　　evoke emotion for people
　　　or nothing; If Detroit goes
　　　bankrupt the museum collection
　　　could be seized…

I stood less
than a foot away
from the painting
van Gogh brushed

302

life into. The awe of it all,
knowing he painted this
bedroom scene to show
his brother, Theo,
how tranquil Arles was,
to see his perspective,
his ever-present blues.

A Spiritual Gift

to *Wheat Fields with Reaper, Auvers* by Vincent van Gogh

Who doesn't reap
a religious experience
viewing a van Gogh?
Step closer, absorb
those forceful strokes –
spiritually drawn,
painted prayers;
regenerate your weary
soul, stained in
social media and materialism.

Vincent's *Wheat Fields with Reaper,*
Auvers is here for the harvest;
repent your detached life
at this art sanctuary, give
yourself a spiritual gift –
anointed with oil:
bold blues, greens and ochres,
cycle of life inspired:

Receive a communion
with van Gogh's nature,
each visit, deepen your beliefs,
"Reap what you sow."

Amen.

Perfectionist

During my neighborhood walk
my mind turned and whisked
through thoughts cobbled by the sun,
searched for rhyme or reason and flit
fast as hummingbirds to nectar.

I moved past sunflowers
who waved and bowed at me,
secretly wishing I were van Gogh,
while monarchs applauded
their own artfulness.

I searched for seeds of inspiration
to grow a poem, dug deep for an idea
like Picasso's, wild and free.
I ignored Monet's gardens
dotting the landscape around me,
much like a painting by Seurat,
and in the process
missed the point.

Consolations After the Death of My Kitten

"After James Tate's 'Consolations After an Affair'"

Chattering at shadows on the ceiling,
my cats run room to room.
They see little Teddy.
As we settle down at night, he visits.
And I can hear peaceful cats purring,
the love that moves me.
I've discovered that I don't need
a lousy spouse, a loan to repay.
I have unfinished paintings
that wait for van Gogh to return.
They know nothing of sangria and Vonnegut.
For them a foggy night in February
is a ghost of an excuse.

Resurrecting Artists in 2017

If Peter Paul Rubens was alive in 2017,
would he succumb to corporate culture
and paint his women as pencil-thin models,
or would he delight in the full-figured,
Rubenesque women that society overlooks?

Would Vincent van Gogh take up
digital painting, discover that a virtual
palette consists of millions of colors
and excel at his new media, or get so
blue that doctors diagnose him
with chronic depression, give him drugs
that make him zombie-like through many
starry, starry nights?

Would John James Audubon stop painting birds
in their natural surroundings, every little wisp
of their intricate feathers; instead pick up
a digital camera loaded with high-powered lenses, shoot
his subjects in living color and aspire to have his birds
be *Audubon Magazine* centerfold –
Beak of the Week?

Favorite Painting

Starry, Starry Night –
van Gogh swirls bright in my dreams:
visual strokes of genius.

For the Love of Sunflowers

Vincent didn't need the peony
or the hollyhock, he wrote Theo,
they belonged to other painters,
all he needed were his sunflowers:
cut or placed in assorted vases,
a series of strong stems arranged,
heads bowed in grace, an homage
to their hand-picked master.

Night Life

to *Night Café in the Place Lamartine in Arles*

It's the overwhelming feeling
when you stay out late, night
after night, and the inside
lights become unforgiving
and bright. It's that dizzying swirl
of ten drinks too many, when
the clock on the wall looks heavy
handed as time ticks too fast
to the music bouncing off
of these red walls of rebellion.

It's the glowing yellow floor,
you're not sure will hold you up.
It's the dark green ceiling
dropping in on your dreams.
It's those other patrons
who look like "ruffians"
with no place to go. They eat
at your life, reminding you
of how this café calls you
night after night ruining
your creative ambition.

Linear Thoughts

to *Young Man with a Pipe*

The contours
of the young
man are clean,
not the wild strokes
of a painter sometimes
thought mad. The watercolor –
soft flesh tones and smooth,
the shaded pencil lines, steady –
not the deep blues,
the wild swirling strokes
that define a van Gogh painting.
This cool drawing exhibits
how this well-known artist
had moments of calm,
and knew how to draw
us to any of his images
over and over again.

An Artist's Dilemma

van Gogh didn't sell art
in his lifetime he failed
to know he was great.

Ndaba Sibanda

How

There was no news about Vincent
No books, no museums, no honour,

You could have been overworked,
You could have been overzealous,

Was it worth all the fanatical love?
Was there any gain worth the pain?

What gain was there to talk about
When normalcy was never silent?

Success was elusive, failure loud
As you quickly gained your footing,

Normalcy was invisible, insanity sang
As you executed your wonderful works,

Were you a painter by vocation
Or an artist by mere avocation?

Now to the practice of speaking
Freely without preconception...

If you were to wake up today
Would you believe your fame?

Would you dump painting
For the pulpit or pursue it again?

How would you deal with love
And your commercial influence?

Of Post-impressionist Paintings and Drawings

an opening with various vacations and unsuitable and unhappy
romances and drinking sprees with disastrous results...

when they saw you copying prints and painting rural life
stuck in abject poverty and in malnourishment and diffidence

struggling with identity and direction and ending up
in Belgium and in France and in asylums and loneliness

who could have thought that *The Potato* and other pieces
will form a fusion of form so compelling and dramatic

and melodically rhythmic and ingenious and poignant
that they would go into the annals of yesteryear

as having laid the foundation of modern art
and crown you the chief symbol of expression?

The Legacy of Artworks

Visual art that speaks of a society's thoughts
and feelings and battles with a saltiness of its life
like --one brave exhibition about atrocities a few years ago
at the Bulawayo Art Gallery—is a rare and worthy artifact

because for the art dealer like Vincent van Gogh and others--
they are the indubitable epitome of misunderstood geniuses
who usually do not get timely recognition and admiration --
instead get arrested as was the case with the heroic Bulawayo artist.

Get Up And Find It

There could be a rumble
Here and there
Because of life's storms

There could be a fumble
Here and there
Because you are human

There could be a tumble
Hard and hideous
Because of a slip-up

Life rumbling at you
Roar at it with vigour
Right the wrongs

Life frowning at you
Tantrums thrown at you
Laugh loudly at them

Life hard and hideous
Hold on and hack
Off all the dents

It isn't always light
Yet seek your light
Life will be bright

For life is but a start
Whose star is in you
Get up and find it.

Sober Up

What is this startling revelation about alcohol and other drugs?
You lived a soaring life today, a crushing life the following day
You were the most feared athlete in the entire world
That all imploded when you were convicted of theft
When you got out of prison, you recovered as an athlete
To the point you won a major world prize
Yet money trickled out of your pockets
As soon as it went in

Then it was bankruptcy
Then in walked disgrace
In walked addiction
You were hurt
In a severe way
Now it is time to drop the baggage in the face of addiction
Now it is time make a full comeback from the jaws of death

Patience Is A Must

I will be calling each of you who have
Come to this earth to remind you that
People aren't electrons and, so don`t
Expect them to behave in the same manner
Under similar conditions, they won't!
Don`t be shocked if you show them love
And they flash at you unconcealed hate
Be glad that at least they're true to you!
Some were taught by parents to smile
Whenever possible, but they frown
Even if it isn't called for and strenuous!
I know you aren't virtuous, either
But try to be patient and people-wise!
Again, I do respectfully and thankfully
Ask for your patience in this regard!

The Other Side Of The Pen

I bumped into an unsung
hero and a brother in the writing community
I saluted him for his resilience and industriousness

Man,
he was still pushing on
against all the odds,
Battling with the fact that
his wife of ten had just decided to
call it a day from their rocky union
citing crippling poverty, since she could
not eat his written 'junk' or sedentary 'laziness'
And his own children long disowned him as an oddity

His plight and plight came in the form of
stark isolation, ridicule and intimidation
Forces of fear dogging him like licentious
dogs hot and heavy on a hit female canine
Unstoppable in the face a series of rejections
he told me of dispatching mountains of
his stories and criticisms and essays
and poems to a variety
of publications

My heart ached.

Tennis Star On The Horizon

I think she is set to break records.
Her heart has been broken several
times by the cynical and silly decrees
and labels and ideas of relatives who
confine her world to her disability.

She has shot out of their little box of
confinement and got some tongues
wagging. How could she ever dream
of playing tennis with such weak arms?
How could she dream big, wax great?

She has refused to wallow in self-pity.
Playing tennis and netball -she has
endeared herself to her teachers
and her classmates. A class monitor,
she commands respect on the court.

Yoby Henthorn

Current Gossip

I've been watching documentaries on your life. Did you know one "expert" said there was so much grit in your paintings because you dried them by placing them face down in the sand? No, I'm serious. Even you wrote Theo about the wind blowing so hard sand grit got on the painting, and in your mouth and eyes.

And, they made a whole documentary about the whore you gave the ear to. Traveled all across Europe and America looking up leads, hints.

Finally found a woman it could have been, but the family said that there was no way she could be a whore, because she was too young, so she must have been a cleaner. Like whores have never lied about their age. Like it couldn't have been Gauguin's favorite whore.

This same woman heard it wasn't your whole ear, which is, of course, what your family wants to hear, but just the lobe of your ear. So why do your paintings show the whole ear bandaged? Finally found a drawing done by your doctor that shows that the whole ear was cut off except for the lobe, and another drawing showing you sleeping with just the lobe still attached.

Do you know how much money they would have spent just to make this documentary?

But cutting your ear off is the one thing people know when someone mentions your name. They wouldn't recognize any of your paintings. In fact, the only painting they might recognize is the one with your bandaged ear, but only because they heard the story.

I have several prints of your paintings hanging on my walls, and a friend asked me if I had painted them!

But, in the 50's and 60's, your paintings, especially the sunflowers, were made into puzzles, curtains, fabric, vases, pictures to hang above couches because the living rooms were gold and yellow. You went from being insane, to revolutionary, to the start of a post-impressionist movement, to being safe wall art within 60 years.

One of your letters to Theo sold at an auction for more than any single of your paintings. And your paintings sell for a lot.

I'm going to tell you this, but don't be too upset, because the ending is marvelous. All the paintings you gifted people often and drawings you gifted people often ended up being burned, or stuffed in attics, attacked by the elements. The young soldier with the red Fez used his for target practice. Dr. Rey's mother took his portrait and used it to patch up her chicken coop. Your mother burned your paintings by the crate full. Yet after your brother's death 18 months later, your sister in law made it her life calling to search out all of your paintings, letters,drawings, anything are still in existence that is about you or done by you. The number of paintings you made was about 900, and the drawings about 1,100. I'm not sure how many of the drawings still exist, but the last I checked the number of paintings was 131. It is good that not all 900 paintings still exist, because after a painter is discovered to be a master, the fewer the paintings, the larger the fame, not for the sheer quantity, but for the beauty, the emotions, the insight. Theo's wife did that for you, saved your work from disappearing, because she loved Theo, and Theo loved you.   Your painting of Dr. Gachet sold for $82 million dollars, one of the top ten most valuable paintings in the world. One of your letters to Bernard sold for $579,212, the letter in which you were writing about your stormy friendship with Gauguin.

In that insane nine week period that you and Gauguin lived together, you two together produced over 45 acknowledged masterpieces, collectively worth over $1.5 billion.

That's saying something, even if most people only remember your ear. There are still art worshipers. And you are one of their altars.

What is your favorite color now?

Art Institute of Chicago

I knew what I wanted to see. As I walked up the marble staircase, there, floating in mid-air was a cloud painting by Georgia O'Keefe. She cut out a large piece of the sky, with the gentle cotton ball puffs of clouds, and put it on a canvas so large it stuck out the end of her garage. I was careful not to stare too long. The first time I saw it, I felt dizzy and almost fell down the marble stairs.

Seurat's Sunday at the park is very large, large as one wall of my living room. I am always very rude, gently shoving my way to the front, studying the patterns of dots. The others are there to see 'art'. I am there visiting kin.

But they are just side visits to see you. They are only an aunt and an uncle. You are my brother.

The blue bedroom must be my favorite. It's a comforting, soothing room, with the serene blue walls, with the warm red coverlet to pull over me on a bad day. I had a room like that once. The walls weren't blue, but in the shade of lilac bushes, with blue curtains that blew and stirred in the breeze, the white walls were blue, and a blue chest of drawers, and a bed with an old red comforter my brother and I would cuddle under when ill, eating chicken soup and crackers.

When you are tortured and drinking too much, I would whisper the alcohol out through your skin, and would hold your smelly, feverish body as you slept, and I'd rock you like I rock myself when the thoughts are bad and too fast and won't shut up, and I would tell you, its only thoughts, its only thinking. Sometimes it helps, sometimes it doesn't. I would only be your dream, like imagining you are teaching me how to see out in the hot, dry, scouring wind looking at trees and fields.

My other favorite painting is what I assume is in winter- pollarded trees, which remind me of the small staked fruit trees in the winter. I am homesick, even for the plainest, most barren sights. The paint still looked wet. I could see every trench done with a trowel or wide stiff brush. It looked like brownie batter. I wanted to touch it, to have it come off in a big dollop on my finger and swirl it off with my tongue. Then I shivered. I was as close, or closer than you were when you painted it. I could feel your breath on my neck.

323

Hypnogogic Dream 1:

A man, dark hair, suit, a knock at the door.

"Enter"

"Sir, here are the next boxes." The woman says.

A strong man in peasant clothes enters the modern office with several boxes which he stacks.

The office man walks over and starts looking through them.

"Geeze, I can't go through all this. All I want is the letters on the yellow house and anything having to do with the yellow house. Don't bring me anymore boxes. You go through the boxes till you find everything on the yellow house."

"Yes sir."

They start to leave, and he stops them.

"Take out all these damn boxes. They suck out all of the light."

A couple of days later they appear again.

"Sir, these are the two boxes on the yellow house."

He opens one, and it is packed with the smelliest long johns, holey socks, worn pants and shirt, all stiff with alcohol, sweat, salt, dirt, and dung. A lot of blood.,"

He tosses them aside, pulls out the papers, and stacks them, and at the bottom finds a wooden box with a sunflower painted on top. Soft rattling inside. He opens it, and inside are the longest, thickest, dirt caked toe-nail parings he'd never even dreamt about.

Hypnogogic Dream 2:

Vincent doesn't know what he did to be in jail. He paces like a tiger. It is boring.

He looks at his shoes. He is a little hungry, and wonders what it is like for really poor people who end up eating their shoes, so he starts chewing and chewing, swallowing in small bits, like a mouse nibbling.

He asks them for a pencil stub to write Theo a letter, but after the letter is written, he can't stop pacing, his thought race making no sense, so he calms his mind by drawing sunflowers on the wall, takes him days, and hours, sharpening the pencil with his bad teeth, and drawing till the walls are covered with sunflowers.

Drawing sunflowers. Chewing his shoes.

Till there is no more pencil stub left. So he bites his finger till they bleed, but soon can't get enough blood to flow, so paints the wall with his own shit, till the whole cell is covered in shit sunflowers.

Theo finally sends the jail money, so when they let him out, the whole cell is covered in shit. Of course they make Theo pay more, give Vincent a sound thrashing, and throw him on the street. They don't even make him clean it up, though they want to make him clean the wall with his tongue. They know he is crazy, and wonder if he'll bite them for paint, or sneak in and steal their shit.

When he gets home, the walls of his yellow house are whitewashed inside and out, and the place is scoured spotless, everything straight and orderly, including his sanctuary, his studio, all his paints stacked by color and squeezed and rolled like somebody with a toothpaste tube fetish, his brushes sorted by size, his painting and canvases stacked neatly, the chairs whitewashed, all the paintings off the wall, his red coverlet replaced by a plain white one. Hearth scrubbed clean with a hob of neatly stacked wood and another of neatly stacked coal, The one pot hung on a peg above the stove, now crud free. No bottle of absinthe in sight.

He falls to the ground and screams! "Mary! How could you do this!"

His landlady scuttles in, backs out because of the smell of paint and Van Gogh's brown crusted hands, and from the door says,

"I didn't do it. It was Mr. Gauguin. He never liked the mess you lived in. He hates yellow. Throw away all your yellow tubes of paint because he said the color made you insane. He said he is only trying to help you get well. He's a tidy man, a clean man, though a whoremonger and a drunk.

He is the cleanest God forsaken sinner I ever met.

"WHERE IS HE?"

"I don't know. He comes and goes. I never know when and I never know where so I just keep my nose to myself. I did see him with the buckets of whitewash and bundles and bundles of old rags and clothes and pails and pails of water. But as for where he went when he'd go, I'd never know, and he'd be gone for days.

Oh, and he said to give you this. Says he knows you never like to throw anything away."

She hands him a box with a sunflower painted on top, and inside are Vincent's toenail pairings. Vincent grins broadly. "At least he got one thing right." He holds the box close to his chest and goes to his room, and lies down on his white bed and pulls the white cover over him with his paint covered fingers, and falls into a deep, deep sleep.

Places to paint that are in bright sun and blistering heat

Hard stick Canyon in the Sea of Brown Grass
A rolling ride
 to the bottom on burros
In the wide, dry creek bed to the light house
A wall of gypsum, silver and gray, shining
Folded like ribbons of Christmas Candy
Flakes of it clear enough to be
Urim and Thumim
I get my vision by dirt and through rock
Sharp knife edge of red cliff
 red like tomatoes
 red like clay pots
 red like good leather notebook
cliff with white band
Too sharp for walking across by fools
Water goes through this red dirt
 this red rock like-
Like whey through cheese cloth
 Like water through a coffee sieve
like water through a cracked pot
like water through your hand

The creeks are blistered, shining tan and gypsum and baked clay red
Gulley washers
Water, when it come, rushes too fast to catch
To swim in
To rescue your car
Is flat and dry by the next day

The red clay beds
Grow stone roses
Grow turtles backs
Grow bottoms of rounded pots

The heat shimmers like
Heat off a boiling pot

Like Hard Cold off of a flash frozen snow field
Like waves of a short, slow waterfall

The water is a seamstress
Shaping Spanish skirts
Ruffle of yellow
Ruffle of red
Ruffle of white
Ruffle of orange
Long skirt sweeping a tan, sand floor
Like a senorita
Thunder claps like canastas

The water and wind worn light house
Warns from
The sad monkey
From devil's slide
From thorny prickly pear
From itchy poison ivy
From scratching mesquite
From fat, mean, poisonous diamond back
Which rattles if you don't pay attention to the light house.

What insanity is like:

Daugherty's new green Wheat field with Thunderstorms
Hot hot
 growing wheat so fast you can hear it grow
Cool air and heat building up billowing clouds
Up, up, up, boiling hot like milk that will bubble over a pot
But up, and up even higher than the Alps
Turning purple at the bottom
Sending dark blue sheets of rain. rain you can see
But are watering the fields the next country over
Mountains moving fast
 boiling purple
boiling turquoise
 boiling grey
Moving over you
You under the swirling center like watching a lid being unscrewed off of
the top
Of this hot /cold jar you are trapped in
Fingers reaching, twisting down to take your house
Your cow
Your daughter
Dashes them to the floor of the next county over

Tim Staley

Alabamian v. Dust Storm

I took my daughter to a birthday party
just this side of Juarez.
Upon arriving, sand was kindly
introduced to our eyes.
The wind capsized a bouncy house
and there were children
screaming in play.

The trees all afternoon just took it:
punched over, throwing up bark,
bleeding leaves. The wind knocked
at the windows with grainy knuckles--
who knows what it wanted--it likes
to hide mountains
with a swipe of its cape.

And still no one agreed to go inside
to the 40 quarts of posole
simmering on the stove,
to *Death of a Salesman*
turned down real low
on a television set seven-feet-wide,
to *The Starry Night* in a plastic frame,
to the faint cloud of steam
rising from a plate of tortillas.

Nature of Marriage

A black veil's been lifted
from the face of my marriage
and instead of a skull
with centipedes in the eye sockets
I find a face of desert flowers
a body in a house-finch-gown
walking on Palo Verde legs
to cross before the dresser
to dim the halogen lamp
to bloom towards me freckled
with promise and surprise

A Worrisome Spill of Mountain and Cloud

My spouse on the sofa
typing furiously on her phone
chewing the inside of her cheek
balancing something sad behind her eyes.

Is she worrying about Lois passing in and out,
is she wishing I was disposable,
is she wishing she was somewhere else--
I can't tell, I'm in the kitchen,
so many human steps away.

If I was her I'd rent a canoe in Arles
and float the Rhône River.
Here's the pictures I'd take: rock,
sand, water, two cigarette butts
forming a T on the pebbled bank.
After two weeks
I'd return lonely enough
to sit down beside her,
to ask her, *what's wrong?*

Following Geese in Equality, Alabama

Now it's news every time
a cop gets shot. I'm living life
on the lakeside,
jogging behind geese
who unsheathe their wings
and threaten to fly.

I wonder how many bullets,
how many wooden crosses
are at the bottom of the lake,
furry with rufous algae.

The magazine said awe
induced by nature
inspires kindness.
I wanted to be friends with the enemy
and my friends made me their enemy.

The clouds seem fluid,
like van Gogh's clouds
rolling and twisting in the sky.

Morning in Equality, Alabama

Nowadays it's news every time a cop dies
but here in the morning dogs stretch out
shaded by pines in the lush Bermuda
and don't even get me started
on the microdramas of the forest floor,
deep in the weave of pine straw,
a hundred million chiggers plotting,
a roach so powerful
trees can read its mind.
It's tacky to call it violence,
all that feverish feeding.
Violence implies conscience.

There's mosquitos rising from the rain
caught in the dimples of every stone,
in the cups of dead leaves,
in the hipbone gullies of dead game.
And it's time for us to rise up
like van Gogh once he put
his parent's dreams down.

Sailing at Saintes-Maries-De-La-Mer

The freckles on her legs sparkle in the sun.
In the sailboat she's pink with youth,
on the shore she's 52.
I work the lines.

My right hand is relaxed,
my left, delicate on the rudder.
I'm working the rudder like a clitoris
aiming thrust just right.

Watch the sail quake, tremble, buck,
the speed's too much
for the rudder--it snaps off in my hand--
the vessel whips in a circle and flips us.

My lover's not fazed
as the water's warm and she's been
thrown from boats before.

Seaside at Saintes-Maries-De-La-Mer

From here everyone is recreating
except those guys flossing a pool
or those guys blowing lawn clippings into the waves
or those missionaries in suits
or those refugees in rags
standing at our threshold
addressing us in the water
letting us swim
saying with their faces,
we hate to bother you.

What Does He Know

I'm speaking to my class
important stuff about commas
when I'm thinking about comas
and this dead dog I saw
beside I-70 on his back
legs frozen in the air
like an upside-down table
in a ballroom of yellow grass
grass the color of van Gogh's wheat.
What should I teach them?
What do I know to say?
That in Corporate America
they'll suffocate as I did
in capitalism's esophagus,
that the best they can possibly do
in this desert town
is pick at a paltry paycheck
like a kid picks at a scab
'til it's completely ripped off. It's hard
not rushing to an open wound.
They're looking down at their phones.
I'm looking out the window
at the Golden Arches across the street
eclipsed by dust and wind.
I'm hungry, sober, sore.
Maybe I'm just bored. I draw
commas on the board
around, *by William Golding,*
and here's a man from Cornwall
stranded on the East Mesa
and they're in phone comas
packaged neatly in their desks.
Sometimes all I want to do
is smack some sense into me.

Everybody's An Artist

16 young artists sit in a circle in the wind
in front of the school, they want to go in.
I have a PHD in the Sandwich Arts.
What's the opposite of fine art? thick art?
even the Grand Panjandrum Rilke
knew you had to burn for it.

AJ has a jacket made from an Egyptian rug,
it's thick, there's dead grass in its fringes.
I can't purchase it on the internet,
it's an intergalactic crisis.
His grandmother made it,
she's terrible at sandwiches.
She's dead now.

Dezzi says everybody's an artist,
she's an artist, you're an artist, I'm a
Sandwich Artist, would you like it
toasted?

Debi Swim

Starry Night over the Asylum

Is anyone in the village below awake?
It is late, late, sleepers in houses dark and quiet.
How can they rest when overhead there is a riot?
Stars and worlds ringing like church bells,
moon ablaze throbbing in hi-hat jumps
a galaxy of milky white tambourine thumps
I cover my ears against the dissonance.
Why aren't there people in the streets
wailing in anger for the noise to cease?
Oh, starry night. Oh, raucous, strident, starry night,
your beauty bellows in discordant din
and I, I fall to my knees in your poignant orbital spin.

Inspired by *Vincent van Gogh, The Starry Night*

Jiving with Chives

It moves herky-jerk
I watch it go
round and round
second-hand time
and try to think of
something to write
about garlic chives
in a flower pot
painted by
Vincent van Gogh
but the tick-tock
has gotten into my head
and I'm thinking
I'll never see that second again.
A sweeping arc
and before I'm ready
sixty of them
have flown away
like the passenger
pigeon, extinct, missed,
ill-used and no more
but not forgotten...
like the painting of
a common thing
immortalized...
perhaps in this poem.

The Night is Richly Dyed

"The night is even more richly coloured than the day. . . . If only one pays attention to it, one sees that certain stars are citron yellow, while others have a pink glow or a green, blue and forget-me-not brilliance. And wit out my expiating on this theme, it should be clear that putting little white dots on a blue-black surface is not enough." — Vincent van Gogh, letter to sister, September 1888

Behold, look up, the night is richly dyed
with shades and hues that glow from deep within.
The midnight sky is sketched so vast and wide
from hemisphere to hemisphere it spins
a tale of Greek mythology
the Ram, Pisces, and the twins
immortalized in paint and pen
on earth and in the starry sky.
An unseen hand with strokes both bold and slight
dipped a brush into a mystic prism
and painted citron, jade, and silver blue.
Behold, look up, the night is richly hued.

Tears of the Snow Queen

It's always winter in the land by the hand of the Snow Queen. She ices the trees, the ground and every dwelling of mouse and fox with a fluffy frosting of ice and snow. The rays of a distant, subdued sun turn the snow into diamond dust sparkling and dancing to the North Wind's tune. A scene of such pristine beauty the Queen herself almost blushes with pleasure.

In the land far away it will soon be March Equinox and time for her annual visit to her sister, Fairy Spring. Though she loves her sister, they are so different; one is cool, reserved and lovely in white and the other warm, dressed in gypsy colors and adorned with touches of gold. The Queen's visits are short for Spring's joie de vivre will begin to thaw her snowy heart.

They part with tender kisses and fond farewells. As the Snow Queen rides back to her country she cries for sadness at their cruel but necessary separation. The North Wind gathers her tears and sows them over Spring's fields of white. The snowdrops grow, brave and vigorous, to remind Spring of her sister's love.

A Visit to Yesterday

All torn down, swept away, nothing remains but memories and they are inaccurate. One short gravel road turned off the main highway... it used to seem so long. Perpendicular to it, near the middle, another short road spun off. There, a row of company houses sat neighborly side by side. The last house was ours and then across the ditch of run ning water (how did it become a creek in memory?) stood the mill. This was the universe, massive, strange, exciting, safe, encompassed within so small a space, like a blue phone booth. It is bigger on the inside.

The world is so large
for little eyes to take in,
little hands to grasp.

The mill was a flooring plant. Stacks of dried planks, big trucks roar ing in and out, loud machinery, shouting men, and the chaos of a busy crew didn't lend itself to curious visits. I stayed on my side of the creek but straddling the one plank bridge that connected our yard to the mill. The dragonflies were plentiful and beautiful. Fairy like iridescent wings and darting motion captivated me. Grandma didn't like us kids playing so near the mill. She warned us that dragonflies doctored sick snakes so we shouldn't hang around them. Didn't work. We just searched for the poor sick snakes.

In the midst of progress
dragonflies fly
nature disregards.

Life Cycle of a Star

Nebulous beginning,
swirling gas and dust merge
a star is born and lives and ages
through stages of fire and depletion
as I have lived, am living...
from my youth too hot, unstable emotions felt
too keenly, unseemly,
burning to a cold hard cinder
or perhaps to a great explosion
where some long day from hence
God's hand will remix me again.
There is a grave yard in the sky
way up high, where stars, like elephants,
have gone to lie amidst the beauty
of a velvet stillness and quiet radiance.
"O starry night, this is how I want to die"
not collapsed within myself
but used up and spent
gathered in a celestial cemetery
of stellar remnants.

There Still Be Dragons

Written after reading the title "Eric in the Land of the Insects"(a novel written by a Dutch author Godfried Bomans)

After I got over my shock of being suddenly small as an insect, I had many adventures and heard amazing stories and histories of the inhabitants of the meadow. One group of peoples I met were the beautiful winged flying creatures. They allowed me to sit with them and listen to an elder speak of their lore and history. This is the story she told...

Deep in a cave there came the sound of sobbing. Odonata, the last living dragon in the world lay trembling in sorrow and fear. Sorrow that all the ones she loved were dead. Fear because she was next. The strong men of Galentia had closed off all exits to the cave and sent their best archers down the tunnel that led to Odonata.

She prayed that she would meet death with courage and grace. The god Leviathan took pity on her and spoke these words, "Because I have loved you, despite your cruel heart, I will not allow your reign to end. I will give you a gentle heart, break your teeth, and give you color and beauty that men would admire, rather than hate, you."

The men came to the mouth of her lair. They expected a fiery death for themselves but they would kill her; they had vowed. But, instead, she rose to stand and bared her heart, her only vulnerable part. In death she would not exact revenge. The arrows all met their mark dead on. She collapsed with a hiss.

At Leviathan's command, Odonata grew small, her wings and body iridescent, delicate, lovely. He gave her the ability to fly gracefully in six directions and to hover. And though he shortened her life span she and her offspring would live fully in the moment with joy and beauty. "Go forth," he said, "Your name shall be Dragonfly."

Waiting for Richard

Crab fresh from the sea, caught by Dinsby's boy this morning, served on Richard's mother's blue ware. A nice contrast I thought, though she would have criticized my choice. A stand of lemons, one peeled, to squeeze upon the meat. A glass of buttery chardonnay pairs perfectly. Crusty bread and a side of mixed vegetables will be filling. Concord grapes, a simple, sweet dessert to cleanse the palate.

I stand back and view the tablescape. The butter knife, with its modern ceramic pattern is a bit jarring but Richard and I received it as a wedding gift from cherished friends. It adds a touch of home though we are far away. The only thing I add are his books and a tankard as a bookend. Perhaps after he has dined, Richard will read some poetry to me by the hearth fire's warm glow.

Star Gazing

I toss and turn, wrestle with cares and the black energy of the day, and then slip from bed pessimistic of sleep or peace. I walk to the front stoop, take a deep breath of stillness… and look up. I find the big dipper and tilt it for a refreshing sip of eternity. Let my eyes follow the stream of stars and gasp at one falling. I wonder if it is as curious of earth as I am of its world. Though I'm not sure I'd be brave enough to fall into its vastness. This fallen star, does it gasp with awe at green, growing things? Does it marvel at living creatures, flying, crawling, running, walking? Does it sigh a longing sigh to be part of such beauty as I long for the stars? I go back inside, to bed, with loose shoulders and calmed mind.

one blade of green grass
one brilliant shimmering star
marvels in between

Never Had a Chance

Soft as the massacre of Suns By Evening's Sabres slain.
--Emily Dickinson / 1127

Like the faintest whisper, *Soft*
fragile *as*
a soap bubble *the*
needle of the fir could *massacre*
Like the melting point *of*
snowflakes under the *Suns*
of Tatooine. Like the brevity *By*
which the Mayfly enjoys *Evening's*
swift kiss then succumbs to *Sabres*
sharp and fleet – love is *slain.*

Sheikha A

Feet in Heels

in response to 'A Pair of Shoes'

the eagle's lips are real, like the salt in a sea

and remembering to carry sweet water to its midst;

it has meticulously arranged a nest on a tree
that grows *jamuns*

where the crows have stopped landing on
its shiny purple gems

and the heads of some of the eggs have begun
to show lines

of cracking, while, me, in my room, on a carpet
untainted

kept clean for prayers, I try out shoes I won't
again wear

for being used to bare-footedness, and my heels
only walked

carpets of all textures, the lines under their heads are

fine, obscure, clean as pink unfilled rivers

taught to heel by the toes, carry weight of just
the body

drapes and lengths of verses I perfected to heart

for the eagle to repeat, moving its lips by feet

that now rest on straw

the strands of which picked under a merciful day's sun,

when it scorched all green matter into usable compost:

all things of gratitude; here, I boast how the sight of

my feet taught the eagle to speak.

Contraption

looking from a window in Saint-Remy-de-Provence

The crow has arrived on its white wings
concealing itself amongst wide leaves
that cannot hold the mass of its growth;
its throat imitates the sounds of the greens
during a spring that hasn't been infested yet
by dry ants on shrinking wood, for that
sort of weather must first grow extra
layers of skin in order to survive the heat-
drenched marrow shrinking down quickly
into a carcass of decomposed pulp. This is
the same kind of solitude that tries infusing
itself for a kill of a good poem like a morgue
of insects feasting relish-ably on a meat
whose skin bore a different trademark –
like the singing crow with the silver beak
and milky wings.

Sanctum

for the umpteen skies Van Gogh painted

The hour grows desolate by the minute
as a boisterous dawn tries to break through
a rigid horizon reluctant to break loose;
it doesn't take long for the night to push
up further (probably trying to break past
umpteen strata of skies) like a mole drilling
assiduously, its hole, disregarding the soil's
consent for permeability; in the same way
the hour is holding still to the clock wanting
to break into a new hour; it becomes apparent
the sun will emerge from a different end,
from over the line of the sea, where the water
has begun to grow warm at the rims of its
sanctity; it doesn't matter if time is ruled by
the mobility of two hands on the dark face
of this wall clock; the dawn can show
its variegated promises but the sky can never
break away from its inherent morbidity.

Jade

'Girl in White'

It's a white walled jungle, frames
of hierarchy. Festivals have commenced
and fountains decorated. Flags of peace
in prayers, freedom of a calling of one's
god, hand-sewn verses on cotton lined
velvets, tall-spouted *dallahs* brewing
scented *qawas*; the market pebbles
stay steady, the one path of movable
consistency. I still remember the
glistening of your dates on a vendor's
bench, leg-loose and errant, as hands
cupped you in bowls to sell at an
expensive dirham – men marketing you
as the pericarp of heaven.

Holy

to finding the higher light

Place a foot in the river, watch the sea
chain your ankles to a spirit. Hear it
call your name to tasks, see a curved
finger rise like a sorcerer's wand.
The different ways in which the word
help is spoken is one: in the eyes
that dull inwards like current unwired.
Lift this weight off the arm that announces
power. There are other mouths to enter.
There is thicker hair to desecrate.
There are drier lips to whip towards
sacrilege. Show my feet their walk. Pour
the vial of silky veins into agape chest.
Teach the spirit to build a gentle noose –
my neck is shrinking on wrinkles fresh.

Being river and sea

when if Van Gogh

the sky has turned green
by sunset's forgotten dance,

the piers have dropped the souls
of their stoop-lights into the water –
a willing caregiver –

the river by a bent of docks
has taken the boats into its arms,

so much is shared
so much can be had

but the sea must learn
to understand constraints,

to know when to enter,
where to hold, what to help,
why to save;

the night is in no rush to emerge
from marine maws, for seashells

haven't slept their fill;
there are no sands waiting

by fertile shores; knowing
the time for every cause

is the sail to completion;
knowing oars of relinquish

is trusting the winds
in deferred sunrise –

Insomnia

Van Gogh to Paul Gauguin

Night oils hang by tenderness,
a chair propped in the shadows

of a dim room is how panic sets in;
re-finding the friend that understood

an aubade was a bat caught in the sun –
its melting wings of wax pouring

thickly on fresh blooms – is like looking
for a needle in a stack of over piled time.

The breasts of wrens are paling in the low
voltage white saver. I can see moonlight

spears ready to jab. My insistency
on pastels is why this every night

the room is a sea of transparent crickets
rising around the mouth of my eyes.

Omen

on 'The Starry Night'

It's easier to fly paper birds. I know
of solitude's sister: loneliness.

The king of distances are sheathed
promises. You live in a castle of

reeds where humming birds sit
on greying stalks of ashes. Scarcity

brought us together, reading too much
into inexistent lines. It wasn't long

until we scattered skeletons across the sea
between us. Forty days of hiding candles

and catching reflections on oil, the earth
still hangs over my head like a scry.

I have run out of salt to throw over
my shoulder; left a long trail I now reverse:

found a sparrow stretch its wings,
then watched a crane take flight.

Purple Honey

the night at Café Terrace

Royal robes on a pauper lantern are shone.
Sister, if you could see the streets tonight;
my indiscriminate lover combing her short
hair after a long day. People are eating
glass out of their hands as if a star's fallen
in. I imagine my body swinging
on the awning that forms a hammock,
looking directly into the violet-spangled
night. In this letter of frozen aesthetic,
I would write a love story that ended
like an untied passionate bull
in a field of acorns. I am drawing bees
in a row of flowers where a thickly
barked tree stings their houses. Tonight's
moon is vague like the amateur fortune
teller across the street handling the cloth
he sits on like a burglar. My lover
moves her lips like in a song into
the yellow light that takes her waist. They
glow like honey, her star-timid eyes.
I rush into a picture of indigo romance.

Intransigence

sun setting in the avenues

It was the mist that unfolded this time

the snow had clotted
like an expert dealt knot

around not fully expanded stones

like an infant is packed
with many layers of clothing;

it made the path appear
like a dotted outline
in a painting before colours
accentuated it

contracted, pinched and held
together as if by a peg

forming an even narrower groove
beneath what appeared like an overlapping

of the path edges, just the type of place

where *they* would breed in clusters;

also, it was seldom
that roads shrunk into crevices

and homes did not simply get
found upon by chance.

Subhadip Majumdar

Vincent, that little Hunger :

Vincent, I know that little hunger
That comes in the night
When you have nothing but a half stale bread and the last sip of coffee
I stand here, there where you become restless and search one by one
from one color to color
It is still seven days to month end
And you have no francs left
The lamp is lit
The light on your long face white beard deep eyes like a hole
I know that it is through this door you walked out
All of a sudden at night in three
Stand below the sky
In the freezing cold, you shiver
You don't care
In the moon light you look a forgotten painter
You laugh
In the wind still there is the smell of canvas
You breathe long
Then you walk towards the closed bread shop and stand for a while
From the road to Montmartre comes down the air
You walk towards it uphill
Then at one time you stand
Before a sleeping girl on road
You stare at her
At her pure face of innocence
Which poverty can never grasp
In the light of the stars
In the silence of the streets
In the glow of faded street lamps
A horse cab passes you
You, suddenly like a mad person start running
Down the hill, towards the road to your home
The cobbled stones makes sound

Your old very old shoe tore away
Your naked hands cold, like death
But then you enter your home
You stand before the white canvas
You pick up the brush
All hunger, now gone
No more worry of just one franc in your pocket
No more the wait of Theo 's letter pains you
No more the chilled winds through the open window make you shiver
It is the time
Now you break yourself completely
Break
Break
Break
In the mirror in the darkness
Your eyes glow
Bright like the moon
You are lost in that world now
Vincent, for which you are born!

2

Vincent at this part of the night I know sleep would not come to me.
It is that same blue restlessness
That sips from the moon
To
My naked body
Keeps me
Awake.
You know that.
As you are that artist
Who broke himself
Every moment
Bit by bit
Part by part
And stand before the dusted faded mirror
Seeing your face
Which would float half in darkness

Half in light
Before completely lost in a vacuum called time.

I stand there near my bed
It is not the room of your Yellow House
But it is still very much
An artist's room
And poverty roams on the place.

So I would whisper to you
It is strange how each night I look at your prints and talk to you
The starry night
The potato eaters
Those line of sketches you did near the mines
I have seen them
So many times
That I know each of them and in the eerie silence
They each as if come out from the sketch
And ask me about you.
How is Vincent?
They would ask.
Some in Dutch.
Some in French.
Some in English.
They still carry the axe with them to work and come back home with
tired black faces
From below the mines
But they would always stop and ask me
Before they walk away again
Lost in your sketch.

What can I say?
When one miner would say me,
'It's been ages and no one has ever cared to sketch us.'
Vincent, the world needs you
Once more
I sit there with all my numbness and like them
Search you

Who made me believe
That you can dream and live and lit life
And with all the shadows within
You would know,
That one day
A night full of stars
Would bestow on you.
That's when
Hidden from the world
You can cry
Unseen by any
Like a man.

Only your work knows
The moments between you and the canvas
Till everything is drawn and done
And gone.
No, it is never gone.
The pain would make it alive.
So alive
That as I stand before your grave
I can only wish
That you made this earth so beautiful
So pure
So innocent
That
Still
The present paints as if with your brush
With colors of your dreams
That only you can see.

Vincent, I read your letters
Again and again
I am that lonely that I love to sip all the images
In your words
Your every hand shake with your brother, Theo
With the women you met
And left

One by one
Well, they never left ,Vincent.
An artist never lose any one
They are all in your paintings
Some with their hands moving
Some in the open park
Some again with faces in haze
Being born is the truth
That truth
Is all
And for that you never cared anything,
Even
Death.

I walk in the streets now far away
From your home,
In Paris, in Hague, in Nuenen, in Amsterdam
And of course in Arles
Each day I count my money
So that I can save enough
To go and see your paintings again
Stand in the queue to museum
Between the bright sun and the floating boats
Of the numerous canals of Amsterdam
I always thought of standing before your yellow house
But that house has gone in Second World war
Perished
Destroyed
But not eliminated
Thus I look at that small postcard of the print of the house
Which I brought from the museum
And within the dark room
Dim lit
With desklamp
Open pages of books
Letters that smelt of fog
I feel that I share with you
One thing

That little pain.

I open the door
Climb the stairs
Come to the roof
And stretch my hands
Towards the sky,
And utter with a gulp in my throat,
Vincent, you are mine!

The Road to Rue des Lepic :

We would slowly walk out of the cafe and in the evening light and go underground.Daniella knows the metro of Paris like her own palm and she explains me the route to Montmarte. Within half an hour when we reached there, I at once spotted the road after reading so much of Van Gogh letters.It is as if my road to home. I asked Daniella to follow me and come to a square where an old man with a beautiful old face with specs seated at the bus stop waiting for a bus.

I asked him, 'Do you know where Van Gogh used to live? '

The old man looked at me and said, 'Do you have a paper with you? '

I only have the metro leaflet with me. The old man brushed out a pen from his pocket and start drawing a map. When it's done he said, 'Follow this road straight. Then turn right. The road name is Rue Des Lepic.'

I thanked him and as I walked with Daniella she grasped my hand and said, 'Now, I can remember the road. To the details. I have come many times here with my father.'

We walked and then turned right and then stopped before a green door building where it is written , "Theo and Vincent Van Gogh".

I don't know but I feel like crying.

Daniella hold my hand and asked what happened? I said,

'It is nothing. I still cannot believe that the dream I have seen for so long, at last I have reached that.'

In the glorious evening of Rue De Lepic I uttered, 'Vincent,I am here. '

We stand there for a while in silence.

A local artist paints on the road.

Someone sings. Young girls visits the bookshop at the opposite side.

This is Paris!

I still in the mood of trance of seeing the Van Gogh's house stand thinking.

Some pigeons fly and they look at me as if thinking what I am doing looking at them. They burble in their own language and I buy a cookie from a shop and throw at them. I give it They immediately start having it with their sharp throat.

'How sweet and simple the scene is! '

Daniella says.

I love to hear her talking.'Yes, looking at the pigeons I think , Vincent must have fed them often. Some of their ancestors must be always there.'

'Yes, it is their home. And they through generations would live here, some may fly away but some would again come back. Like me.' Daniella slowly said.

I stared at her.

She looked at me and said,

'Yes, like me. Some one who has left her home gone to England for study, never can settle there and now back in France.I wish my father had not sold the home. If I have a home now.. '

I with my eyes on the pigeons again said, 'Yes, I know the pain of losing a home. It continues with you where ever you go. And my old home often comes back in my dreams, as if the grills , the walls, the doors, the windows asking me, 'Why have you left us? And I know I have no answer.'

'I am like a wind you know.' Daniella says.

I hold her hand and smiled,

'Yes that French wind that has always called me from across the seas and oceans and mountains to come below the Eiffel and lie and live and find a girl named, Daniella.'

That night with the Christmas moon shining we stand after a long Paris walk below the Eiffel and kissed deep.

Then we spent the night lying on the grass making love just in the French way.

Carol Alexander

A Dish of Sun

What I love is citrine, stones and old straw,
the warmth of absinthe and a pooled yolk
and the goddess who serves in a yellow gown,
her skin golden from infancy in the fields,
solid planes of wheat where weevils drone.

What I crave is the blue above Auvers-sur-Oise
and the Sun's eye and olive leaves.
I've prayed without ceasing by the churchyard
and millrace where boys tempt the current.
Once, in a fever, I see a child drown.

       *   *   *

Sorrowful yet always rejoicing, I distill
in my sunflowers the gist of a body
nursing the soil. In this summer heat,
composed of tiny, spiraling dots, skin crawls.
Electric shocks goad the rain.
A word is spat out from the mouth of God--
all His honey and His fire.

And work is a sermon, the umber sheaves
scented with the sweat of laboring men.
A woman is pushing her wheelbarrow.
Spears of the cypress trees carve up heaven--
and oh this impasto, grass licking like flames,
scintillating weft of his ministry.
Let me not be verbose; there is enough paint still.

       *   *   *

"They have tilled the earth themselves with these hands

they are putting in the dish...they have thus honestly
earned their food."

If I cannot preach, I can pray.
The potato eaters husband their oil. They know lack,
they have tilled the earth, breaking its stones.
What they eat has the color and form of stones.
If I cannot pray, I can paint.
What I do is no less than what they do.

      *   *   *

Brother, remember the mill. How we talked!
I have kept joy, the black wings and harsh cries.
One mislaid a pitchfork in the hay,
and it flamed in the sun like the holy rood.

      *   *   *

I am in the portrait of a yellow chair
when I fear the muddy river teeth
and doubt the strength of the bridge.

I wait for his return, paint myself into the chair.
There is a rush seat for him, if he will return.

      *   *   *

The countryside stirs with the beat of crows,
which I make as a child might--three quick strokes
over tufts of grain. The land abuts heaven
while a sick soul takes comfort
in the swoop of feathers massing cloud.
Let them do my restless bidding, *bien bien*.

      *   *   *

What I know of want lies in the poppies,

a red I have spared only for her.
The models have disappeared, seeking gold.
But the poppies--still, they have life.

      *   *   *

A poet wrote he was neither well nor ill.
De sterrennacht swirled in my head
when I propped a canvas against the wall.
My disease, says the doctor,
is hyperbole. Swirling like tongues
that have sipped deep of absinthe
the stars swim, their trails of phosphorous
having something marine.

When I hear my father preach, I hear the God
of economy, the moderation of the Dutch.

Father trudging home through the snow
is struck down in winter's mindless gale--
through night's excess the steeple breaches,
a solid form binding the starry night.

      *   *   *

When he shoots me, I pray for him
as I'd knelt for the men gone down the mines.
Two days dying, lapped in moon glow,
belly of a woman cupping my seed.
The boy, who's mocked me through the town,
hands me this perfect suicide. Down, heart.
It's enough to be given the light,
these colors that have built a church.
See how the houses tile the hills, how a spire
ballasts this aching blue.

Redux

The yellow blooms of Auvers, stippled in the grass.
This warm morning of his last spring, in a field
that has defied March to the teeth, sprawl the hasty stems
and the girl child with eyes of Frisian blue.

Noonday dress stained with sunlight and orange oil,
butter sheen of her cropped fringe, reddened cheeks;
she takes the lunch of a *midinette*, glimpses protean clouds
like the ferny tresses of singed saints.

Guidebook to the cities, our speckled passports,
espresso beans, crumbling cakes of of almond paste--
the train runs past Auvers, seen through the lunette.
Redux all journeys, that a painted child may tongue
a taste so sweet, to quell the fear of death.

Heavy-bellied cows with harmless horns
munch garlic in the field, ignore our train.
Their milk will be no good, and soon it will storm.
The girl has bitten the orange now: she's all sugared breath,
grass streaking the crown of her head. She is a touchstone
of something found. But this doesn't need to be anywhere at all.

Self-Portrait

Blue stones are his eyes, or brown. Or green.
They change with whatever light he sees.
Today he wears a cloth cap trimmed with fur,
a loosely buttoned smock. His soul keeps passing
through his hands, into the fast, dark strokes
of his peculiar signature. He peoples the gallery
with myriad selves. We have no right to mourn them.
He is always reworking an innocent prayer,
and his scumbled iconography, the ages of man
as martyr and saint, the way the blue of iris
threads into the blouse and coat, the way
he could drink and go down to the river
where the peasants fished for their late supper,
how he changed his coat from blue to brown,
his drawn face livid or flushed by northern sun--
here, said my old father, who painted every day,
was the man, he suffered, he worked on.

Refusal

What are those birds like sparrows,
but smaller than sparrows, oh the redwing blackbirds--
drab females of the species daubed with finger paints,
hardly black at all--flock to the steeple of the church.
I think of his crows, and wheat fields beating with grasshoppers
while the thin soup jells. And the lemons on the plate
pooling in green shadow-- a trace of nothing,
wiped from the sleeve. He dresses himself in shadow.
And later on, the brushes cleaned and quiet,
he eats from the white plate and potatoes in the yellow dish,
just enough to keep away that final gust of the cold.

Jonny Huerta

Van Gogh vs flying ergot

Van Gogh ate paint chips
mixed with lead
He painted wheat fields
For some odd reason
And tiny pieces of flying ergot
That seemed to resemble crows

Van Gogh vs Joe Montana

I had a dream I found a portrait
of a young Joe Montana
Van Gogh painted
after he won his first Superbowl
at an estate sale in San Francisco
when I asked the old lady
how much it would cost
I didn't have the five bucks
to buy the damn thing

Van Gogh vs van Gogh

Van Gogh died
Before his first
self-portrait
dried

Van Gogh vs. The ice cream man

I remember when they used to burn
old tires along the trail
to the top of Tortugas Mountain
and would walk up that shit barefoot
holding a statue of a plastic jesus
I once hiked up old Tortuga
On three hits of Starry Night acid
and heard the ice cream man
from the top of a giant waffle cone

Van Gogh vs coyote fence

Alligator Juniper
Adobe walls
coyote fence
Alfalfa fields
maybe if
Van Gogh
Was born in
the Southwest
he would have
sold more than
one painting
before his
Untimely

death

A horse named van Gogh

He was a wild painted horse
Never meant to be broken

Too volatile to ride
And too majestic to be put down

We set him free on the llano
And never saw him again

Some roughnecks say they
See him in the distance

Between the oil pumps
And the mirages of
West tejas sunsets

Van Gogh paints a tombstone

You did real good, son.
Just Let It Go.
Won't you let the Angels
call you home?
Tonight's sunset
Will have to be
your tombstone.
It has your name
written all over it
and will go down
in the record books
as being the most
Brilliant and colorful
As if the ghost of
Vincent Van Gogh
Was allowed to paint
A catron county sky
just one time.

Montagnes á Saint-Rémy

I heard a story once
about a guy who found
a Spanish breastplate
hiking in the Sandia's
late last summer.
My buddy found an
old Apache bow
In a cave in
the Chiricahuas
earlier this spring.
I read In the newspaper
that a Pennsylvania hunter
found a perfect
Henry repeating rifle
leaning against a tree
a couple autumn's back.
Well, this winter I found
true love up in
the Mountains at Saint-Rémy
and that's more precious
than any rare find.

Lisa Wiley

On the Fifth Floor of MoMA

I bump into *The Starry Night*
accidentally like my sister-in-law
who didn't know it was here either —

she'd only spied the painting in textbooks,
sobbed when she first saw van Gogh's masterpiece.
Not larger than life. Just real.

Anne Sexton created her own version:
The night boils with eleven stars.
Oh starry night! This is how I want to die.

And she did. Wearing her mother's fur coat,
she started the engine in her garage.
On these unforgiving February days

full of fake sponge candy hearts,
when I want to unlock the gun cabinet,
I crawl to the treadmill instead,

run until I see those swirling stars.
Sweet release like a heroin addict,
I don't need needles to reach that hot sky.

The Last Time I Saw Her

—for my next door neighbor

The last time I saw her
she was walking her dog, beloved Yogi,
with all the patience in this world.
She waited for me to pull out the driveway
veiled by perpetual pines.

The last time I saw her
her smile shone like a young girl's.
She wasn't going to work,
kept private what lingered in her lung,
tended her purple irises instead.

Her chocolate eyes warm, full of light,
her spirit sparkled through the whole block.
The last time I saw her,
wish I had grasped her hand —
now I see her irises everywhere.

Does She Glide in a Gondola?

1.

My dead neighbor's name typed in black.
Glossy AAA travel insert
with two gondolas and red flowerboxes
arrives in my mailbox instead of hers.
Promises of discounts and odysseys,
gleaming and alive.

2.

Jubilant to go on a movie date
when she finishes reading
Under the Tuscan Sun,

Shelly flutters like a songbird.

I want to return her mail,
talk to her about Italy,
what wine to pair with dinner.

3.

Did Death guide the mailman's hand?
Was I buried under a featherbed
when he knocked — climbed her stoop instead?
My cloudiness frightened him,
her soft soul an easy catch.

4.

She slices tree branches *like butter.*
Look how easy this gizmo works.

Her son's banana curls bounce,
stacking the branches.

5.

Does she glide in a gondola?
I still walk the sidewalk.
She's in an urn with cobalt blue butterflies.

6.

Serious little girl,
her daughter sits at the sill,
dark eyes survey the neighborhood now.
No replacement for mother's love.
Just slow melting, simmering sauce
on Sundays when her aunts come by.

7.

I want to have a word with Death.
Scold him. Tell him he's all wrong.
What about the neighbor behind her
who complains about their dead pines
every chance she gets *What if they blow over?*
Might kill me.

8.

Shelly lives in bold brushstrokes —
her front door, lilac; her son's room, crimson;
the family room, magenta.
I long to sit on her celery-colored porch,
dip pitas in hummus, watch the traffic
with her laugh raising the roof.

9.

She tells me *It's okay,*
I see everything now.
I know your darkness
when your baby was born.
I know you tried your best.
Please bring my daughter flowers for her birthday.

10.

Spring will shoulder her way in,
bring buds to the dogwood
and rows of purple bulbs.

Now, her husband plows our sidewalk,
the motion methodical, medicinal.

Poetic License

I can turn the grass blue,
change willows into strands of licorice,
conjure a pterodactyl to devour
your worst snaggle-toothed nightmare
or lasso the moon instead of a lightbulb.
*Your poetic license trumps reality
most of the time*, you say.

No need to wave a wand;
you always took my breath away
like seeing the Grand Canyon
for the first time at sunrise.
I knew all your layers in every light.
Your eyes my storm shelter —
safe even running through a hurricane.

Bob Kunzinger

Bumping Into Vincent

I put out a blanket and some wine, a few glasses, and we sat in the afternoon summer sun just outside Auvers, France. I wanted to go to this spot since the late '80s or so after studying fine art at university. Then there we were, with wine, and a beautiful summer sun though the wind was bending the wheat well past the breaking point. I had to hold down one side of the blanket.

A skinny, red-haired man walked past and since we had extra wine I offered him some. He graciously accepted, though his voice was weak, almost a sigh, and since I handed him the glass while he sat down, he—or I, I'm not certain—spilled the wine on his shirt. I poured him a new one, apologizing, to which he didn't make any remark except to smile. Still, he spent the rest of the afternoon holding his left side with red bleeding from his shirt and onto his hands. I felt so bad.

He asked why we were there and I said, "Well at this moment it is to talk with you and get to know you! Tell me my dear new friend, what have you been doing with yourself today?"

He took a sip of wine, waited, and told us of his afternoon:

I took to a field outside the village and worked there on a somber painting. There were crows, many of them. And the wheat fields balanced the flight into the wind by bending the other way, with the breeze. Had a boy been passing through I could have taken the scene for *The Sower*. But only I was there. I brought my palette, canvas and brushes with me, and also the revolver. Sometimes the crows slash down toward the painting and I use the gun to scare them away. I'd just as soon be left alone. Well, today the crows didn't seem to matter. I retrieved the revolver between strokes, shot, but missed my heart. The bullet lodged instead in my side.

I was walking home when you kindly offered to spill wine on me.

I assume they will send for the local physician, which is fine, but I insist on Dr. Gachet. I much prefer to be pronounced dead by someone I know; it is a cold enough occasion. Still, I doubt they can do anything for me since it will be impossible to remove the bullet, and matters must be allowed to run their course. Interesting that I suddenly wish to draw the good Dr. Gachet.

Do you mind if I smoke my pipe? I find in it an old and faithful friend and we never part. I hope they can reach my brother Theo. Perhaps he will remain by my bedside the entire time. No one needs to convince me that both doctors are good and perhaps might even be able to prevent further attacks. It isn't the attacks that concern me, though. At least during them, as out of touch as I might have been, I wasn't aware of the contempt in people's voices toward "pour Vincent."

Oh, yes, I apologize. I am Vincent.

Anyway, I admit they can save my life, and with the stretch of the imagination they may be able to prevent further attacks. But the sadness will always remain. I feel Theo understands that death is perhaps not the saddest event in a painter's life.

Listen, and please be clear about this: Properly speaking I was not a madman. The paintings I did in the intervals of attacks were not inferior to the others. I simply acquired an illness. But art is jealous; she does not want us to choose illness in preference to her, so I did what she wished. This is the completeness with which she overtook my life. I find no error in anything I did; perhaps some in others' views toward me, which I cannot blame them for. But the roots of the mind run deep and cannot live without occasional watering. I fear I have dried up.

People never understood that I was just trying to leave some sort of souvenir out of gratitude for being able to walk on this earth for some time. And I wish not for anyone to believe that I shot myself in spite of the life I led, or because of it. Suicide was always something I completely denounced. Look at me, though! I was much younger once and the life that exploded from me then would have filled a thousand canvases. But by the time I started to paint, the enthusiasm for life was declining rapidly. And no matter how enthralled we become in our work, how enthusiastic we are in doing what we believe to be the voice of our soul, without a complete love of life, the work is pointless. The work will only create illusions. I had that love of life for a complete twenty-seven years, from the days of my youth in Zundert right through my preaching in the Borinage outside of Brussels, I was alive.

Then I painted. I guess the entire outcome would have been different had I managed to intertwine the two. But if there was always a certain undercurrent of vague sadness, it was certainly difficult to define. Perhaps my life never caught up with my desires.

I would love some more wine. In the glass, thank you.

It is not always the colors we see that make a painting beautiful, and so in life. I boarded a carriage that I believed to be mine but nobody told me the bridge was out. Ha! When you dedicate your life to one thing, one idea, one line of work, you expect the faith of friends, if not their support. Family and loved ones may not agree with you and may quite the contrary believe one to fall dead on one's face, but the burden is easier carried with even the *slightest* faith. Only Theo understood this.

As a child art was in our family. But so was the Gospel, and that is what found its way into my heart. And what is at the bottom of one's heart stays there.

I had an older brother, you see. His name was also Vincent van Gogh, also born March 30th, but in 1852. But he died almost immediately, and exactly one year later I was born and named for him. I, too, born March 30th to a preacher in the small village of Zundert in Holland. I was registered in the hospital as number 29, as was the first Vincent. Odd. Oh, and what is today? Well, the 27th, yes. Perhaps I should hang on a few days until the 29th to die. That would indeed be say. But, believe me, the saddest account of my youth which perhaps never left the bottom of my heart is the daily walks to my father's church, where at the front gate was the elder Vincent's grave.

Yes, please, look at me; I desire to die, with all the sadness which remains. But until today, you must believe, I desired to live.

After a while he picked up his materials and I helped him stand. His shirt was now soaked red throughout his side and even down into his pants. I offered to give him a ride but he insisted upon walking the rest of the way. He was kind enough to leave the painting he was working on, one of a wheat field with crows. But the paint is still wet.

Mary Ellen Talley

The Teen with Down Syndrome Volunteers to Teach Art History to the Speech-Language Pathologist

or Starry Night

Stray threads of words
she cannot read
she walks the high school halls
clutching her dad's thick book
of Van Gogh's glossy paintings
sashays past my office
and I invite her in with other students
to point out landscape   horizon   portrait
indigo swirl and curve
The Olive Trees
Wheat Field with Cypresses
Rosebush in Blossom
what he saw outside the window
Show the master's self-portrait
straw hat or guess
at instructions on surgical dressing
as if we're all able
to sort the several Starry Nights

She heads downstairs to show her art teacher
Van Gogh's famous colors

same as if she's off to take a trip
because she says she wants her own
bedroom at Arles
lavender walls to soothe jitters
(the red faded and now
the room looks blue)
sunflowers and cadmium orange sunshine
at the window
Her several reproductions –

one-a-day she copies his fierce flowering
cochineal lake, vermillion highlight
squeezed tube of French ultramarine
on bumpy jute
He – (ever spending the brain
down to the last guilder) –
for paint tastes so delicious
although Theo implies it's self-defeating

As if in straw hat jaunt
she heads toward her bus
holding a thick stemmed yellow daffodil
flipping it across her body to the right
with one footstep
and to the left with the next
Van Gogh asks if it's edible –
she says a flower's not for eating
If he loves the color
swallow sunshine
ride a bike with wide tires
down a pebble path
to jump on a Big Wheel
watch the wide North Sea
She says to face your fears –
colored lights shine
their variance
on the night sky palette

To an Elusive Ear

hear it:
follow the fold,
your ear canal
narrows
to elastic stretch.

the anvil chorus
of a thousand
strobes of sound
will bounce
off that taut membrane,

pulsing onward,
space of sound across
miles
or days of one person,
light and sound,
so many missed intentions
coursing through the inner ear.

do not hesitate
to count the fractured spectrums
that never made it to Arles
needing to row
through fluid thrumming fields.

look at that face,
that rambling message
coveting synapses
of each dream vision
field of sunflowers.

electric connections fly
within a voluminous cavern,
spiral staircase
of hair cells clicking on and off

rods and cones so fast light cannot flicker
as something akin to sight
glistens inside cortical crevasses.

word pictures cannot strike
past the Auditory nerve
alerting optical synapses
beyond the round window
if made of shifting sands.

Our Daughter's Teen Age Foray into Home Décor

So we nix Van Gogh's Starry Night swirls
on the bedroom ceiling
fearing only half an evening would forever
rise above us when we sleep.

God knows why she doesn't want something
a bit simpler
like the original lavender of Van Gogh's Bedroom at Arles
before the curious incident of his ear.

We leave her with $100 and free rein
in our bathroom.
Ah, the lavender walls when we return,
blue walls sponged nearly white.

Lavender ribbons woven through curtains.
No major changes
but the directions say just place the white tiles
above the old floor.

Upon return, we notice the Care Bear tattoo at the base
of her spine as she bends
over the floor quizzically realizing that each self-stick
square tile keeps sliding.

Dad and daughter bonding scraping even the old
linoleum to start over
replacing all tiles, deft cutting around the toilet.
One tile remains askew.

Our daughter now lives 3,000 miles away, leaving us
her impressionistic zeal,
lavender ribbon looped through lace curtains
at our bathroom window.

Jay Passer

Brothers

her name's Asia
she strips at the Deja Vu
my brother is obsessed with her
now I see why
long and lean,
finely formed
with a wide mouth and dancing green eyes
and a jaunty jut and strut on the stage
acrobat on the pole
every man in the place salivating
in the disco ball-speckled darkness
I pull my old stingy-brim
lower over my eyes
if my girl knew where I was
she would assassinate me

Asia gyrates a last time with a coy smile
heads into the back as
Motorhead's *Ace of Spades*
fades to black
Vinnie is obviously agitated
I order a couple vodka sodas
and walk over
damn Teddy, where'd you come from?
quit sneakin' up on me!
I smile and hand Vinnie his drink
so now I'm stalking you?
well at any rate it's
good timing bro, can you spare 20 bucks?
when can't I?
I guess never
I look toward the stage
so that's Asia

yeah, that's her
Vinnie starts to light up
he gets that way, gesticulates in crazy arcs
his eyes blazing rebellion
his psyche demanding revolution
I got a good feeling about Asia
he sings
she's a goddess disguised as a strumpet
my brother the dichotomist
what're you gonna do, use her as a model?
I'm working on it
but she's not too keen about it
she thinks painting
is obsolete
she wants to star in a porn flick
well she's got a point
painting may be lucrative for the painter
but the star will always circumnavigate the cosmos
oh thanks for that, brother
how very encouraging
how 'bout that Jefferson?

a couple days later
I get an email
it's from Vinnie
describing the color of mustard in a pale sunset
as unsettling and vulgar
the faulty mechanism of cobalt
blue worse than the black and blues
entertaining suicide on the face
of a maudlin drunk
why don't you just text me bro
if you want to talk
but my brother is possessed
with Asia
and sunshine and broken buildings
squealing, jerky buses burdened with
the working class

and the squalid streets
and the faces
all the faces of the wretched and destitute
the bodies lying prone across sewer grates
steaming with the productivity of industry
meet you at the Deja Vu
being the daily mantra
the last several paintings
shocking the common public
those with no problem serving
shit sandwiches to the wedding party

I can't complain
my own girl keeps me in line
it's Valentine's day daily with my girl
plus she's planning on
pregnancy
Vinnie tries to hide it
but he's jealous
even while I fork over cash for supplies

Asia I hope
Asia I dream
Asia I freeze
Asia I objectify
Asia I sigh

nothing to lose sleep over, right?
there's gonna be a day I choke to death
looking after your best interests, bro
I thought
but couldn't bring myself
to say

she sure looks hot up there though
straddling that pole
maybe a condescending moment
ensues
but dawn awakens, 6 AM
and down the street at Vesuvio's

the bartender hasn't even brewed the coffee yet

Asia
her eyes leaking emerald ink
saves the entire existence of humanity
with a swift smile
and spandex cross-legged
we huddle together on the second floor
looking out over the cold bustle of
Columbus
but I'm the third wheel so I
down my shooter
as my cell vibrates
gotta take off, duty calls
Vinnie perks an ear
under that jaunty Panama hat
sell something will ya?
preferably of mine?
Asia devilish
swirling her fruity vodka

the image of her
as I let myself into the gallery
projected on the future of my life
in 3-D
not a good day for happy commerce
they're betting under
while my brother
being the best painter of the bunch
is dissented and obfuscated
maybe it's the Panama hat
from that stint in Mexico City
the corn cob pipe
you know he scents his skank with lavender?
some funky rebel
ass under control, I got it made
most of my quiver shoots straight
it's nothing to lose your cool over
but then there's my
brother

he causes me endless torment
genius is like that
I get on the line to the Hague
to Prague
an important lady in Philadelphia
places like Los Angeles, Melbourne
Tel Aviv and Tokyo
meanwhile Asia
whose real name is Ariel
or Annabelle or
Abigail
swirls her fruity Stolichnaya
re-crosses her legs and twists
her finely sculpted foot
toenails painted
cherry red
like ten tiny sunsets
my cell vibrating again
eloped to my ass via
my back pocket and
galvanizing my
stupor

sure thing
I'll take that early Mark Tobey
we talked about, and
the Jenny Holzer neon
the David Hockney pastel
the Cindy Sherman selfie
and the Francis Bacon print
the Keith Haring Porsche
if you'll throw in
the Deborah Butterfield
statuette

done deal,
back to the firing squad
as Vinnie always says

camped out in the frozen morning
with his frame and easel
capturing
a street scene enveloped in fog
hitching to Monterey with
stops at sequoia groves
In-N-Out Burger
pumpkin patches
and the bleak majesty of the Pacific
always at his heels
dozing on the beach
at Half Moon Bay

some say he's mad
that he ought to be committed
that he can't be trusted on his own
that painting harasses the dark matter in his head
wearing that crazy hat ringed with candles
sucking down the absinthe
which isn't even made
with wormwood anymore
his pornographic women
and crabbed insistence
on the eternal reward
he'll be the death of me
since I couldn't stand living without him

but it's back to
business
then a bite to eat,
some dim sum at
Yee's on Grant
where guess who struts by
Asia
undoubtably
on her way to catch some Z's
with Vinnie in tow
careening only mildly

happily oblivious to my presence
I watch her ass
the ass of Asia
so enchanting
receding down the sidewalk
Asia
is hotness personified
but in the end
nothing to lose an ear over
still
I'm waiting for the day
Vinnie paints her
to the nose of his F-4 Phantom

Judith Berke

Dance Hall

Once everything was geometry.
So that a philosopher
who once would have been a geometer—
would have looked at this painting and said
See, what did I say? Almost everything in this scene is geometrical:
each section of balcony a rectangle;
each hanging light like a tiny sun—
in fact, the face of almost every woman there
is a sun..." (though someone else
might say their faces are too flat
to be suns; are *imperfect circles*, or freeform
shapes, or triangles . . .)

"Time is a straight line
(leading into the future,)
he'd have said, though now we know
there is no future (and no past either) . . .
But try telling that to the woman
with the feather like a scarlet bird
in her hair;
who's thinking she's been waiting
for one of those stags to come speak to her
forever . . . or try telling one of the stags
himself -- who is looking forward to midnight
so he can go home (and the dance
hasn't even started yet!) Who seems to sense
what we know now--

that time (and space) are wavy
wobbly lines, like the line of people in the back
of the dance hall, that seems to undulate

like a sea that might suddenly crash into

the people who mill in an orderly
fashion in front; who are able to wait
for whatever pleasure they'll get there—
if not dancing, then maybe just pressing against
people, smelling that strange mixture
of perfume and sweat and fear
that seems to pour out of them in a place
like this; or maybe that unusually tall
man, with closed eyes and bent head—
who seems to have a more sensitive (bigger) nose

that most, and is sniffing around
all over: that cat-in-heat
smell (more like a beautiful black panther
in heat, he likes to imagine)
that seems to come from the woman with black
hair; that marigold (or is it a yellow rose)
smell, that comes from the woman with the yellow-orange
hair as if this were not a dance hall at all, but a zoo
and a garden . . .

Fourteenth of July Celebration, Paris

Why is so much of history about terror?
You'd think the two were conjoined
twins; you'd think those were American
flags and banners is this celebration at night in Paris—
but that's because they're just mad dashes
of color; there's no shape, no pattern
to anything there

like that wild celebration in Cannes
that night, when a rifle
suddenly went off near my ear . . .
There was a woman knitting
there too; though not as grim
as the one in the green doorway
in Paris—a Madame Defarge
if I ever saw one –

though the painting is not about
history (or a story based
on history); that woman with the yellow
 parasol might seem to float up
off the ground, even if this were not
the 14th of July; in fact, there is so much

excitement and joy
there, it seems those red, white and blue
banners are rising, flying like giant birds
into the sky, having somehow been freed
from the poles, the ropes, the strings
they were attached to!

Field of Flowers

A child lies in a field on her back,
feeling it breathe under her
like a great soft anima.
She does not know that the place is beautiful.

She only knows what her body knows.
How a leaf feels, falling cool on her face.
Something sticky crawling up her leg.
The sweet smell of the flowers
that makes her feel faint.

Then, when she's older, she sees the painting
and says, *This is the place where I was,
and it's beautiful.* her body and mind
come together
like twins that had been separated.

Then she forgets. Till years later she sees
the picture in a book. By then ther is
 so much pain and pleasure
packed insider her, she's not sure.

She lies on the bed and tries to remember.
How old she had been.   Where the place was.
All she knows is that
she was looking up. That something cool
was on her skin. And the smell, some

sweet smell that made her feel she might die
of joy or pain, or both.
She doesn't remember.

Two Fish on a Piece of Yellow Paper

These are not the divine fish, the water spirits,
becoming more and more human—
    half fish, half man.
Not the fish of fecundity,
each with its thousands of eggs,
mediating
between earth and sky.

These are not the fish of the word,
each a god with a trident,
or the fish of the devil, or the golden
ones that came to eat
from the priest's hands.
These are not the fish of sex—
sometimes a male, sometimes a female;

not those that were scribbled everywhere—
illegible to almost everyone.
Not even the everyday cloud-
fish we see in the sky.
There are only two, not enough
    for a trinity;
facing opposite directions

like the fish of astrology;
like John and I
each thinking the way we faced
was the only way.
So streamlined, so swift
you'd think they'd never get caught
as we do, who carry the water inside us.

Bowl of Potatoes

It isn't *every* vegetable that has its portrait painted
and *no* other vegetable was used for a holy wafer
when there was no wheat. "Give us this day
our daily potato," the prayer should have said—
but the potatoes didn't let it go to their heads—
they were too much part of the earth for that—
though this was a bit much, so many jammed
together in that earthen bowl, like the "huddled masses"
in American, where they had come from in the first place
before being sent to Ireland, and then back to America
again, and well, they were just everywhere—
so why did people speak of them as if they were clods:
the poor lowly, homely
potato, they said, forgetting the French Charlottes with caviar
and cool, elegant potato soup; and that King Louis XVI
had worn their flowers in the buttonhole of his coat!
Oh the joys and chagrins, the highs and lows
of such renown! It was enough
to make a starchy vegetable long
to be some thin, green, leafy one,
that wouldn't give enough nourishment
to a flea! to make the, the potatoes, long
to be not picked, to be just left under the ground
where they started. Would people e sorry then!
Mightn't they wish they had spoken better
about them, the potatoes? Just thinking
about this made the potatoes in the painting feel like weeping:
In fact, with all those eyes
all over them, it was hard not
to weep: dozens of eyes in these potatoes
made mostly of water anyway,
and every one of them weeping.

Young Woman in Her Garden

Is there such a thing as too much
abundance? asks the young woman with the question
mark for a hat, gesturing with her almost
translucent hand at the garden growing so wild
around her . . . *No, you tell me,*
I say, thinking there must be some-

thing she could say, about controlling
things, about being able to be
perfectly still while everything around you
runs amok. . .
Even if the painting gives her
only a profile, and no mouth at all

with which to answer.

Night with Stars

I can't imagine what I'd have thought
(what I'd have felt) looking up and seeing
that enormous spiral galaxy
in the sky, that night in 1889.
If I'd seen how it was surrounded by other, smaller galaxies,
each with a black hole, like an eye
at its center—
all of which look close enough to collide
with each other, with us,
though they're actually millions of light years away—

And imagine what people in that small village
would have thought, who knew even less than I
about astronomy, about the universe,
who had only that giant cypress
to protect them, or the mountains
they're surrounded by; who wouldn't understand
that the sky is full of dust ad gases
and also something called "dark matter,"
which bends the light passing through it

so that if they could see through it,
it would be like looking through at telescope
so they could see it closer—the patterns
of it—so maybe it wouldn't be so overwhelming,
almost frightening, seeing that whirling, spiraling
sky, that the painted has painted, as if he
was our telescope that night,
our dark matter (with its dark energy)
magnifying everything, making it clearer.

Portrait of a Poet

If you asked the tapeworm (which has no alimentary
canal of its own) why it has lodged in this poet's
body, it would say it didn't know but if you asked it
its name, it would say Art, would say the act
of creating . . . There it is, inside him, its long tubular
body a worm but its mouth the open beak
of an innocent (ravenous) baby bird
crying *Feed me!*

And this bird (this worm) is always hungry;
if the poet opened his mouth you would see its
beak (which might instantly swallow you up,
so you'd better watch out) open inside it, screaming
for food; even though it easts almost everything
the poet eats, till the poor man looks like one of his own
poems: pared to the bone, not a smidgeon
of extra flesh on him . . .

Not only that, but this worm, this stomach inside
his stomach, seems to have swallowed everything
around him; appears to have swallowed his whole world--
so that he seems to be sitting black, empty space
all alone, except for those few stars (which we see
in the portrait, above him); which this thing inside him would
like to suck down and swallow, too, but it can't; these stars
have their own, more powerful gravity, and prefer to remain

in heaven.

Five Portraits (Same Pose) of Madame Ginoux

How can you live
in a world that's so confusing?
Peel away that handsome powder pink mask from the face
of this woman, and you might find a different
mask underneath.

People thought my friend was aloof,
maybe because she held her eyebrows
like this, so they arched way above
her eyes. I hear this woman called
to the painter, and all he did was paint her.

If I had called out
somehow to that man, would he have seen me?
Even if I sat turned away
as she does, her cheek in her hand?

In one picture she seems to be close, intimate
with the painter. Then you see in another
she's looking right past. Hiding behind
that table, those books.

How can you be sure of what you see?
Her dress I thought was black is really blue.
Her eyes I thought wistful might just be sly.
The portrait I thought most authentic is a fake.
And vice-versa.

A Pair of Shoes

In his trillion-page essay
the famous philosopher concluded
that these shoes belonged to a peasant in a field;
only they didn't. They were the painters—
probably not a left and right
shoe--you had to be rich
to afford that. Otherwise, you wore just two
shoes, generic, and hoped they would somehow take the shapes of
your feet,
the way you'd try to fit opposite sides of yourself
   into one dream.
It was at this exact moment
he began to paint what was inside his mind
more than what he saw just with his eyes.
Or maybe through a film of color (passion) over
what he saw. These fantastic blue strokes
the shoes are wrapped in. A sad
color. So gorgeous
you don't even mind the sadness.

Still Life with Grapes

A mother tells her child she loves him
but then treats him as though she hated him.
so is it any wonder
the child has no faith in words?

As for this painting, it's called "Still Life With Grapes,"
but it certainly doesn't look
like life—

purple grapes don't glitter like amethysts,
green grapes don't glimmer like greenish white pearls—
and it certainly isn't still, either—
not with the grapes looking as if

they might leap right up off the platter.
Aesop's fox, if it could see
this, would go crazy
trying to eat these grapes!

Then there's the tablecloth
that swirls like a whirlpool
  beneath them,
as if trying to suck
the grapes right down into it—

which couldn't be the way it really was,
could it? Even if some physicists say
it was; the painter must have just
made it look that way—
otherwise, how could we stand it:
    a world where everything that
s supposed to be still
jumps and jitters and whirls,

where the table holding it all up
(like the grapes) isn't solid—

that collection of atoms
that we tell ourselves

is a table, that we *must* see
as a table.

Somewhere There is a Field Where the Birds Will Die for You

I once saw a very beautiful picture. It was twilight and the grasses in the fields combed themselves towards the gnarled pear trees. The sky didn't exist but the birds did. Their blue wings filled the air. Feathers rocked from the sky and covered the fields in a blanket of indigo. There was no way to know if it was day or night. In the middle of the field stood a man. He stared down at the feathers. He looked tired. I thought of my tiny bedroom in my yellow house. How warm my bed is at night. My walls are blue like the feathers. The man in the picture is familiar.

* * *

The man comes to visit me at night. He is tired and asks to sleep in my bed. His body is cold as he curls up next to me. He whispers, _the journey is very long to the end of the road._ Outside my little window the birds begin to murmur.

* * *

I woke up in the field of feathers. They floated up and then down every time I breathed. Standing over me were two young boys. They held their hats in their hands. Their faces were smeared like drying paint and I couldn't make out their features. One boy held a gun. _We shot the birds from the sky,_ the boy said. He pointed the gun above him and I saw the sun. It rippled its way over the black branches of the trees in waves of orange and yellow. The feathers around me began to burn. The boys did not move. It was quiet and I heard the sound of footsteps on the road. I heard the sound of the bones in the feathers crunching as they came closer. I knew the man was coming for me. He was cold when I left him in my bed.

Claus Ankersen

Just like van Gogh

My father looked just like van Gogh. Except for the fact that he actually didn't. But my father had a beard like van Gogh. And he once presented himself as the great painter. It was in his youth. My mother and him were attending a fancy party on some castle. A lot of upper echelon peeps standing in line, as my father discovered – It was all a charade. Nobody really cared who anybody was. And so, given his turn, he paraded the entire line of honorables, shaking their hands and presenting himself: "Hello. Van Gogh. Nice to meet you".

My father never cut off his ear. But my mother was his first and greatest love. They never really got over losing each other to the swinging wife-swapping free love tyranny of the seventies. He never cut off his ear. But he axed his hands numerous times. All the wounds would heal naturally. He'd barely rinse them. Just leave them be. My father was strong as an ox. Almost just as stubborn. After the divorce, he took three extra jobs to feed my sister and I, keep the estate and everything going. He taught me about world religions. Everytime he said 'nirvana' there would be such a longing in his voice and his eyes would water.

My father spent his entire professional life as a teacher. He loved children more than adults, and he loved the children nobody else loved more. He insisted that he was a darwinist and an atheist. But he was afraid of ghosts, and the neighbor told me that he dreamt of going to the Himalayas and spoke about it often. We, his children, had no clue. He never mentioned it. My father needed time alone every day. Just an hour or two. He'd be outside. Summer or winter. Fiddling with something. Mending, building, fixing or doing. He liked to restore old furniture and carve delicate spoons out of old wood.

My father wanted to become a writer, but he stopped himself dead before he began. Instead he became a savior for so many lost children. Always helping the lost and spending his entire life in selfless service, as per custom, his death was sudden, unjust and unbearably tragic.

He was hospitalized with a minor ailment, contracted a hospital infection and died miserably and lost, unable to speak and move, after just 21 days. All he wanted was to go home. So I had him brought home. For eight days he lay in his coffin on a table in the big living room. Every morning I would lift off the lid, kiss him and have a coffee and a date with him. I'd eat his date as well.

At night I'd lift off the lid and talk about the day. We talked through tarot cards.

My father was eventually taken away to be burned. I wanted to embalm him and have him stand in a corner, so I'd have him close by always. But this is illegal here. Almost everything is. A friend of mine took my dad's photo to Nepal, where a lama came down from a mountaintop and performed a great big puja. My father appeared before the lama, but didn't trust him. The lama asked my friend if my father was a Christian. My friend said he didn't know. When the lama assumed Christian form, my dad wanted to talk. The lama said that my father was a Boddhisattwa, because he had lived his entire life in selfless service to his fellow man, and that he were free to do as he pleased, to be reborn as animal, human, deity. Or to end his incarnations on earth and proceed into the western heaven. He chose the western heaven.

My father is everywhere and nowhere. We talk with tarot cards. Somewhere in the western heaven of the buddhists, my father could be attending a party, perhaps high up in a castle. Even in the western heaven, he will probably be the only one with long hair, as he will shake the hands of every one of the other honoratiores and greet them:
"van Gogh. Hello. How are you?"

In the memory of his flesh

Some proof is carved into the meaty part
of my lightbody dreamt.
Haste and impatience zigzagged
as a white mark on my left shin. A relic
from headdiving through a shopwindow
at age seven, because the schoolbell rang
while I collected stickers in a jeans-shop

The gravel grinding in my shoulders
a reminder of the mile in the pool
I swam everyday, a drifter
stinging in my lower back, courtesy
of swift moves and sloppy measurement
a bartender, a late night, a small puddle of olive oil
and too many Christmas beers. My lower ribs
hamstrings, and the infrequent pain in my butt when I sit,
a testimony to my yogic aspirations
along with brittle wrists
a tale of the seven seas and the drink
I sailed on. My eyesight, mysteriously
blur my vision of the all too white
hair of which I have no clue. Wisdomteeth
and the chabang, silent as my dead parents.

Will I be like you. Will I die
like you. Some proof is carved
into the meaty part of my lightbody
The rest
remains
to be seen.

It was that summer
our wings grew through the screens
our talons mirrored and reflected
in the white
our eyes glued to the smart screens

glued to our hands, glued to our hearts
slurping and smacking invisible lips.

We cut of our genitals and grew extra titties
as we shared the flesh of the last softskin, standing
tall in a circle of flat flat and so cold
screens and chips and devises, making light
dance on our scaly skin
inked to match
the alligator-green inside.

It was that summer
that last one
before our time began.

Time flies

Time flies
and stands still
because eternity is so long
it almost never happens
first and last breath
the same, scream, shiver, sigh
Impossible to catch
it's too long, eternity
simply
so long, eternity
always was and always will be
never was and never will be
those immeasurable moments
all those seconds, one
of never ending bliss
heart-ache, marching in patterns
doubles only discernible
from breathing, after fifty
a triple bypass or a freak accident
when the orange sun
and the end of days
rise in the west.

Inside the eyes of a star in flight
the emptiness of a deer
caught in some headlight
time flies arrowstraight
into the crooked lines of your heart
a complex infrastructure
of smooth superexpressways
conjoining jesters and days into one last laugh
time stand on one leg, dancing
motionlessly
a babyface on an old mans shoulders.

The Walk

They should have told us
we would walk alone
They could have let us in
on the secret
that we are animals
and each our own
But they kept it a cabal
that parents are people too
shrouded in youth revealed
after four turns
in the labyrinth of crossroads
we walk their walk
two-legged cephalopoids
doomed to keep discovering
the same
walking alone.

They should have told us
they would take their leave
They could have told us
we would be abandoned.

**Dan Sicoli**

a razor of doubt

as if you offered housing
for the sadness

as if the remains
suggested a forever

as if it only made sense
in the mixing of oils

as if theo could
bring you water

as if any of the gentle women
could brush the bristled fire you wore

as if the thickness of your mark
drew life from nature

as if you were longing
for the sadness

as if the voices
could be lopped off

as if serenity
borne of poverty could endure

as if your chest
was a breeze-filled mountain

as if all your ornaments
could absorb the unintended sadness

as if the clouds drew arms

that reached out to caress you

as if you could become
all the things you created

as if the intensity of light
could cure the shadows

as if the warmth of the vineyard
could ignite the genius of vigor

as if the day your chest deflated
we all recoiled in silent hallucination

impasto

you found a way
to tell your own lies
borrowing secrets
of invented technique
you made the braille useless
and all the bridal walks obsolete

you stole sky and earth
you stole the ghosts of beauty
and signed your name
to every starlit night
and every bright thing that shined
among the human company
folding into your life
stirring the brighter light
into chlorophyll
                cobalt
                    saffron

Dr. Marianne Szlyk

Home from the Oncologist

Parking her car, Thelma counts the crows
balancing on the roof of her house.
The birds are almost as big as chimneys.

She tries to remember whether crows mean death.
No. Maybe owls or ravens are the auguries
out West where trees tower over houses.

But she knows Van Gogh's last painting,
the murder of crows in the cornfield
a day or two before he died.

She will ask her friends.
She cannot ask her husband.
He's been dead two years.

Thelma watches the crows fly
off to the neighbors' large house.
Crows are just birds up there.

On her roof they loomed like bad omens
from nights swirling with coal dust and
cigarette smoke, throbbing with nausea,

from another painting whose light
is just a smear of yellow and orange
oils trapped behind black lines.

She pictures her family's ghosts hovering
over her street, trying to find where she lives.
Once they find her, she must join them.

After Café Terrace at Night

Van Gogh's painting reminds Thelma
of her trip to Europe, of
wandering around Germany at night.

She and Casseau didn't want
to waste waking moments inside
the tiny, high-ceilinged hotel rooms

with sheets that reeked
of cigarettes they didn't smoke,
with windows that opened

onto a street noisy with football fans
or a sluggish river whose black waters
she could still taste.

Outside stars sizzled, yet
summer nights were cold enough
for her to wear his jacket,

the sleeves hiding her hands.
Its faded leather smelled of
cigarettes from college, years ago.

It did not smell of him.

She staggered, tipsy
from one sip of beer.
The stars fell like snowflakes,

a blizzard seen from behind
cobalt glass. She shivered despite
his warmth.

They stopped at the café,
its blaze of yellow light

promising the absence of cold.

That night the trees' leaves
fluttered like streamers. She imagined
palm trees, beaches further south,

the next stop, next time.
There was no next time.

At home she sips decaf coffee,

fingering the cracked leather jacket
that smells of him now,
not cigarettes.

She remembers that in Germany
stars burnt holes in the cobalt
sky.

Here at home they are
so far away from her
now.

The Starry Night

A retired schoolteacher from Arles happens to see Van Gogh's The Starry Night in an exhibition.

I know that view. Perhaps I saw Van Gogh paint.
But I assumed I was alone that night.
The stars were bright,
and the trees had been wrung of green,
the filthy color of frogs and algae.

I stood in the swirling grasses
and read the stars' fine print,
ordering them into constellations
of science, not myth.

At dawn, I prayed for all the patient astronomers
keeping watch in Arles, in France
before I joined them,
the drained, red-eyed men
among fat, drowsy children.

To these students and this artist,
the madman, the ex-preacher,
the stars were supposed to be firecrackers,
cartwheeling, yellow and oranging,
sparks on the sky.

Explosions and shockwaves crossed
that night over the watery town.
The townspeople slept
that night, fat children hugging
pillows.

This painting shows a ripped sky
and old cypress trees like daggers.

Perry S. Nicholas

The End

None of us Atlas.
So I envy those who manage
to hold the world, gently, at bay.
I never would, even if I could.

Leaving it all out there, love,
I've nothing to show, blurry
visions like cried-out irises.

Where did Ramona go?
Her phrasing a soft snow.
Perhaps she is buried
with the ear of Van Gogh.

A *Starry Night* in 1888

We cannot get to a star while we are alive, any more than we can take the
train when we are dead. --Van Gogh

It just is so matter-of-fact, the way
the houses exhale Japanese lanterns
onto the water with slightly imperfect
symmetry on this first night of dreams.
Above begins a trip to the heavens
achieved only through death, a route
reflected across the body of France,
lonely dots connected by funeral trains.

But stars need more than one man's longing.
Why choose to focus on his sky, when
the two small figures demand attention,
yet barely seem to notice the show
bursting right over their shoulders?
Majesty, and at the same time, it just *is*.

Old Man with Head in Hands

On the painting by Van Gogh

One of the lost, he cradles his head
in his hands, weeping, as if pained
by the rough knuckles, paws pressed into
his own eyes. This doesn't help him accept
his place any more than he did the previous day,
when he sniffed out where his morning meal
was coming from, where he might find
a bed that night. Craving to know answers
to questions his hunch creates, we
don't understand how to pose them—
he is not a matter of duty, but an orphan
forgotten until this painter awakened him
with his cracked strokes of public service.
In the centered blackness of the lithograph
lies our forgiveness for the splintering artist,
braced to face his own social brokenness.

Doctor's Notes
Drs. Upar; Rey; Peyron & Gachet– File of Vincent Willem van Gogh

V   **V**egetarian:

V. will not ingest meat. Eats frugally; smokes far too much. Manifests
Malnutrition in Stomach Ailment, Muscle pain, Poor concentration, Gener-
alized Weakness. Depression and Mood Swings unmanageable. (Severe
Protein Deficiency)?

A   **A**bsinthe:

Thujone Poisoning? V.'s Abuse=causation=Porphyria, manifesting in
Depression; Hallucinations; Seizures, Severe Stomach Pain. (Symptoms
exacerbated by concurrent Lead Poisoning? See "O").

N   **N**urture:

V. claims a childhood without Nurturing, describing it "cold; with-
drawn"; and relationship with Mother Anna, tense. Rejected by her in
favor of an ideal to which he could never measure up (dead brother
Vincent, whose grave was marked with his own name and exact birthday,
and to which A. took V. to weekly to decorate with flowers). V.'s lifelong
quest to replace Mother's love obsessive. (Seeking the haven of womanly
companionship to counter the Ills of the World?)

G   **G**onorrhea:

Burning during Urination; gonococcal Lesions. Mercuryl Chloride pre-
scribed (Proper Calomel Form of Dosage, since the raw Specific is far too
potent for the constitution, and can lay waste to the body). V. instructed
to Abstain from Alcohol during Medication—to no avail.

Effects of such Treatments? Mental irritability noted; Impaired Cognitive
Skills, Sleep Disturbance, Memory Loss, Confusion. V. complains of Severe
Chronic Headaches; Cramping of Bowels.

O   **O**il Paints:

Saturnism; Lead Poisoning. (Minium; Sugar of Lead). V. forbidden to lick
his brushes, or eat his paints. He disobeys. Symptoms of Exposure persist.

Seizures Increase; worsening Nervous Constitution. Hallucinations; Night Terrors. Delirium; Mental Epilepsy.

G   **G**od; **G**enius:
V. undisputedly a Force unto himself. His Early Religious Studies provided him Clarity of Vision regarding Nature: for him, the Truest Manifestation of God. His eloquence; his interpretation of God through Paint and Canvas; his Articulate Correspondence all support his Genius. See "H".

H   **H**istory:
V.'s Genius will be Proven. Speculation as to the Causes of his Medical Complaints shall continue until Body can be Analyzed. It is Our Contention that his Mental Condition was Exacerbated, if not Caused, by Physical Phenomena. History will Prove his Life; History cannot Hide his Death.

~~   ~~   ~~

Sources:
http://www.umich.edu/~ece/student_projects/remedies/mercury.html
History of the Medical Treatment of Gonorrhea; Thomas Benedek, University of Pittsburgh
https://en.wikipedia.org/wiki/Vincent_van_Gogh's_health
Vangoghletters.org
https://blog.oup.com/2015/06/vincent-van-gogh-motherhood/
The Van Gogh File: The Myth and the Man, by Ken Wilkie

Impasto

This letter was recently discovered, carefully concealed within the lining of a greatcoat belonging to Theo Van Gogh, brother to Vincent. It has been authenticated by Museum Experts.

My Dear Theo—

I send you one last note, impassioned; hot blue words on yellow paper – yet hollow, as most confessions are when the confessor is dead! You must know that, apart from your name which my fevered lips thanked so often for intervention on my behalf, there's another name I kiss...

Forgive me! I write you this in my final hours, in much pain... but also with the nagging ache of deceit. Life's desperate, brother! Well you understand how I suffered intolerable insults from Zundert to Paris, how they sneered at me throughout my life, scoffing that I was more pig than painter. Yet—*you* believed in me, even when I did not. You – and another, whose name I'll reveal in a moment. But you must pledge to conceal this name beyond death, as I do, and ignore the wild conjecture that may spring up surrounding my demise. You must know that everything that gossip surmises will be false. I trust you will fly to my side, dear brother, since I implored Dr. Gachet to send for you immediately – but by the time you arrive, I shall be beyond mending. I sit here, smoking, but not for much longer. I'll start my story from the end, and work backwards to where it all began... And when you have read it, you must burn its proof.

Do you recall what a beautiful evening it was yesterday? Radiating with fading, apricot light.

I stumbled through the vibrating green tones of the whispering corn, clinging to life like a sparrow to crumbs—yet still managing to observe the colours of my wound! It bled magenta and red, in impasto gouts, onto a canvas of death.

Dragging myself upstairs to my room at the Auberge Ravoux, I asked Dr. Gachet to send for you, and placed myself in Destiny's palm. And because I insisted to Ravoux that I'd tried to kill myself, and told the two *gendarmes* who questioned me this morning not to accuse anybody, the rumours will instantly blossom and tumble over themselves in profusion like the flopping heads of over-reaching peonies. *Vincent, in a fit of fury or flux, has done himself in with a gun!* Even you now probably believe this to be the truth?

Wrong.

You know how often we have discussed suicide; know full well that the intensity of my response to Nature makes me a terrible coward! And I have always viewed suicide with distaste – as sinful and immoral. I've been having good health lately since I stopped drinking, doing better work than before! My nightmares have all-but disappeared, and I've been loving life very much. How the paintings have been flying out of my brush! And yet, understanding that my previous malaises caused glorious peaks followed by the deepest pits of hell, I assure you faithfully that my low spirits when you arrive this fateful day has nothing to do with my old condition. And here is the reason.

Early yesterday morning, leaving my easel in the fields, I went to meet a skinny Jew—the jeweler I heard of who has a little shop off Rue Daubigny. I purchased from him a small gold ring with the demurest diamond, the intent of which illuminated my soul far brighter than any starlit sky! I couldn't contain my pace as I walked—no, raced! to my angel's pale green door. She opened straightaway, and seeing the ecstasy upon me, became anxious for my health. I assured her I was well; better, even! She allowed me into the house, and I knelt before her.

In this manner, I proposed to Marguerite.

SHE is my secret, brother! She is my savior. Marguerite, Dr. Paul Gachet's gentle daughter, the most brilliant star in my heavens! After I was discharged from *Saint Paul-de-Mausole*, fully recovered in my faculties, you assisted me to settle in Auvers-sur-Oise, and meet Dr. Gachet. I can confess now that since we met, she and I have grown into a deep, mutual understanding. She found a light in me which I long since thought had been burned out by the intensity of too many zealous suns—the brightness of Eugenie, for example; Christien and Kee... not to mention that business with Margot. I thought myself burnt out. But she, sweet angel, rescued me; and I painted her in the Doctor's Garden, dressed as my bride. When I wrote you:*"But we're still a long way from people understanding the curious relationships that exist between one piece of nature and another, which however explain and bring each other out"*, I was speaking of her, and myself.

Marguerite and I made secret plans to be together—but not before she found employment, since her father was dreadfully against our communion. I do believe he's almost as ill as I am... But after I left you in Paris, I am sorry to say I regressed awhile, cleaved apart as I was from her;

watching time stretch to an infinite horizon from the restless blackening misery of my mind. The midsummer sun, too, beats upon one's head so fiercely it makes one crazy… I became torn in two with the waiting, fearing my miserable soul was not worthy of my Guiding Star, and she would change her mind. This is the time I wrote you that my prospects grew darker, and could I see no happy future at all… Of necessity, I resorted to my old nemesis, absinthe.

But then she sent word she'd found a decent engagement; and was ready; and now, here she was before me! Now, filled with the clean, rapturous air of love, I almost blew her over! She set to crying; and accepted; and we embraced; and entire constellations danced before me in colours so divine, I ached! I could scarcely believe myself in such good fortune.

But Theo! The heavens turned on me, as they always seem to in the throes of joy. Marguerite's brother Paul-Louis had returned to Auvers after leaving the University, working odd-jobs in order to finance his desire to be a great painter (calling himself Louis Van Ryssel. I do not think much of his talent. His work is pretentious and I find him more eccentric than his Father, and spoiled. He's an odd duck, with the bearing and comportment of a deranged stork). And now suddenly, this same Paul-Louis burst in upon us, his youthful countenance inflamed, ranting like Hade's demons. The reason? He'd seen me at Rue du Bout d'Aeles. Yes, the brothel…

He was hired to repair the front door of that miserable place where I, in absinthe and shame after visiting you in Paris, frequented the whores. (But what alternatives had I, in my search for comfort?) I have but a faint memory of seeing Paul-Louis there at the time, since I was drinking to ease the terrors of both soul and stomach, even though the doctors insist I must stop. With this foul portrait of me in his heart, he went berserk, cursing me for a crazed, syphilitic knave, cursing me to wretched sinner's nameless grave.

He stormed to a dresser and pulled out a pistol, preparing to shoot me. Marguerite screamed for him to see sense—then he, after remembering I usually take Ravoux's pistol to the fields (to scare off the crows), along with my easel, challenged me there and then to a duel. And I – for pity's sake, what could I do? To the fields we went, doomed.

My beloved Marguerite continued pleading, half-demented with anguish, weeping and dragging upon his jacket, for him to change his course, certain she would surely lose one of two people she loved. But alas – her begging was in vain. He would not be swayed, vowing to tell all to his father; avenge his sister's honour. I was not permitted to plead for clemency; he waved his pistol wildly, cursing me to hell; bellowing at me to shut my disgusting mouth.

We assembled in the field, a triangle of misery. Black crows rose up from their cover, screaming, warning the skies of disaster. Time halted for me. The wheat swayed in a sweet breeze; and here and there, sunflowers nodded, as if they were already bestowing forgiveness. I raised Ravoux's pistol, unable to bring myself to fire. But Paul-Louis had no qualms. Such is the impetuosity of youth.

When his bullet found me, Marguerite fell, swooning, and could not be roused.

Instantly I recognized our fate. What reason did I have to impugn my love? What reason to incriminate her brother, for whom I'd previously held no ill will? Therefore, in the cool of the evening, I entreated Paul-Louis to remove her straightaway home, and to swear an oath upon my blood that not a word of this terrible day would be breathed to any living soul. He returned after seeing her settled. Propping me with his skinny shoulder, we stumbled some distance together towards the Auberge, one awkward stork and one wounded pigeon; after which I managed the last few paces on my own while he returned to the fields to remove all traces of our presence.

The rest, brother, will be written. The busy bush of Conjecture daily grows a new flower, and the buried potatoes of rumour grow new eyes. Soon they will all rot. So shall it be. In the distance now, I see the cypress trees turning black. They have always been omens of death.

I plead for your forgiveness. My mind is peaceful, at last, relieved of its tedious burden of confession. I die praising heaven you finally have the truth of my mysterious demise. Those young lads, joshing me about, were not responsible; nor is it suicide. I trust you to kiss my Marguerite, and beg of you this promise: that you swear upon my grave, and on all we have meant to each other, that you tell no living soul of our unhappy story; and carry it, unspoken, to your mortal end. The idyllic tale of love; of contented hearth and home was never mine; never meant to be. *La tristesse durera toujours.*

Ever yours, dear brother—

Vincent

[Author's note: Story inspired by *Wheatfield with Crows*, by Vincent Van Gogh, circa 1890. Some scholars believe this was his last painting. The circumstances of his death continue to be speculated upon. Marguerite Gachet suffered a nervous breakdown after Vincent's death for which she was briefly institutionalized. She never married, and rarely left her father's house until her death in 1949.]

Sources:
Vanity Fair, Nov. 2014
Van Gogh: The Life, 2011, by Naifeh & Smith
The Van Gogh File: The Myth and the Man, by Ken Wilkie
The Last Van Gogh by Alyson Richman
Van Gogh in Provence and Auvers, by Bogomila Welsh-Ovcharov
http://www.visual-arts-cork.com/famous-artists/van-gogh.htm
Vangoghletters.org

Huang Xiang

Van Gogh

Translated by Andrew G. Emerson

The painting holds high like torches
Sunflowers turning high-heaven's blazing
Sun
To burn up the magnificent painting spirit stopped by a bullet
To burn down the brilliant temple of golden yellow
Opaque color-dabs like clots of
Blood
Gush fiery tears
Struggling lines feverishly erupt, twitching like raw nerves
The back-view of a giant
Reappears
This man has his back towards you
The center is a palace of many hues
Over his life he used every color to erect his sacred empire
He is a sovereign who never opened his stronghold to common people
He himself its only subject and only guardian angel
His imperial territory extends like rays of sunlight, expanding in the souls of
men
Vomit the sunlight
That forms a memory of swallowed fire
A whole life in the painting
Explodes
Flesh and blood fly out of the picture
More than man can endure, causing panic
The sunflower's multiple star-bursts
Disrupt the canvas night-sky
Every painting is dynamite that upsets the viscera
Every painting hung on the wall stares like a
Stalking tiger at the steaming
Silence

Suffering epilepsy, your nerves already now show the effect !

You're exclusive in the extreme,

Reject everything

All celestial bodies are but heads you have smashed, dashed to smithereens

Because people love you, they shout out:

"Kill him!"

Your paintings are in the grand posthumous skeleton temple to your
magnificent life

Magnificently sacrificed for the paintings

You are buried in your picture

The yellow leaf of your severed ear rasps like a cicada

You leave your painting to shoot across cosmic space

Glowering at the Death God like an angry

Raven

Turn your face towards the setting sun

Wheat-fields and beech trees brush your blue-and-black peasant smock

Wild beasts in the painting make

Still-wet

Footprints

You feel the arid puff of a woman's gaze

irritating your back

At a glance it becomes a fogbound cypress. Mute shouting fingernails
pierce the somnambulant canvas. Sallow dusk's pallet is as smooth as skin.
The

evening sun's shimmering light descends unprovoked. A startled
paint-spotted rag.

Love is so Simple. Like death, like a simple

Cross

The first time to receive a woman's love, for a crude man who sought no
female pleasure.

Hugged close to the skin like a devils' spells, like a soothing salve

Wild kisses break through life's mysterious waves

The blank canvas deep as the dry well of your vision

Violence torments the silence

Mania! Mania! Mania! A mania roiling you

Roiling a batch of

Lemon

Yellow

He who worships the fireball is himself a fireball

441

Sun's golden-yellow colors blister you, bum you, like flames
Sputtering on your face
Sun! Sun! Sun!
The sun is near kin to revolution
The sun is a scintillating
Fission
The sun is the pounding windstorm's
Embryo
The sun's bloodline starts with
Madness and Wildness
A portrait of a great life without pretense
The shadow cast by the sun behind
Is also the shadow of the leading sun's
Funeral procession
Because of this, your every painting digs
Your own grave
You paint a sea, you could be swallowed in an instant by a water bird
You paint a tree, you might be hanged from a crotch that you painted,
You paint a star, you might discover it right in the dark of your leg, or in
the countless indistinct cells of your bone-marrow
Rising falling in infinity
A masterpiece is really the face of a devil
That has been expelled from the Church of the Common Man
To the discerning mind, it is another
Coming of Christ
In religion's impotent place
Blending the juices of the Gospel
One who dishonors God embraces God and
Sleeps
Morals are but soured fruit
Love a worm-eaten coffin
The wine of life
Puts falsehoods in perspective
To disclose a sensuous dawn
The blazing sun's
Tyranny
Paint' s savagery gets savaged by a violent sun
Sunlight whiplashes you, burns you

Leaving slashes and burn-marks on your body
Your
Whole body badly sunburned
Hoping for freedom your eyes are
Blinded
You cannot escape this despot sun
The despot sun bloodthirsty by nature
Sunlight time and again raises up
A high tide of epilepsy
When it hits, it spatters a golden foam
The light's quick pulsations, like destructive yellow silk
Tighten on heaven's clear
Sulphur-colored pigment, squeezing out clusters of sunflowers
Sunlight's
Hands dance, feet stomp
The mountains seem color-blind
The sunflower's yellow sun
The sunflower's virgin
Rising sun
Every ray's delicate measure emits pain and suffering! Emits destruc-
tion!
So aggressive the sun's outburst
You cannot take the blows, your body mangled
Your whole body badly sunburned
You want to paint the whole cosmic space yellow
Van Gogh!
You are extremely golden-yellow
Hopelessly golden-yellow
You the idol's mortal enemy
Honor golden yellow as an
Idol
Your popped-rice and grape-juice body
Nerves all like a return volley of arrows
Faces the sun
That huge magnet of a heavenly body
Flashing and vibrant
Like a violent rage poured dazzling out of an empty vat
Sharp as razors, the suns rays dripping blood

Cut apart your
Solitary soul
Silently stinging
A shadow quietly sobs
Dare like a concealed stare
Beautiful but awesome
The only opportunity of all one's life is to die
So the whole of one's life is but a
Preparation for death
You are buried in the painting's smoldering ashes
Skeleton consumed in the conflagration
A magnificent star gone far away
Content, the tranquil flames have no fight with the world
Bitter wailing
For a
Testament

November 26, 1990
Hands gesticulate, feet stomp
Laughter fierce, insane
Sobs and tears fall down
Dash the pen, the poem is done
(The original poem covers a whole length of wide paper in wild cursive style)

梵 高

畫幅如火把高舉
向日葵轉動高空放火的
太　陽
燒死了被一顆子彈中止的偉大畫魂
燒毀了黃顏色的金光燦爛的色彩的神殿
色塊濃濁如淤血
色　彩
流出火焰之淚
掙扎的線條熱病猝發，抽搐如神經
一個巨人的背影
重　現

此人是背向著你們的人
中心是色彩的皇宮
終生用各種顏色堆砌他的神聖的帝國
他是一座凡人永遠達不到的城堡的君主
它的唯一的臣民和唯一的守護神
他的帝國的版圖綿延如絲的陽光在每一顆人類的心靈中擴張

嘔吐陽光

成為飲火的記憶

整個生命在畫幅中

爆　炸

構圖血肉橫飛
令人無法忍受和驚恐萬狀的
向日葵群星閃爍
騷動畫布的夜空
每一幅畫都是攪翻五臟六肺的炸藥
每一幅畫都是挂在墻頭的
虎視眈眈絲絲冒煙的

靜　默

癲癇病患者，此時你的神經已發作！
你這個極端的排他者
排斥一切
所有的星體都被你砸爛腦袋、撞得粉碎
人們因為愛你而大聲叫出：

“殺　死　他！”

你的畫在你的身後矗立偉大生命恢宏教堂的骨架
偉大的殉畫者
你葬入了你的畫
刺耳的黃葉如蟬噪鳴
你從畫中奔出宇宙大房間
如一隻怒氣衝衝地瞪著死神

鴉

把臉轉向終局的太陽
麥田和山毛櫸拂動你的農人般藍黑相間的衣衫
野獸在油畫上踩出
未乾的

蹄　印

你感覺一個女人風吹日曬的眼光
搔癢你的背
一筆眼光化成霧中的絲柏。啞叫的指甲掐入夢游的畫布。黃昏的調色
板光潔如皮膚。留下一絲擦不去的夕陽哆嗦的光線。一陣驚恐的油彩
沾滿抹布。愛是多么簡單。如死亡，如一個簡單的

十　字　架

一個不討女人喜歡的粗魯的男人第一次擦開女人之愛。
擁抱如貼身的著魔的符咒，如寧靜的香膏
狂吻鑿開生命神奇的微瀾
空白的畫布深如目光的古井
狂暴揉傷一片寂靜
躁狂！躁狂！躁狂！躁狂滾動著你

445

<pre>
          滾動著一團
            檸   檬
                黃
火球的崇拜者自己就是一個火球
太陽金黃的色彩燒灸你、灼傷你、火焰般
            濺滿你一臉
          太陽！太陽！太陽！
          太陽是革命的近親
          太陽是一場蠕動的
                裂變
          太陽是震顫風暴的
                胚胎
            太陽的血緣來自
            瘋癲與迷狂
      拒絕偽飾大生命的肖像
          後面的太陽投下的背影
          又為前面太陽的背影
            送   葬
        因此，你的每一幅畫都為自己
          開掘墓穴
你畫一片海，你頃刻就會被水之鳥吞噬，
你畫一棵樹，你就會吊死在自畫的枝丫上，
你畫一顆星，你會發現它正在你的黑暗之腿或某滴茫茫骨髓的細胞中
            浩瀚升沉
一幅杰作就是一張魔臉
被驅逐出庸人的教會，
它在慧眼中是又一次
基督降臨
在宗教無能為力的地方
融解福音的果汁
          猥褻天地者摟抱天地
                睡覺
道德是發酸的果子
愛蛀空死亡的棺木
            生 命 之 酒
          透   視   謬   誤
            呈現性感的晨光
          陽光輝煌的
                獨   裁
色彩的肆虐狂受到太陽狂暴的肆虐
陽光鞭笞你、烙傷你
在你身上留下鞭痕和火印
                你
          遍體鱗傷陽光
        眼睛因渴盼自由而
</pre>

446

刺瞎

你這太陽的暴君逃脫不了
嗜血成性的暴君的太陽
陽光一次又一次涌起
癲癇的高潮
一觸即發的金黃飛沫四濺
急速的光的脈搏如災難扭成的黃綾
勒斷天空的澄清
硫磺色的顏料管擠出一朵一朵向日葵

陽　光

手舞足蹈

群山如色盲

向日葵的黃太陽

向日葵童貞的

日　出

每一絲光的纖維的韻律都流泄痛苦！都流泄毀滅！
咄咄進遏的陽光暴動

你不經一擊，粉身碎骨

遍體鱗傷陽光

你要把整個宇宙的大屋都漆成黃色

梵　高！

你是極端的金黃

絕望的金黃

你這偶像的死敵
奉金黃為

偶　像

你爆裂谷漿和葡萄汁的人體
每一根神經都如密集回射的箭簇般

朝向太陽

巨大磁石的天體

錚亮而旺盛

如空缸擲出眩目的暴怒
剃刀一樣鋒利的陽光血淋淋

割開你的

孤　魂

寂靜螫人

影子低聲嗚咽

黑暗如隱秘的瞪視

美麗而恐怖

一生唯一的一次機會就是死亡

而全部生命都祇是為著

準備一死

你葬入炙熱的畫灰

烈火散去厄運的骨骼

一顆偉大的星球遠去

淡泊寧靜的火焰與世無爭
悲　　　號
如
遣　　囑

1990年11月2₆日

手舞足蹈

瘋癲狂笑

聲淚俱下
擲筆成書
（原詩為整幅大紙，以鬥筆狂草）

David S. Pointer

Young Painters

seized
by
14 sunflowers
unveiled
by flash dancing
Nazis
at the thoroughbred gator show
with complimentary velcro saddles
where youth movements ride free
draped over next gen vein openings

Sanctioned

      by earlessness
      by hallucinations
      by absinthe
no longer capable of storming
the ground floor for supplies,
the brothers catapult to outsville
leaving *The Potato Eaters* alone

Entrenched

                inside
                well behaved
                art scandals
remaining a designated survivor
on Route 66 as a helicoptor convoy
transports the Van Gogh collection
with Moulin-Rouge performers riding
as security shotgun escorts

Rambling Diatribes

                  following our hero's
melancholoy
                 marvelously adept
at psychic neuro-cartography finally
touching down
              inside cranial headwaters

***

bleeding on easels
gifting earlessness
onto the world

Easel to Easel

        the artist
in bondage
        stitches him/herself
back together again with purse-
string sutures....
removal of diseased portions
of flaking paint or painter
should be rectified and closed up
with transverse anastomosis,
tissue or artshow celebrations.

Primary Reason for Primary Colors

Something about absorbent gauze
                              dressings
cloaked over 800 paintings captivating
post-modern globe
                     ligated with art
appreciation classes or creativity
that allows all these pathological
indications, vibrantly to keep, keep
clawing out to call us up as friends

***

fish scale beach
concert pianist
finds guitar pick

***

strangler fig tree
even the old python
moves somewhere new

***

ground level wind
whispering sky secrets
to everybody

***

hood sunflower
punctuates
the gunfire

Ally Malinenko

Just One More Day

It could have been the jetlag
or the head cold
or the vodka's before dinner
but I started crying
again
last night
over Anne Frank
and Vincent van Gogh.
Over these long dead ghosts
who never found out
what they would meant to the world
as if that
meant anything
and I know I sounded
like I cared about the wrong things
instead of just creating art
or that I knew my clock
has been foreshortened
by disease
but what I wanted you to know
love
is that I just worry
that this one life
isn't going to be enough
that no matter what we do,
I'll go unsatisfied
begging the night
desperately wishing
I could stay.
Please
just
one more day.

Su Zi

4 V

1

That small room
   modest window
   simple chair
  dense with dizzy scents
   turpentine
   linseed oil
   buttered pigments

How could one not swoon.

2

A century of children
  will eddy around,
  the docent's voice a blur,

They will see the rich touch
  of color.   those bold harmonies
  the familiar depicted
   beyond dare

In some cobby corner
   of their most fitful confusions
  will be this dense rectangle
    the sure patience of your fingers.

3

Momma implied your sanctity
  hers was a vocabulary of emotion
   a tidal force of passionate cursing
   a confusion of your life and your work

knotted.
I read your letters when I was just learning blood
  such painful poverty
  such pragmatic choices-- food or paint --
   echoed down my own....
Still and now
   when the owls' twilight opera
   ever reminds of other worlds.

4

Your cafe is eternal
  clean, lit, empty
Each table lonely in the night.

How good is the coffee?
  is it deeper in flavor
   when the lamps are ringed in mist?

This is the painting not shown much--
   it's quiet, elegant
  a study in optics; how light lives
  a memory of subsonic triangles and circles
  a transmission from beyond wherever we sit
now barefoot
  from you
   a love letter to the misty evening
   and a come hither midnight
    that whispers still.

John Grochalski

and the radio d.j. won't quit talking about the beauty of the sun

another day comes on like a virus
in this box that has no plot
i look at pictures by van gogh and feel nothing
look at author photos
on the backs of novels
that should've been declared D.O.A. on arrival
and feel the cold passage of wasted time
there isn't much to do really
except sit and listen to symphonies from the dead
passing between the news of horrors
in a violently redundant world
suffer the inability to carve words from the air
as the talk of chipper fools outside my window
leaves me salivating like the damned
people here have been stupid, ignorant and self-serving
for hundreds of years now
why should today be any different?
sometimes it's an emotional battle
just going to get the mail
because you worry who you'll run into
another sad suck stuck in the mouse wheel
of doing the same thing every day
i think of all of the places in this world where i could be
and none of them stack up
to being wrapped inside the sheets on the bed
prostrate and numb
days like this are still births
and to think of all of the people who've gone too soon
while here i sit soaking up the oxygen
with my indolence and complaint
life is madness and miracle
life is random and cruel
it's good parking on a saturday afternoon
a wreck on the highway during a hangover morning

it's the next line that won't come
as the dogs begin barking a harbinger of doom
and the old cat hacks her warning
while i kill another fly as the coffee turns cold
think about cutting off my ear
and the radio d.j. won't quit talking
about the beauty of the sun.

starry night

the crowds
are gathered around *starry night*
as if it were the only painting in the world

what sad irony, huh vincent?

none of them seem to be looking at it
just taking pictures of the work and walking away
to find the next masterpiece

maybe there is nothing to look at anymore
but the idea of standing in front of something
that once held beauty and meaning

one guy is leaning into the painting so closely
with his tongue out frat boy style
as if he's trying to lick those van gogh clouds

jostling for space
with hordes of sticky kids
who are touching the golden frame

as their parents laugh
and snap away more digital memories

nodding blindly at the guard
who keeps yelling about the sanctity of art

and how no one is supposed
to use flash photography
in this museum.

drooping sunflowers

i look at the cut sunflowers
at the entranceway to the grocery

three for seven bucks

only they are already drooping
in their big, scratched plastic vase

how depressing to see sunflowers this way!

i think of van gogh's sunflowers instead
the tranquil feeling of monet's painting as well

how many people have stood in front of them
from peers to people with ipads
who take their quick tourist photos
and then move on without really looking

those immortal sunflowers on canvas
always vibrant and full, never heading toward decay

i think those museum pad-holes deserve
to look at these grocery sunflowers
instead of those painted by the masters

let them take their photos of these dying monstrosities
and post them onto facebook or tumblr or instagram

for people no longer experience anything
as the general course of their life

but must always be the focus
like everyone has become a three year-old child

so they might as well save themselves
the twenty-five dollar museum entrance fee

461

there is no hope for these sunflowers at the grocery

some will get bought
most will get tossed with the expired meat and eggs

i think of drooping sunflowers
wilting in the late summer sun
then i go inside the grocery store
to buy two ripe pink lady apples
from a cashier who looks so angry

like i ruined her day just by saying hello

or perhaps she's bent out of shape
about the sunflowers dying too.

to my co-worker whom i bought ten dollars of christmas candy from

that was a magnum bottle of red wine, lady
a six pack of GOOD beer
or three rounds of swill at the local pub
albeit with no tip
that was a pizza lunch for two days
a potato and egg hero on a wheat bun
this week's copy of iron man, batman, and wolverine
that david ruffin CD i'd had my sights on
a donation to hurricane relief
or a pint of cheap scotch donated to myself
that was the paprika needed to spice up my life
it was gleeful drunken purchasing power on itunes
cat treats by the bushel for the beast
who keeps waking me at three a.m.
fancy coffee or gourmet tea to sooth hungover mornings
a small print of van gogh at the MoMA
a knish and a soda for the wife in central park
vanilla ice cream cones in the cold of brooklyn
two days of bus or train travel
a brand new winter hat or gloves off of a street vendor
halal food with the change leftover for the homeless dude
in washington square park
LAUNDRY MONEY
or a couple of packs of topps football cards
some used books on philosophy from the strand
¼ of a membership to the american freedom from religion foundation
or a subscription to rolling stone
it's two weeks of the sunday new york times
a movie ticket if i stay away from manhattan
that ten dollars that i gave you
for christmas candy that i won't even eat
you know, what i call your yearly extortion money
could've been any one of those things that i listed
or a bunch of stuff that i haven't even thought of yet
instead of something that i'll be tossing

in the back of the cabinet
to collect a copious amount of mold
before i throw it away at easter time
next year.

peacemaker

i have to be the peacemaker
i have to make this peace
6 ½ hours stuck in traffic
from gotham to new england
with angry cops
and toll booths omnipotent
only to arrive here
at my brother's house
to suck down his light beer
in the presence of domestic disarray
i don't even know what happened
but they expect me to make the peace
like some old western officer
like some wizened philosopher
who isn't battling his own demons
but he's sitting on the couch
and she's yelling at him
threatening to take away
his three-month old daughter
and they are both looking at me
and there is nothing for me to do
except drink his beer
and think about traffic and toll booths
as they fight
fade into the walls from embarrassment
wonder about the holy madness of van gogh
try to navigate
around the edges of their hate
say something thoughtful or funny
even though i am at the bottom of myself
on this ungodly night
play the peacemaker in this house
throw the gauntlet of harmony down
when i'd always rather
watch the world burn
as i have done many times before

over and over again
every time that i come here
by train or plane or car
when all i ever want from anyone
is to be left
alone.

say something that'll attack the sun

if you have to think too hard
about the act
if you have to fake it
then maybe it is time
to turn off the machine or put down the pen
because the words should never be forced
and the memories or inspiration
should never be beyond the fingertips
you see
we as humans are attracted to the banal
the mundane
the rudimentary
and the severely repetitious
this is why we have art and artists
to shed some light and hope on all of that dark
it is called giving the world
a little meaning and beauty
if you don't believe me
just go and ask van gogh.
but it should never be forced
so if you are sitting there tonight, writer,
and the thoughts on your next set of words
are taxing your brain
if you can think of nothing to say
that'll make someone get up
and want to attack the sun
or make love to the moon
then please, for the sake of us all... just stop
pick up a magazine, join a bowling team, get married,
or go and start a dull profession.
we already have enough writers
who are fakers and fornicators in this game
to last another dreary lifetime
and there's not enough money or time
left in it for someone else
to drag us deeper

into the depths
of this dying sea
wasting nights playacting
waiting for inspiration to hit
when they never had it
in the first place.

art collector

my wife and i
are in an art gallery in soho

i don't like soho
because there are always too many people
walking the streets

celebrities and tourists

buying things that no one can afford

i don't believe poverty and thrift exist
when i am in soho

maybe i come to soho too much

but my wife wants
to see this exhibit in the gallery

it's on brian froud

he draws elves and faeries
did design work for jim henson movies

this is a pop art gallery
and froud is interesting enough

he's hanging up there with seuss
and bob kane drawings of batman

charles schultz panels of snoopy
and good ol' charlie brown

the prices are outrageous for this stuff
thousands upon thousands of dollars

i don't know a single person
who can afford them

but that doesn't stop the gallery clerk
from coming over to us
trying to show us various paintings and the like

she must be nuts or desperate

this woman must have one hell
of a sense of humor, i think

i shake my head and we make small talk
but i just want to get away from her

call it the philistine in me
but people like her make me uneasy

they make me feel less than i am

my wife senses my discomfort

we keep trying to move away from this woman
but the more we look at the art work
the more she keeps coming at us

with questions and comments
with suggestions and anecdotes

everywhere we go she seems to be

she asks me if i collect
rather what i collect

baseball cards, comics, and debt
i want to tell her

picassos and van goghs by the dozen

you must have me confused with somebody else
i think to say

because my haircut is free
and my boots only cost forty-dollars

but instead i tell her nothing

i stand there and sweat
play the role of assuming art collector

let her think what she wants to think about me

as i look at black and white prints of the grinch
the last of the frouds
watch the city move
outside the windows of the gallery

the streets of soho
fill with more and more people

carrying bags emblazoned
with expensive names
and very little taste.

Norman J. Olson

a painter's view of Vincent van Gogh

Vincent van Gogh, everybody knows his story.... it is, in fact, the arche-typal story of the visual artist... in the Western world in the 20th and 21st Centuries... a young man from a barely middle class family, who just does not fit in... he is awkward and sincere... he tries to please his family, tries to become a minister (his dad is a minister) in the Borinage coal mining region in Belgium... we all know the story how he gave away everything he had to the poor miners and wound up giving up on religion and decid-ing in illness and abject poverty, to become an artist... how he beat his head, literally, against the wall and by sheer force of will taught himself to draw and later paint.. then he fell in with the avant garde in Paris and tried his hand at everything from Japanese prints (painted in oil) to Seurat pointillism... and then moved to the Midi where the sun was more intense and he could find the models he needed to fit in with his theories of color and harmony... he chopped off part of his ear and gave it to a prostitute (his relations with women did not run smoothly at that time or ever), went nuts, scared the pants off of Gauguin with the razor and the sliced off ear and after time in and out of the nut house, committed suicide by shooting himself in the stomach, which in those days virtually guaranteed a horribly painful and lingering death which he did have...

the story is wonderful and achingly romantic... how can you not love this poor man who suffered so much for art, was not much appreciated in his own lifetime and was later canonized as the first modern artist of monumental, unquestioned genius... i have read many biographies of Van Gogh and believe me, there are literally hundreds out there and i know and love his story... reading his collected letters is enough to reduce the most hardhearted prick on the planet to tears... and i cry like a baby when i read his final letters to his beloved brother Theo...

interestingly, while Van Gogh was living out our fantasy of what an artist is and should be, he was also making paintings... the history of these paintings is interesting in that after the seminal 1913 Armory show of "Modern Art" which introduced European avant grade painting to the USA, the art war between traditional academic art and so called Modernism was quickly won and the impressionists, expressionists and later abstractionists became valuable and collectable while Bougereau and Millais were by 1950 pretty much worthless, Van Gogh, Cezanne, et al were quickly accelerating in value... those 19th Century academic masterworks which had been worth vast sums of money in 1880, 1890, 1900, and were painted by successful academic artists who lived in huge mansions, became the subject of scorn... Van Gogh and Cezanne had far surpassed them in value by the late 1960s when i started art school... and while the market for academic art has rebounded a bit, you better have a hundred million dollars in hand if you want to buy a decent Van Gogh...

and, of course, along with this vast increase in pecuniary value has gone virtually unanimous critical acclaim... only among the flat earthers of the Classical Realist movement or other radically out of it sectors will one hear even a hint that poor old Vincent was anything but a great and immortal genius...

so, when i think about Van Gogh, it is hard for me to come to the art clean, so to speak... to see the art without considering the above three factors... when i see a Van Gogh on the wall of the Minneapolis Institute of Art i know that i am seeing a small object that is worth a vast sum of money... enough to buy the biggest mansion in Minnesota and have enough left for a garage full of Ferraris a substantial donation to Save the Children and a fat stock portfolio... i know that the greatest minds in the field of art history and criticism have the opinion that i am staring at a work of great genius and, i know the sad romantic story of Vincent's terrible and heartbreaking life...

so how can i form my own opinion, as i would form an opinion on some lesser work by some barely known artist, someone who has not been canonized as the greatest of the great... i guess that most people would say, "why do that? who cares" and truly, why care if my judgement is biased by the three factors above, Van Gogh's sad biography, the vast worth in dollars of his work today and the unanimous critical acclaim? well, the truth is probably that such an effort to form an opinion of the work itself without considering the artist or the current market and the opinions of others is probably doomed...

but, why not give it a try... first the easy part... i think that in spite of his eccentricities, Van Gogh was a very fine and quite traditional land-scape painter... his heavy use of impasto paint was not unprecedented in landscape where Dutch artist have for centuries been adept at making blobs and strokes of the brush look like trees and clouds, buildings, wheat fields, etc... Van Gogh took the conventions of landscape as he found them in the later years of the 19th Century and moved landscape paint-ing into a new world... he looked at the sun and painted it lemon yellow not because he was too stupid or nuts to look away but because he loved those bright colors and he really wanted to capture some of the magic he saw when he looked at a landscape... his letters make it clear that color was constantly on his mind and he often describes to his brother the bril-liant colors he was using in Arles...

anyway, i think his landscapes are wonderfully alive and can really open my eyes to the brilliance of color as we perceive it in this world... and i think that even if i did not know a thing about them or the guy that made them, i would learn from looking at them... and delight in how they are painted...

as a person educated to the modern aesthetic, i can appreciate the sumptuousness of the surface... the pure sensuality of the paint so rigor-ously and lovingly applied... also, the intensity of the artist's vision is com-pelling and clearly expressed in the landscape paintings... the patterns of brush stroke so evident in so many of the landscapes as in the whirling cypress trees of Arles, the star halos in night pieces, and in his treatment of grass and leaves are incredibly intricate and show to me the role of human vision, in creative interaction with reality as well as in the act of image making... as a landscapist, Van Gogh did not go for the easy hit but dug in with his brush and paints to make a statement for example, about a tree limb with layers of twisting grey and black paint...

although less conventional than the landscapes, Van Gogh's still life paintings are right in line with the tendency of the impressionists toward broader handling of paint... a Van Gogh still life is like a Bougereau still life painted with a pick and shovel... color defeats form and paint de-feats verisimilitude wherein the still life is an excuse for a color explora-tion where details of a sunflower head for example, are implied in heavy ridges of paint with Rembrandt's concern for light torn from Rembrandt's concern for shadow...

so, it seems to me that if i were around in 1885, i would have responded to the landscapes and still lifes as being sort of what the impressionists were doing but with bolder and heavier handling of oil paint...

i am not so sure that i would have liked Van Gogh's portraits nearly as much... in the 19th Century, academic artists considered these works to be clumsy and very poorly done... in portraiture, they thought Vincent Van Gogh was trying to paint a portrait like Bougereau would paint a portrait (with a smooth surface and a photographic likeness)... and just could not pull it off... no crime there, academic portraits are pretty hard to do which anyone who has tried to do one could tell you... but modern critics take a different view... they see that the distorted portraits are the way they are because that was how Van Gogh wanted them to be... or at least that he honestly painted what he had to and could not have painted the swirling form of Dr. Gachet, for example as a smoothly illusionistic academic portrait...

i would give some credit to both theories in that, having started to make serious art rather late in life, Van Gogh originally strove for representational mastery that he saw in artists he admired like Millet and Messionier... I believe that at some point early in his development, maybe while painting *The Potato Eaters*, he began to accept that this "clumsiness" was more accurate to what he saw than the smooth finish of a Messionier could ever be... and once he started down that road, he became free somewhat of the shackles of representation and came to trust his hand and eye to make a compelling visual image which more or less represented what he saw in front of him...

well, whatever the reason, he found his "look" very early on and although he changed in color and style to some degree, it is seldom difficult to look at a painting and say it is or is not by Van Gogh...

so, i guess at this point i must admit that i enjoy looking at the work of Van Gogh for all of the reasons i have mentioned above... i enjoy seeing this work as a part and projection of one of the most interesting and

475

unique lives that i know about... i like to look at his work and i feel like the work invites me to look at it as a part of his life... everyone breaths, Van Gogh breathed and painted... and i think that getting to know this guy who has been dead for all these years, who thought deeply about life and art and who chose to make these strange paintings just enriches the experience of taking a walk through a hanging of his paintings... plus, even though some of the images seem crude or forced to me, they always compel me to come back for another look... I love to look at paintings and although the impressionists and expressionists do not interest me much, i will go out of my way to see a Van Gogh... and on some level the paintings always seem to say to me, "if you are not willing to paint with this level of commitment, give it up!!!"

  i must also admit that i am starstruck to the degree that just being near to these paintings that are worth such vast sums of money moves me... considering that having our art become valuable and cherished by the culture is something that most of us who do art secretly, in our heart of hearts hopes for even though it is very poor form to admit it... so, i look at a hundred million dollar Van Gogh on the wall and wonder if any of my paintings will ever be hung on such a wall or worth such a sum of money... i guess i am admitting here to being a very shallow person in this sense and so, well, there it is... seeing a show of Van Gogh's is in this sense like taking a drive through Beverly Hills...

  i also enjoy reading about the paintings and hearing the modern critics explain how the composition and color speaks to the alienation of the creative mind or some such gibberish... critical discussion always of necessity comes after the art and in the case of a very successful body of art, is usually about the critic finding some reason why the art is as wonderful as it by popular acclaim said to be... and again, i personalize it wondering if anyone will ever write about my art and try and fit it into the culture of the 22nd Century for example...

  and this really is the role of Van Gogh to other artists... the message is even if you are a total failure, sell only one painting in your lifetime, have only a handful of people for an audience (and them mostly relatives), earn your living by something totally ignominious like waiting tables, factory drudgery or mooching off your brother, receive no critical attention from the art establishment and seem to most people to be a bit more than half crazy, you could be the next Van Gogh... someday, your works could be worth hundreds of millions of dollars and you could be universally acclaimed as a great genius while Jasper Johns or whoever, (the Bougereaus of today) would be as forgotten as Fredrick Leighton and all his friends are today...

Doug Mathewson

Purple Bears

My friend from work, Kitty Wang, wanted to get together so I could meet her new boyfriend. She'd had a few over the years but nobody she wanted to show off like this guy. It's hard to imagine she'd be looking for my approval but who knows? We work out of the same office, just she's not around much. Kitty has that same thing with time that Billy Pilgrim had where you just become "unstuck" and get moved through the years back and forth with no warning. That's where her old boyfriends had come from.

From all different eras, distant places in time. I guess that's why I never got to see them.

So we meet up at this hip new place Kitty likes. She always catches on to the trendy-trends. This place is micro-brews, kale salads, with strange and exotic paninis. It's nice to see her. Like I say, we're friends but she's not around work all that much. She's with this guy who she introduces as "Vincent". She says he's a painter and doesn't speak much Americanise. He seems nice enough, a little odd maybe, but so what? We order and sit down. Me on one side of Vincent and Kitty on the other, then I notice he only has one ear. As you might imagine Kitty has put herself on the side with the ear and is filling it up with gushes and giggles in something I don't speak. He's smiling and flirting right back so I'm odd man out and start drawing on my napkin. That's what I do at work. I draw (not on napkins usually) art for some of the books and comics we publish. Mostly I do science fiction and fantasy. Maybe horror or romance if we're slow. Anyway I'm drawing spacemen and moon maids and old Vincent gets real excited and starts drawing in all this amazing background stuff. Big starry night skies behind my guys with ray-guns, and pin-up girls riding six legged purple bears.

We were both laughing like crazy and shaking hands, when the food came and Kitty told us quit it. Knock it off and get back to lunch.

Donald Armfield

Figures from the Undergrowth

1.

Overlooked at first, just a second coming
of disappointment and embodiment
devised from the first, idolized and preserved
in her own subconscious.
Rejected by mother,

Reaching out from beneath the undergrowth
of melancholia, abandonment and loss
for a nurturing love I dearly desire.

Am I just the underbrush for the larger picture?

Impasto street art in varieties of blue sorrow
Starry Nights dripping off the edge of the ville.
Just a dab of primary brightness, lighting up the skies,
before bleeding into the Rhone.

The darker shadows drag at my feet,
a juxtaposition hunch of embarrassment.
The dilemma builds, but nothing is high enough
for the less importance.

Or is it a darker image, looking for the brighter side?

I try to hide in the gardens
amongst the abundance of growth;
sunflowers, daisies, red poppies
and the crown imperial fritillaries
centering myself with bright colors.

Hopeless, only confusing the disturbed chameleon
 as it tries to adapt to the pain that lingers within.
The fluctuated madness continues to flicker

and a diligent effort to escape this forlorn sorrow.

Am I just a secondary color lost in it's own mixture?

2.

It's the Postman, that guides me
into the fields of Arles.
Where the still giants, bleed into the horizon,
I see myself perched along the branches
of the Almond Blossoms and
the Mulberry trees that bloom in Autumn.

Avoiding the sunlit hours
that sometimes dazzle with;
featured sapphires or turquoise skies
molded by the clouds,
 the orange stroke of noxious
blinding sulfurs from the sun.

Should I leave the day to sleep?

Devoting my nights to a thrown stone,
trails of sparks rippling the skies
like a disturbed pond.
A bird's eye view over an idyllic village
as the day comes to rest.

My reflection looks up at me from within the glass,
the contents drown my sorrow. The little money I have
keeps my reflection barely visible
my unkempt beard damp from the last sip.

and that was the night THEY came...

3.

Outside the white dots scattered
along the black surface of the night sky.
A certain brightness shines over the sidewalk, from

the vibrant glow of the lantern hung in the Night Cafe.

To the back of the Cafe, they stood
coupled at the elbows,
funeral attire black as soot,
the treeline pulling apart
like a handful of dry clay.
White wildflowers along the ground
prune into piles of confetti.

Is this the premonition of a death?

Like watching a ferocious paint brush
in the hand of an angered artist
black out an entire treeline.
Placing a pair of sickly standing cypresses
over the newly formed path,
the couple remains...

The figures unclench, from each others grasp
like an identical morphing symmetry
they fly to the adjacent cypresses.
Sleek black feathers, perched up high
calling out to the open air,
for the murder to arrive.

A spectrum of chromatic laws
lights up the sudden day break
like a bleeding garden.
All within the blink of an eye
dusk returned with it's violet shade,
before nights black curtain dropped.

The crows gathered, crowding the sky
innumerable amounts of silhouettes
crossing over the luminous glow of the moon.

Did the night sky just swallow me whole?

4.

Fresh oil paint, swirls around in my skull
lifelike portraits of acquaintances
bleed onto their very own canvases.
Haunting reminiscences
told from the glare of every soul
displayed in my mind's eye.

The subject of my watercolor
shows the worthless rags
hang on the street corners.
I seen the beauty in them once
even their sorrow needed love.

Lastly the bullfighter, victorious
presenting self mutilation to the audience.
The beautiful intended to see
fainted at the grotesque attempt
to woo.

Shall we meet in the wheat fields?

Whether you hold in your cry of anguish
blow off rejection, ostracism or
feel like a financial burden to one.

The old tattered boots
and a journey to ones solitude
high in the mountains,
may not show it's beaten path

A darkness should never hide
your true colors
or lie beneath a figure
in the undergrowth.

Marc Pietrzykowski

Ici Repose (Name) (Date)

I first saw Vincent Van Gogh eating half a meatball sandwich from a garbage can next to a hedge bordering Prospect Park in Brooklyn, NY, back before Brooklyn became famous for the third time, when it was just Podunk Junction, a place to hunker down beside the cocaine and hedge fund glitter bomb that was, and still is, Manhattan. We Podunks were quite fond of it, vagabond Podunk and Podunk-born alike, we liked it and our tribe grew, swaddled in second hand overcoats and basement dance parties, and Vincent seemed to fit in, at first.

Vincent was nine-tenths hysterical, young and bitter and bruised but funny, also clearly not sleeping enough and thus prone to see cats slinking about where there were none, like on the bus. He appeared rarely but seemed omnipresent, his short, hairy arms reminded us of what we suspected men looked like in olden times, rough and blunt and covered with dark hair. He was also lazy, and unkind at times, and generous the way one who cares nothing for his fellow humans can be.

"That's a famous name," people would say when they met him, myself included. "I'm a famous guy" he always replied, and he was. He was famous for saying that, we would watch and wait, those of us who knew, and we would introduce him to everyone, just to re-enact our own indoctrination.

It was a goal of mine to take Vincent to see Vincent, MOMA had some, the Met had more, but he always had something better to do, like scaring the pigeons in park 'til they leaped into the sky, then settled again a dozen feet away, or digging abandoned half-cigarettes out of cracks in the sidewalk, but only when he had a full pack and knew some prig was looking at him.

****

Everyone knows the story: Van Gogh died poor, unrecognized as an artist, by shooting himself in the chest with a revolver in 1890. The headstone of his grave, beside that of his brother, Theo, reads "Ici Repose." The poet Frank Stanford also shot himself in the chest with a revolver, in 1978, and died much more quickly than Vincent, I assume because guns now are much more efficient than they were in 1890. One of Van Gogh's paintings, *Portrait of Doctor Gachet*, sold in 2015 for 151.2 million dollars. Frank Stanford's 542 page epic poem, *the battlefield where the moon says I love you*, is back in print and can be purchased for 30 dollars. I wonder if there is a room, somewhere in the world, where a copy of Stanford's poem sits on a coffee table, ready for reading, beneath an original Van Gogh. I suspect there is no such room, but I can imagine there is one, and that is the most human thing, to imagine that something which does not exist might exist.

Part of Stanford's poem goes like this:

*just like another blind singer the men come down to see with their equipment
they get his song they pay him twenty dollars and he don't hear from them ever
again except sometimes in the mail on Christmas when one of them might send a
five dollar check there won't nobody cash oh tell me brother how do the old men
feel who were young as purple flowers from Hawaii once when they listen to their
songs coming in over a borrowed radio tell me don't they take up a notch in they belt
don't they tie another knot in they headband don't they wring that sweat out
have mercy Jesus deliver me from the lawyers and the teachers and the preachers
and the politicking flies can't you hear them buzz can't you hear them bite another
chunk out of me oh brother I am death and you are sleep I am white and you are
black brother tell me I am that which I am I am sleep and you are death we are
one person getting up and going outside naked as a blue jay rolling our bellies
at the moon oh brother tell me you love me and I'll tell you too I want to know
how do they like it when the ones who sung shake they leg on the Television
I want to know Jesus don't a blind man count no more some by signs others by
whispers some with a kiss and some with a gun and some with a six bit fountain
pen whoa lord help me and my brother help us get through this tookover land*

I can't help but imagine Vincent Van Gogh, the painter, and Vincent Van Gogh, the Brooklyn scrounger, would have loved this poem. I imagine all three of them drinking wine in a shabby, crooked room some where, talking about the way women move, and about the ocean, and how similar the two seem when lots of wine is drunk, then later there would be a fight and a chair would get broken.

Poetry is not an investment for rich people, but books are, like the copy of Blake's *Book of Urizen* which sold for 2.5 million, or a first edition of *Canterbury Tales* that fetched 10 million. Books are too private for conspicuous consumption, or rather, they are of a more rarefied sort of showing off. Where does one display a copy of a first folio? As guests enter the party? Above the couch? But of course the insanely wealthy probably don't bother showing off their art or their books, they put them in hermetically sealed safes to appreciate. I am having trouble imagining this, because I don't know any truly wealthy people. They are another species, and will become moreso as genetic modification and cybernetic enhancements proliferate until they are what they always believed themselves to be: better humans than the rest of us. And they still won't be able to look at *The Potato Eaters* or scan Canto XX of the *Divine Comedy* and feel anything but pride.

J. K. Rowling, Harry Potter's creator, sold a hand-lettered copy of *The Tales of Beedle the Bard* for 3 million dollars. The profits of the sale went to Rowling's charity, which serves orphans worldwide. The book was purchased by an art dealer on behalf of a corporation, Amazon.com, which also distributes the book you are reading. Wu-Tang Clan, a US hip-hop collective, sold a single copy of their recording *Once Upon a Time in Shaolin* for 2 million dollars on an auction website. The purchaser was Martin Shkreli, the CEO of a pharmaceutical company notorious for purchasing drugs whose manufacturing licensing had lapsed and raising the price astronomically, because he knew people need the drugs and will die without them. I like picturing Rowling and the Wu-Tang Clan having brunch and discussing their plans for making their art valuable. I like picturing Martin Shkreli in jail, and since he is rich and well-connected it is a nice jail, but while he is there he begins to have visions worthy of Blake:

In fierce anguish and quenchless flames
To the deserts and rocks he ran raging,
To hide; but he could not. Combining,
He dug mountains and hills in vast strength,
He pilèd them in incessant labour,
In howlings and pangs and fierce madness,
Long periods in burning fires labouring;
Till hoary, and age-broke, and aged,
In despair and the shadows of death.

And a roof vast, petrific, around
On all sides he fram'd, like a womb,
Where thousands of rivers, in veins
Of blood, pour down the mountains to cool
The eternal fires, beating without
From Eternals; and like a black Globe,
View'd by sons of Eternity, standing
On the shore of the infinite ocean,
Like a human heart, struggling and beating,
The vast world of Urizen appear'd.

Shkreli would not know what to do with such visions. Rowling probably would. Wu-Tang probably would. Van Gogh and Stanford would, and did, all their lives. That is why the rich will never be what they always believe themselves to be: better humans than the rest of us

****

There was another Vincent Van Gogh, the one stillborn to Vincent's mother a year to the day before the painter was born. Vincent was a replacement child, his grieving parents even gave him the same middle name, Willem. His other brother, Theo, also named his son Vincent Willem Van Gogh, and six months after he did, Vincent the painter killed himself. There is, according to the white pages, a Vincent Vangogh currently living in California, and another in Illinois. There is also a Vincent Troung Vangga, also in California, which is close enough to be interesting, and to make me wonder what kind of art that Vincent makes.

Much has been made about the effect the stillborn brother had on Vincent, on his art, on his life and his struggle. Everyone who has written and thought about this is wrong, of course, but only in the sense of being not correct, which is not the same as being not right. *Bedroom in Arles* is not correct, but it is right, in the sense that I can feel what it is to sit there, what it smells like, what noises the walls keep out, and be completely wrong in this feeling, and also perfectly right. Names are imaginary things, too, they are counterfactual: the person, Vincent Van Gogh, is not the name Vincent Van Gogh, it is an imaginary designation meant to help us navigate a world with the faulty equipment of our bodies—faulty in the sense of being wrong, and also right.

Names are words for people, and words are, if I remember my Kenneth Burke, titles for actions.

When the Mongolian Communist Party took over the country in the 1920s, they had the citizenry get rid of their surnames, to help get rid of old clan rivalries and facilitate tax collection. In 1997, this became far too confusing—people were getting married without knowing they were related, for example—so the government told everyone to choose a surname. The cosmonaut Gurragchaa chose Koсмос, the Mongolian word for "cosmos," as his surname. I imagine J.K. Rowling is happy with her name. I think Martin Shreki should change his name to Martin Lubberwort. Van Gogh has become more than a name, simply saying it conjures up the tortured artist, the swirls of color. I asked a librarian for a book about Van Gogh, pronouncing it correctly, like Van Clock, and she said, "you mean Van Go?" I knew it was supposed to rhyme with clock because an art historian once corrected me, so now I have been corrected twice for saying his name, I suppose both must be right, and I am not right no matter what. Which is a state to cherish, in my world.

****

I never actually met a person named Vincent Van Gogh. The person I described at the start of this essay, or zuhitsu, which is more what I am aiming for, is actually a composite of people I knew and of the self I was, twenty-five years ago. I could call the one in California, I suppose, or the one in Illinois, but I'm sure they are tired and resentful of their name and would just hang up. Or maybe they are jovial, and love the attention their name grants them, who knows. I could also visit the Van Gogh Hair Salon, or the Van Gogh cafe, the Wine Shop, the half dozen little galleries that have incorporated his name, but I would rather imagine the painter, feeling edified at the truly monumental success of his work, at the multiplicity of businesses his name decorates, at the way even the most artless people instantly react to his name, the title of his life and work; just as his vision of the sky was more than the sky, his name has grown beyond a name, though it still sits there on a headstone in Auvers-sur-Oise, saying nothing until it is read. And at the same time I can imagine him scoffing at the whole churning, bloody mess, squinting through his glass of absinthe, telling the owner of the Van Gogh Day Spa ("Your Body is our Canvas") to piss off. Unless, of course, she moved like the ocean.

Heller Levinson

in the hand of Van Gogh's The Sower, 1888

connubiality   tender   generating tender-nesses
tenderizing   effulging seed
   sun halo sower sanctifier
h a n d   d e n s i t y
mitt, paw, flipper, -- this hand-gigantism bellows volumes, reeks lamb-like,
reeks of a palm saturated with tears, tears for all sentience, for all that
profits from support & nutrition, for all that could use a "helping hand,"
. . . .
yet
you wouldn't want to cross this hand, with its curious overlapping of
sensitivity & brutality, that fragile border where mink-glove cushioning
can morph into a bludgeoning maul at a moment's notice, . . . hand
become signal, semaphore, --
salvation

hand become
seed spread – *ministerial sprinkling, holy water* – a hand you would want
to leap into, the thumb constructed to nourish a muzzle, to assu(re)age ...
a hand you would want to salve you,
in no particular manner

Horses on the wall in the Chauvet Cave, I fasten on their muzzles, nuzzle
to
their muzzles, the Sower hand & the muzzle, shaped from the same
earth-matter, the same clay, if we brought that hand to the cave
wall, placed it there, the haunt that *they exist f(r)o(m)r each other* .....
commingling eternalities —
muzzle spun into hand   hand into muzzle
in the nuzzle of muzzle

 a disposition   acclimatization
perforce   lapping   swallowing   licking
killing

articulation   where speech forms   noise factories
expression gardens
letting the go(o)ds out
thrivery

muzzle like ambrosial hand
survival tools   from hand to
mouth
that which feeds   fundament
collecting feed – fundament
dual providers
antiphonal nurture

a muzzle is a plant growing from a hand

hand like ambidextrous muzzle

the hand is a mouth without fingers
boca   bouche   mouthing mouth   merry-go-round
merry mouth mongoose muskrat mosquito suck blood bath   bathe
the hand in muzzle nuzzles (the four horses on the cave wall come forth,
bathing hand)
(((((((((((((((((((((((((
dentition hand   ((on hand
a hand with teeth
                    -- fang-hand
hand-some
the hand that bites
(don't bite the hand)
hand is the property of
eat

VG created over thirty works on this theme, the Sower, but in this
painting the hand collects his very soul . . . a *being* swarming, opening ...
give ▯ spread, ... inviting animal, human, living matter, a hand caressing

the earth, soothing original pain ... a hand that is both a lamentation and a corrective.

VG disapproved of the polished hands painted by his academic contemporaries. He wanted hands gnarled, hewn, peasant hands that make, that work, hands like the Sower hand, — gigantic Hand Bosoms, dripping Milk-Seed . . . .

Deleuze & Guattari talk about traveling from the armchair. Imaginatively jolting into a place, environment. I am all for it. While not contesting the general sweep of this persuasion, certain occasions require hands-on confrontation. Personal intimacy. Case in point: The Sower. You can contact VG, even graft VG, without ever embarking upon a voyage of this sort. But you will never en-counter, come to know, the hand, the thumb, in the Sower. These are Site-Specific Identities. They can be conjured, but not Seen. Not Absorbed.

Returning with Van Gogh

Returning to the states after my immersion in VG, entering the elevators, walking the NYC streets, — people looking Down, immersed in their "screens," De-Evolving from becoming Erect, . . . I imagine Vincent beside me, . . . how would he react? I am on 79th Street between Second and Third Avenues. I count 11 out of the 12 people on the street looking down at their screens. I view them as passive cattle being led about by Evil Rulers from foreign galaxies, by Steve Jobs, AT&T, Verizon, Microsoft, Google, & Co. They exalt in their gadgetry. Securitized by gadgets. Soothed by these comforting Teething Toys. Clueless as to how they are the lifeless players in a vast prosperity plot.
Vincent didn't look down. Was not led about. Vincent looked Out. Outward. Upward. Toward the Sun.

I am on the Second Avenue bus going downtown. Sitting at a window seat. Behind me, a teenage girl is on a cell phone talking to her friend about how boring the Botanical Gardens is, couldn't they find a movie to go to instead. Standing above me, a man blares loudly into his cell, "I'm on the bus, . . . I'll be home in about ten minutes." To the rear of the bus, yammering in a heavy New York accent, an older woman reschedules her doctor's appointment. The man sitting next to me phones someone . . . they talk baseball. How so and so is going to do this year. I only want to look out the window, enjoy the city, be peaceful, linger in scenery, but I am bombarded by annoying, grating vocalisms. I have no phone urge. None at all. I wonder if there is a pill for improving one's lack of phone urge.
Mr. Baseball is getting louder and more passionate, something about the Dodgers not having a chance. That's it. That's my limit. I reach into my backpack, grab my phone, and call Vincent: 917 – 246 – 5501.
"Hey Vincent, buddy, ..." I am purposely loud and hail-fellow to mirror bozo's discourtesy. He gets louder and talks of innings. I block him out and concentrate on my exchange with Vincent.
"Boy, you really threw them for a loop with that crow picture, didn't you ... what? ... you laughed too when you heard they thought it was death coming to get you, ..." I chuckle along with V, "... well, that's part of the fun, isn't it?" I say, "seeing what they're going to make of our excruciations? Yeah, I knew you were a crow, a black dot on the green

492

lawn of color ineptitude, I knew you were leaving earth, sick of the earthlings, their numbskullery, having to feed upon their garbage, their leftovers, their no-talent assessments, pushing you, a nurturer, to the margins, who wouldn't want to take flight, be part of a colony you had always lusted for, . . . imaginative, winged creatures, fanning out, flaming, grabbing the sunlight away from humanity's greedy unappreciative undeserving soul-dams, draining them of their arrogance ..." Vincent laughs, taking obvious pleasure in my complicity. "Sure, I knew what you were doing, while they're thinking some obvious metaphor could stand in, could translate your profundity, ... well, it's good for some chuckles, when in practice you were . . . . ▢

"pistoning to carcinogenic heat
in tribal dignity
we, the Crow Nation, rise
                              -- an umbrellaed cancellation
hosting backwards
uplifting in planetary retreat
flanking in the syrup of a voodoo nation
these flagging contagion wings
ripening in the retrolight of annihilative bloom

VACCINATION
                              OPACITY!" I scream emotionally.

I push the red button and close the phone.
The bus has emptied considerably.

493

Nina Bennett

Love, Vincent

I start to delete the e-mail from Vincent, not knowing
anybody by that name, when I realize the address
is my father's. Last week he had surgery to remove
a squamous cell growth from his earlobe. As I read
his brief morning greeting, I again see his ear
swaddled like a miniature mummy, his hazel eyes
dulled with pain and fear. I type a quick reply,
better Van Gogh than Picasso, and sign it
your sunflower.

Floyd Salas

Cast Out on Earth

The magic of his childhood
stains his canvas
painted in brush streaks
that shimmer like tears in the night sky
a bursting rapture
his trembling spirit
swirling across his heaven
powerful
as God

Maja Trochimczyk

Into Color, Into Light

—after a painting by Vincent van Gogh at the Norton Simon Museum,
   "Winter (The Vicarage under Snow)"

Board the train from Paris to Avignon,
Flow through landscapes in TGV comfort
Move from the opal grey mists of urban rain
Into the intense fantasy of color and light
You never thought existed

Scarlet roofs, violet fields of lavender
Gold sunflowers turning their dark faces
To the yellow eye of the sun in the azure
You have never seen such phantasmagoria
Of hues you never thought existed

You will know why you have to stop
At the threshold of the museum, frozen in place
By the flaming branches of a mulberry tree

Now, you know why it is so hard to listen
To the song of the old man bent down
Beneath darkening winter sky

the shovel, the shovel,
the shovel, the snow
It's heavy, it's heavy
it's heavy, it falls

You look across the hall at the grey,
Soft snowflakes at dusk, helpless
Against the darkness of bare soil
Trees covered with a blanket
Of wet snow, precariously balanced
On the blackened limbs of winter

A man has to do what he's told to do
To eat, to earn a cot in a cramped room
In a soot-covered hut

the shovel, the shovel
the shovel, the snow

Darkness and light, night and day
You know why, now, you do know why
This longing for freedom

The Mulberry Song

—after van Gogh's Mulberry Tree at the Norton Simon Museum

I am the mulberry tree, ablaze with color
before the last day of autumn

I came into being in a flurry of brush strokes
on a cardboard, under the azure expanse of unfinished sky

turquoise – into cobalt – into indigo
green – into chartreuse – into amber – into gold

buds into blossoms – into fruit – into earth
to fall – to fall not – to end – to end not –
to begin

The brightest star, an ancient supernova,
I am aglow but for a moment

I outshine reality with artifice
exploding off the canvas

paint – paintbrush – swansong

leaves of the earth – ripples in the stream – crystals in the air –
aflame, all aflame

I make magic of the mundane shape of the world
sic est gloria mundi

it is – it will be – it is willed to be –
once captured in a frenzy of light, becoming

time transfigured into swirls of awareness
crystallizing at the edge of oblivion

I am the mulberry tree – I am the alchemist tree –
let my song fill your day till it glows –

become pure gold with me

Azure

—*after , La Méridienne oú La sieste, d'apres Millet*
by Vincent van Gogh

The harvest noon – the sun's polished
Disc above broad fields of yellow.
Half of the day's work is done.
She curls into a ball by his side.

He stretches up, thinking of the bread
Slices they'll butter for children.
They rest together, two pieces
In a puzzle of ancient wisdom.

She picked the first stems, a fistful,
Solemn among the rolling waves
Of wheat ocean. She pleated the straw
Into a figurine, placed high up on the fence

Overlooking the fields. She learned it
From her mother, her mother before her,
Mother before mother, back to that first
Handful of grain, droplets of milk and honey
Spilled in offering to the Earth Goddess.

After weary strides of the harvest
Under the sky's eye – wide open
In an expanse of blue, cornflower, azure –
They rest in a rich wheat shadow.
Their chests rise with each breath
of the heavy scent of the loam.

Noon rays dance on the straw
Silenced by the blades of their sickles.
They moved together, in consort,
They rest together, in comfort,
Blessed by the white gold of silence.

Karen Greenbaum-Maya

"Still Life with Anemones"; "Room at Arles"

Now tendrils writhe up from the canvas, spill
across the yellow frame in arsenic green,
his telltale color for what wants to fill

and crowd him out until there's only vines.
They halt his brush, then overrun his face.
Too late, now, for the vase's heavy line.

Bed washstand chair: the doctor's house at Arles.
There is no way to walk across the room.
Each shabby piece has warped this smallest world.

His eye advises him not to assume,
not to rely on any point of view.
The chair, the bed, the window do not dream

the same great yellow field to hold them all,
and where they don't agree, the air bleeds out.
He cannot step across. The floorboards fail

to guide him where he never can arrive.
There is no place to be, no way to leave.

Connie Ramsay Bott

The Café Terrace on the Place du Forum

He comes to my café most nights,
sits at a table alone.
You can smell the linseed oil,
see paint under his nails, yellows, greens, blues.
Sometimes his anger wells up over nothing
on grey days when the sun doesn't show.
He says he's fuelled by colors,
can't wait for the light of day
so he drinks too much wine to drown the night.
On hot summer days he burns as well,
joy that seems like rage.

I've seen his paintings.
They don't sell.
Too much in a rush
to slap down his passion,
his craziness on canvas,
but I smile at him.
What else can I do?
He's a customer.
He comes to my café most nights.

Vincent's Self Portraits

a dozen different likenesses
each holds me with contempt-cold eyes.
I imagine him staring
from mirror to canvas
and back again
jabs of hot flat colors
no shadow no shade no relief
never letting go of his anger
what he saw when he looked at himself

A Minor Van Gogh

Our little museum is proud of its Van Gogh
even if it is considered
one of his lesser works.

It's led a difficult life
you see by the crackled surface,
the chipped paint here in the corner.

Let's be honest, if it was pristine
it would hang in some great gallery.
The insurance would be out of this world.

I know a bit about the man –
how he lived with a damaged soul
such beauty from imperfection.

Composition

He saw beauty in
the common things
around him

burned brightly
in his need to create

was fed by his anger
at the blindness
of his fellows

wore his poverty
like a badge of honor

left behind
a priceless legacy.

Peasant

He sees me
paints my rough hands
worn clothes tired eyes.

I'm told there are fine places
where they hang portraits
of fine people.

I have never
left this farmland
but can be sure

the painting of a poor peasant
will never hang
in such a place.

From the Detroit Institute of Art

The paperback guidebook cost $3.95 in 1971.
The cover was one of Van Gogh's self-portraits
straw hat blue jacket ginger beard
the rather sharp nose   canny eyes.
The severe strokes of the brush
his trademark in his later days.

Inside we had two hundred or so pages
prints of paintings   photos of sculptures
stone and tile reliefs   all reduced
to the size of half a page
with a description to tell you
what you can just about see.

After page 24 we moved to black and white.
On page 163 among the Post-Impressionists
was a work from the last year of his life:
"Bank of the Oise, Auvers".
You'd know it was his by those brush strokes
thick dashes of paint for the water the boats
the people   and the gray greenery.

The book was all they would let me take home.

Aunt Margaret

lived in Detroit
with my uncle and four cousins
where the men worked in factories
and the women kept house
or had jobs at stores or restaurants.

She was kind but sharp minded
did people's income tax for them
dressed in shirts and shorts,
sweaters and slacks
made shrimp salad for Christmas.

She knew people like us
didn't get above ourselves,
shouldn't show off or try to look clever.
That would make you an outsider
in the only home you could hope for.

On the wall of her small living room
hung a print – a vase of sunflowers,
sharp strident yellow
a nod to another place another time
a world where she'd never belong.

So the Stories Go

We know so little –
try to stick scraps together
turn them into theories
explanations why
he is so loved now
and wasn't
in his own time.

Maybe his intensity
was frightening.
If you get too close
all you see are the
slashes of paint.

Back away a bit.
See what you see.
It's more than enough.

Vincent and Me

He wouldn't have liked me
would have found me
dull and too careful.
He would have laughed at my sincerity
and fear, wouldn't have given me
a second glance.

I would have had no patience with him
his outbursts, his anger
the drama of it all.
No doubt, I would have run a mile.

But maybe, just maybe
I would have been the one
to please him, calm him down,
distract all the passion
that fueled his great mind.

In Our Time

We have him safely diagnosed.
He's that poor insane artist
who saw swirling stars
in his sky, put them on canvas
deep blue and gold.

Back then no one told the world
it was okay to love the chaos
in the beauty he saw and shared.

Now his art has been ratified.
He has been labelled and understood.
It's safe to let him carry us away.

Contributors

William Rock is a sculptor and painter. His art has been exhibited internationally, where he has spoken and taught extensively on the nature of creativity, mysticism and art. He also has had the opportunity to study, as well as teach with, Tibetan and Chinese monks as well as artists, writers and poets of the various spiritual and philosophical disciplines. William Rock is the founder of Art and Inspiration International, a non-profit organization that promotes the arts, creativity, education, dialogue and cross-cultural collaboration. williamrockart.com

Huang Xiang is considered to be one of the greatest poets of 20th century China and a master calligrapher. He is a multi-nominee for The Nobel Prize for Literature. Huang Xiang spent over twelve years in communist Chinese prisons and was tortured and put on death row twice for writing his lyrical, free-spirited poetry and for his advocacy of human rights in China. He has been described as a 'poet on fire' a human torch who burns as a lamp of freedom and enlightenment. Twenty of his books have been published in several languages. centurymountain.com

Ryan Quinn Flanagan is a Canadian-born author residing in Elliot Lake, Ontario, Canada with his other half and mounds of snow. His work can be found both in print and online in such places as: *Evergreen Review, The New York Quarterly, Word Riot, In Between Hangovers, Horror Sleaze Trash, and Red Fez.*

Catfish McDaris won the Thelonius Monk Award in 2015. His work is at the Special Archives Collection at Marquette University in Milwaukee, Wisconsin. He is listed in Wikipedia. His ancestors were related to Wilma Mankiller from the Cherokee Nation. Currently he's selling wigs in a dangerous neighborhood in Milwaukee. Van Gogh and Catfish were both born in '53 and Vincent died on his birthday July 29th. Cat's hometown is Clovis, New Mexico, Gauguin's father and son were named Clovis.

Mendes Biondo was born in Mantua (Italy) in 1992. He is a journalist and he published two books: the novel Trappola di cotone (Nomadepsichico, 2008) and the collection of short stories and poems Amanti bendati (ExCogita, 2010). He is the Editor-in-Chief of the cultural blog RAMINGO! (https://ramingoblog.com/). His English poems were published by Visual Verse, The Plum Tree Tavern, Scrittura Magazine, Poetry Pasta, Angela Topping – Hygge Feature, The BeZine and I Am Not A Silent

Charles Joseph lives and writes deep in the heart of New Jersey. Peppered by a battery of life experiences—good, great, bad, and worse— Charles is the author of NO OUTLET (a novel), five poetry chapbooks, and Chameleon (Omnibus Unum 2012-2016) a collection of poems and short stories that will be released in the spring of 2017. Visit him at www. charlesjosephlit.com

Daniel G. Snethen is a poet naturalist teaching on the Pine Ridge Indian Reservation of South Dakota. He has conducted research on the Federally endangered American Burying Beetle for over twenty years. Snethen coaches oral interpretation of literature and poetry recitation. He has coached two students all the way to the National Poetry Out Loud Competition in Washington DC. Snethen also coaches drama and has produced over 35 plays. Snethen serves as the Vice-President of the South Dakota State Poetry Society. His favorite piece of literature is The Rhyme of the Ancient Mariner. He owns a pet rattlesnake named Witten.

Bryn Fortey is a veteran of the British 1970s Speculative Fiction scene. He was later seducedby poetry, editing OUTLAW, a post-Beat magazine that attracted many American contributors.
His poem 'A Taxi Driver on Mars' was placed first in the Data Dump Awards for Science Fiction. Poetry published in the UK in 2009. After a break due to family bereavements, he returned to writing and had MER-RY-GO-ROUND, a collection of both fiction and poetry, published by the Alchemy Press in 2014.

In August 2015 **Alan Britt** was invited by the Ecuadorian House of Culture Benjamín Carrión in Quito, Ecuador as part of the first cultural exchange of poets between Ecuador and the United States. In 2013 he served as judge for the The Bitter Oleander Press Library of Poetry Book Award. His interview at The Library of Congress for *The Poet and the Poem* aired on Pacifica Radio, January 2013. He has published 15 books of poetry, his latest being *Violin Smoke* (Translated into Hungarian by Paul Sohar and published in Romania: 2015). He teaches English/Creative Writing at Towson University.

Rona Fitzgerald was born and educated in Dublin. She has been living in Glasgow for 21 years.
Beginning with six poems in the Dublin based Stinging Fly magazine in 2011, she has been published in UK and Scottish anthologies, in Scottish Book Trust publications and in both print and online magazines
Her most recent publications are in Aiblins: New Scottish Political Poetry, Three Drops from a Cauldron Midwinter special and Oxford Poetry XVI.iii Winter 2016-17.

Dr. Sudeep Adhikari, from Kathmandu Nepal, is professionally a PhD in structural engineering. He works as an engineering consultant and part-time lecturer; married, and staying with his wife and family. A music junkie and an obsessive reader/writer, Sudeep believes in dogs, chilled beer, trees, and ultimate meaninglessness of existence.

Prolific Americana songwriter and poet, **K.W. Peery**, is the author of 'Tales of a Receding Hairline' and 'Purgatory'. 'Tales of a Receding Hairline' was a semifinalist in the Goodreads Choice Awards - Best in Poetry 2016. His upcoming 2017 releases include 'Wicked Rhythm' and 'Ozark Howler'. Peery is a regular contributor in the Australia Times Poetry Magazine. He writes about personal life experiences. As he grapples with morality and mortality, the unvarnished truth is breathtakingly obvious. His unapologetic vulnerability is neatly embedded within each work. Peery is most well known as a founding member of the Marshall/Peery Project. This collaboration produced four critically acclaimed studio albums from 2005 to present. The Marshall/Peery Project frequently appear on the Roots Music Report and Americana Charts. Their songs are in regular rotation in the United States, Germany, Australia, Japan and the United Kingdom. Credited as a lyricist and producer, Peery's work appears on more than a dozen studio albums over the past decade.

Clint Margrave is the author of *Salute the Wreckage* (2016) and *The Early Death of Men* (2012), both published by NYQ Books. His work has been featured on Garrison Keillor's *The Writer's Almanac*, as well as in *New York Quarterly*, *Rattle*, *Cimarron Review*, *Verse Daily*, *Word Riot*, and *Ambit* (UK), among others.

Brenton Booth lives in Sydney, Australia. His book 'Punching The Teeth From The Sky' is available from Epic Rites Press and all book sites.

Ali Znaidi (b.1977) lives in Redeyef, Tunisia. He is the author of several chapbooks, including *Experimental Ruminations* (Fowlpox Press, 2012), *Moon's Cloth Embroidered with Poems* (Origami Poems Project, 2012), *Bye, Donna Summer!* (Fowlpox Press, 2014), *Taste of the Edge* (Kind of a Hurricane Press, 2014), and *Mathemaku x5* (Spacecraft Press, 2015). For more, visit aliznaidi.blogspot.com

Wayne F. Burke is primarily a poet who dabbles in prose. His three published poetry collections, all from Bareback Press, are WORDS THAT BURN, DICKHEAD, and KNUCKLE SANDWICHES. His chapbook PADDY WAGON is published by Epic Rites Press.

George Wallace is Writer in Residence at the Walt Whitman Birthplace (2011-present), first poet laureate of Suffolk County LI NY, and author of 30 chapbooks of poetry. An adjunct professor of English at Pace University, he is editor of Poetrybay, Walt's Corner, and co-editor of Great Weather For Media. In 2015 he was named laureate of the Beat Poetry Festival. Wallace maintains an active international schedule of workshops, lecture presentations and poetry readings. In 2012 he visited Velsen, ND, the ancestral home of Walt Whitman's maternal family, where he presented the city an official copy of Whitman's Leaves of Grass.

Kerry Trautman's poetry and short fiction have appeared in various journals, including *Alimentum, The Coe Review, The Fourth River, Think Journal,* and *Third Wednesday*; as well as in anthologies such as, *Mourning Sickness* (Omniarts, 2008), *Roll* (Telling Our Stories Press, 2012,) *Journey to Crone* (Chuffed Buff Books, 2013,) and *Delirious: A Poetic Celebration of Prince* (NightBallet Press, 2016.) Her poetry chapbooks are *Things That Come in Boxes* (King Craft Press, 2012) and *To Have* Hoped (Finishing Line Press, 2015). Her chapbook *Artifacts*, is forthcoming from NightBallet Press in 2017.

David R. Cravens lives in Farmington, Missouri. He received his B.A. in philosophy from the University of Missouri, and his master's degree in English literature at Southeast Missouri State University. He's won the 2008 *Saint Petersburg Review* Prize in Poetry, the 2011 Bedford Poetry Prize, and was a finalist for Ohio State University's *The Journal* William Allen Creative Nonfiction Contest. His work has been published extensively in literary journals throughout the U.S. and abroad. He teaches composition and literature at Mineral Area College.

Adrian Manning lives and writes in Leicester, England. He is a Pushcart nominated poet who has had hundreds of poems, articles, reviews and interviews published in print and on-line around the world. He is also the editor of Concrete Meat Press.

Eve Brackenbury, Kansas City poet and suburban bookseller, is the author of three books of poetry, and has been published in various anthologies and publications. Although much of her work is found in print, she prefers spending time with her audience. She's a frequent guest and host for poetry readings and public speaking engagements.

Richard Wink is a writer from Norwich, England. Widely published, his latest book 'The Last Days of the Worm' co-authored with Ryan Quinn Flanagan and Ben John Smith is out now. You can contact him at rich.wink@ yahoo.co.uk

Guinotte Wise has been inspired by Vincent van Gogh since art school. He welds steel sculpture and writes at his farm in Resume Speed, KS. His art can be found at www. wisesculpture.com. and his books are available on

Amazon and other outlets. His poetry and fiction have been featured in over fifty literary reviews. His wife has an honest job in the city and drives 100 miles a day to keep it. Wise would like to be Poet Lariat to any outfit that would have him. He knows it's Laureate, but he's a rodeo poet

Chigger Matthews is a word artist living in the American Midwest. He has toured with the Cringe-worthy Collective from Buffalo, New York, is the host of Free Chigger Matthews presents, and is currently an artist in residence at the Osage Arts Community in Belle, Missouri.

Bob Holman's latest book is The Cut-Outs (Matisse) (PeekaBoo Press); "Van Gogh's Violin" appears in Sing This One Back To Me (Coffee House Press). He has published seventeen books, taught at Princeton, NYU, Columbia, Bard and The New School and is the Founder and Artistic Director of the Bowery Poetry Club. He is the host of the PBS documentary, Language Matters, an investigation into endangered languages and poetry, and a founder of the Endangered Language Alliance in New York.

Robert Lee Kendrick grew up in Illinois and Iowa, but now calls South Carolina home. After earning his M.A. from Illinois State University and his Ph.D. from the University of South Carolina, he held a number of jobs, ranging from house painter to pizza driver to grocery store worker to line cook. He now lives in Clemson with his wife and their dogs. His poems have appeared in Tar River Poetry, Xavier Review, Louisiana Literature, South Carolina Review, The James Dickey Review, The Sow's Ear Poetry Review, and elsewhere. His chapbook, Winter Skin, was released in 2016 by Main Street Rag Publishing.

Neil Ellman is a poet from New Jersey. He has published more than 1,400 poems, most of which are ekphrastic and written in response to works of modern and contemporary art, in print and online journals, anthologies and chapbooks throughout the world. He has been nominated twice for the Pushcart Prize and twice for Best of the Net. His latest chapbook, Of Angels & Demons (Flutter Press, 2016), is based on the paintings of Paul Klee.

Victor Clevenger's latest poetry collection is titled *Congenital Pipe Dreams* (Spartan Press, 2017). Selected pieces of his work have appeared in a variety of places online, & in print. He spends his days in a Madhouse & his nights with his second ex-wife, together they raise six children in a small town northeast of Kansas City, Missouri.

Lisa Stice is a poet/mother/military spouse. While it is difficult to say where home is, she currently lives in North Carolina with her husband, daughter and dog. She is a Pushcart Prize nominee and the author of a poetry collection, *Uniform* (Aldrich Press, 2016). You can find out more about her and her publications at lisastice.wordpress.com and facebook.com/LisaSticePoet.

James Benger is a father, husband and writer. His work has been featured in several publications. He is the author of two fiction ebooks: Flight 776 (2012) and Jack of Diamonds (2013), and two chapbooks of poetry: As I Watch You Fade (EMP 2016) and You've Heard It All Before (2017). He is a member of the Riverfront Readings Committee in Kansas City. He is the founder of the 365 Poems In 365 Days online poetry workshop, and serves as Editor In Chief of the subsequent anthology series. He lives in Kansas City with his wife and son.

Lylanne Musselman is an award winning poet, playwright, and artist, living in Indianapolis, IN. Her work has appeared in Pank, Flying Island, The Tipton Poetry Journal, Poetry Breakfast, The New Verse News, Ekphrastic Review, and Rat's Ass Review, among others, and many anthologies, most recently, the Nancy Drew Anthology (Silver Birch Press, 2016). In addition, Musselman has twice been a Pushcart Nominee. She is the author of three chapbooks, with a fourth forthcoming, Weathering Under the Cat, from Finishing Line Press. She also co-authored Company of Women: New and Selected Poems (Chatter House Press, 2013).

Ndaba Sibanda was a 2005 National Arts Merit Awards (NAMA) nominee. He compiled and edited Its Time (2006), and Free Fall which has been accepted for publication in India. The recipient of a Starry Night ART School scholarship in 2015, Sibanda is the author of Love O'clock, The Dead Must Be Sobbing and Football of Fools. He has contributed to more than twenty-five published books.

Yoby Henthorn is a recluse living in Alaska. She is currently writing a collection of poems, "When Icarus Falls", also a book on her journey through Bipolar disorder, and has been nominated for the Pushcart Prize for her poem, "Cereberus".

Tim Staley was born in Montgomery, Alabama, in 1975. He completed a Poetry MFA from New Mexico State University in 2004. He's served as publisher of Grandma Moses Press since 1992. His debut full-length poetry collection is Lost On My Own Street (Pski's Porch Publishing, 2016). His newest chapbook, The Most Honest Syllable Is Shhh, is forthcoming from Night Ballet Press. He lives with his wife, daughter and two mutts in the American stretch of the Chihuahuan Desert. His hobbies include thinking, nachos and waiting. Find him online at www.PoetStaley.com.

Debi Swim lives in West Virginia (USA) with her husband Kyle. They have three children and six grandsons. Debi has been writing for most of her life but only seriously after joining a writing group about ten years ago. She was fortunate to be mentored and encouraged by Salvatore Buttaci, a fellow poet and good friend. She has been published in several online journals and locally in the Bluestone Review several times

Sheikha A. is from Pakistan and United Arab Emirates. Her work appears in over 100 literary venues, both print and online, including several anthologies by different presses. She is the author of a short poetry collection entitled Spaced [Hammer and Anvil Books, 2013] available on kindle. To know more about her publications, visit her blog sheikha82.wordpress.com

Subhadip Majumdar a writer poet from India. He is certified in Creative Writing from University of Iowa. He also edited for a long time a reputed Bengali poetry journal. Wrote a short novel as Tumbleweed writer in Shakespeare and Company, Paris. Two poetry books published and one novel in process of publication.

Carol Alexander's work appears in anthologies including Broken Circles (Cave Moon Press), Through a Distant Lens (Write Wing Publishing) and Proud to Be: Writing by American Warriors, Vol. 1 (Missouri Humanities Council and Warriors Arts Alliance). Her work can be found in journals such as Bluestem, Canary, Caesura, Chiron Review, The Common, MadHat Lit, Mobius, Poetrybay, The New Verse News, Red River Review, Split Rock Review, and The American Journal of Poetry. She is the author of the chapbook BRIDAL VEIL FALLS (Flutter Press). Alexander's full-length collection of poems, HABITAT LOST, is due out in 2017 from Cave Moon Press.

Jonny Huerta is from Portales, New Mexico. He is the author of posole with benefits and Acid & Menudo.

Lisa Wiley is an assistant professor of English at Erie Community College in Buffalo, NY. She is the author of two chapbooks My Daughter Wears Her Evil Eye to School (The Writer's Den, 2015) and Chamber Music (Finishing Line Press, 2013). Her poetry has appeared in Earth's Daughters, The Healing Muse, Medical Journal of Australia, Rockhurst Review, Third Wednesday and Yale Journal for Humanities in Medicine among others. She serves as regional judge for Poetry Out Loud and has read her work throughout New York state.

Bob Kunzinger is a professor of arts and humanities in Virginia. His work has appeared in magazines and journals throughout the world, including Ilanot Journal, the Washington Post, St Anthony Messenger, World War 2

History and many more. Several of his works have been noted in the Best American series, and he has published seven collections of essays.

Mary Ellen Talley's poems have most recently been published in Typoetic. us and Kaleidoscope as well as in recent anthologies, The Doll Collection, All We Can Hold poems of motherhood and Raising Lilly Ledbetter Women Poets Occupy the Workspace. Her poetry has received a Pushcart Nomination. She has worked for many years with words and children as a Speech-Language Pathologist (SLP) in Washington public schools. Her art experience has included serving as art docent for her children and grandchildren's elementary classrooms.

Jay Passer was first published by Caliban magazine in 1988 at the age of 23. Since then his work has appeared in print and online in scores of publications spanning the globe. He's authored 8 chapbooks and appeared in several anthologies. His most current collection is featured in The High Window Press's *Four American Poets* of 2016. Jay holds a degree in Culinary Arts, employed in the service industry for 30+ years as barista, soda jerk, line cook, pizza maker, and sous chef. Passer lives and works in his native San Francisco.

Barbra Nightingale is **Judith Berke**'s literary executor.
Judith Berke, a Miami Poet, died in 2014. Her first book was published by Wesleyan University in 1989, only eight years after she started writing at the age of 49. She had a chapbook, Acting Problems, published in 1993. These poems are from her manuscript on Van Gogh. Her poems have been published in The Atlantic, American Poetry Review, Poetry, New Republic, Paris Review, and many others. She has received grants from the state of Florida and the National Endowment for the Arts.

Barbra Nightingale has had poems published in numerous poetry journals and anthologies, including The Liberal Media Made Me Do It (anthology), Sonnets Out of Sequence (anthology), Rattle, Sacramento Poetry Review, Kalliope, Southern Women's Review, The Kansas Quarterly, The Missouri Review Online, InterlitQ, The Eloquent Atheist, Many Mountains Moving, Narrative Magazine and City of Big Shoulders. Alphalexia, her newest book just came out with Finishing Line Press (2017). Two Voices, One Past was a Runner Up in the 2010 Yellow Jacket Press Chapbook Award, and was published in September, 2010. Geometry of Dreams (2009) a full-length collection of poetry was published in 2009 by Word Tech Press, Ohio. She has six other collections of poetry, and a yet unpublished memoir, Husbands and Other Strangers. She's a professor Emerita with Broward College, and an advisor Emerita with Phi Theta Kappa. She lives and plays in Hollywood, Florida with her two and four-legged menagerie.

Hillary Leftwich resides in Denver with her son. She is co-host for At the Inkwell, a NYC based reading series. She organizes/hosts other reading events and fundraisers around Denver. Her writing has appeared or is forthcoming in Creative Coping Mechanism (CCM) "A Shadow Map" Anthology, Hobart, Matter Press, Smokelong Quarterly's "Why Flash Fiction?" Series, The Review Review and others.

Claus Ankersen is a Danish writer, poet and artist. He is the author of eight books. He performed in 19 countries around the world. Selected material is translated into 11 languages. Claus Ankersen works with literature, art and hybrid expressions, often with a focus on systems critique, activism, esoterics and transformation. He loves to do site specific commission hybrids in the public space and won the juryprize 'Fencepole' for best public work in Copenhagen in 2013. When he is not writing, Claus enjoys cooking and works on developing a new system of yoga to be taught in his mystery school.

Dan Sicoli lives just south of the Canadian border. He is the author of two poetry chapbooks from Pudding House Publications (Columbus, Ohio), Pagan Supper and the allegories. In addition to co-founding/co-editing the literary press and magazine Slipstream (www.slipstreampress.org), he can sometimes be found in local dives, saloons and barrelhouses banging on an old Gibson with an area rock'n'roll band. In late summers, he oven-dries home-grown plum tomatoes.

Dr. Marianne Szlyk is the editor of The Song Is... , an associate poetry editor at Potomac Review, and a professor of English at Montgomery College. Her second chapbook, I Dream of Empathy, was published by Flutter Press. Her first chapbook, Listening to Electric Cambodia, Looking up at Trees of Heaven, is available through Kind of a Hurricane Press. Her poems have appeared in a variety of online and print venues, including The San Pedro River Review, Cactifur, Of/with, bird's thumb, Truck, Algebra of Owls, Setu, Solidago, The Bees Are Dead, and South Florida Poetry Journal. Two poems have received nominations for Best of the Net and a Pushcart Prize respectively. Recently she was artist in residence at The Wild Word.

Perry S. Nicholas is a Full English Professor at Erie Community College North in Buffalo, N.Y. He has published one textbook of poetry prompts, three full-length and three chapbooks of original poetry, and one CD of poetry. He has hosted four poetry venues in the WNY area. See his work at perrynicholas.com.

Autodidact & incorrigible optimist, **kerry rawlinson** gravitated decades ago from sunny Zambian skies to solid Canadian soil. Fast-forward: she now follows poetry & art's muses around the Okanagan, barefoot. She's won contests (e.g. Geist; Mississippi Valley; Postcards, Poems & Prose; Fusion Art;); features in literary publications—often with artwork—eg. pioneer-town; The Centrifugal Eye; CanLit; Main Street Rag; Minola Review; right hand pointing; 3Elements Review; Section8 Magazine; WAX poetry & art; amongst others, and in Anthologies, e.g. Forgotten Women, by Grayson Books. Photo-artwork's out there, e.g. Qwerty; AdHoc Fiction; Adirondack Review; Five on the Fifth. Visit: kerryrawlinson.tumblr.com and @kerryrawli

David S. Pointer has been writing and publishing poems for over 25 years. Currently, David serves on the advisory panel at "Writing for Peace," and as Assistant Poetry Editor at "As You Were: The Military Review." David currently lives in Murfreesboro, TN with his daughter and cats.

Ally Malinenko is the author of the poetry collections The Wanting Bone (Six Gallery Press), How To Be An American (Six Gallery Press), Better Luck Next Year (Low Ghost) as well as the novel This Is Sarah (Bookfish Books). She lives in Brooklyn and tweets a lot about David Bowie.

Su Zi Master Arts Lit Loyola. Publications, gallery and art event exhibitions, performance ...including Chicago, LA, NOLA, Tampa et cetera.

John Grochalski is the author of The Noose Doesn't Get Any Looser After You Punch Out (Six Gallery Press 2008), Glass City (Low Ghost Press, 2010), In The Year of Everything Dying (Camel Saloon, 2012), Starting with the Last Name Grochalski (Coleridge Street Books, 2014), and the novels, The Librarian (Six Gallery Press 2013), and Wine Clerk (Six Gallery Press 2016). Grochalski currently lives in Brooklyn, New York, where the garbage can smell like roses if you wish on it hard enough.

Norman J. Olson is a small press poet and artist. Since publishing his first poem in 1984 after many years of rejection, he has published hundreds of poems and art works in the literary press in 15 countries and all over the USA.

Doug Mathewson likes to stay home with his wife and their two cats and do as little real work as possible. He is known as a writer and editor of short fiction. His stories have appeared here and there, now and then, in publications around the world and perhaps beyond. More of his fiction can be found at www.little2say.org, an online journal of "True Stories From Imaginary Lives". Much of his time is spent as Editor of Blink-Ink, which is a quarterly print publication of 50 word fiction. More information at www.blink-ink.org

Donald Armfield has a deadpan style of adventure. His genre bending style has scored him spots in over a dozen anthologies. Get a glance of his active imagination of whimsical horror, interesting sense of humor or out of this world strangeness with a poetic touch of prose of vivid imagery. Google the name or check out his links:
amazon.com/author/donald-armfield
https://www.facebook.com/donald.armfield/

Dr. Marc Pietrzykowski lives and works and writes in Niagara County, NY, USA. He has published various and sundry poems, stories, and essays, as well as 8 books of poetry and 2 novels. His most recent book of poems, So Much Noise, and book of short stories, Monarchs of the Undertow, are available now. You can visit Marc virtually at www.marcpski.com.

Heller Levinson lives in New York where he studies animal behavior. He has published half a dozen books and his work has appeared in over a hundred journals. His publication, *Smelling Mary* (Howling Dog Press, 2008), was nominated for both the Pulitzer Prize and the Griffin Prize. Black Widow Press published his *from stone this running* in 2012. *Hinge Trio* was published by **La Alameda Press** in 2012. *Wrack Lariat* is newly released from Black Widow Press. **tenebraed** (Black Widow Press) is being printed currently. He is the originator of **Hinge Theory**.
hingetheory@gmail.com

Delaware native **Nina Bennett** is the author of Sound Effects (2013, Broadkill Press Key Poetry Series). Her poetry has been nominated for the Best of the Net, and has appeared or is forthcoming in publications that include Gargoyle, I-70 Review, Reunion: The Dallas Review, Bryant Literary Review, Yale Journal for Humanities in Medicine, Philadelphia Stories, and The Broadkill Review. Awards include 2014 Northern Liberties Review Poetry Prize, and second-place in poetry book category from the Delaware Press Association (2014). Nina is a founding member of the TransCanal Writers (Five Bridges, A Literary Anthology).

Floyd Salas is the author of nine books: five novels, three volumes of poetry and a memoir. His first novel, Tattoo the Wicked Cross, along with his memoir Buffalo Nickel, is featured in Masterpieces of Hispanic Literature (HarperCollins 1994). He was 2002-2003 Regent's Lecturer at University of California, Berkeley, staff writer for the NBC drama series, Kingpin and the recipient of NEA, California Arts Council, Rockefeller Foundation, and other fellowships and awards. His work is archived in the Floyd Salas collection in the Bancroft Library, UC Berkeley. www.floydsalas.com

Maja Trochimczyk, Ph.D., is a Polish American poet, music historian, photographer, and author of six books on music, most recently *Frédéric Chopin: A Research and Information Guide* (rev. ed., 2015). Trochimczyk's seven books of poetry include *Rose Always, Miriam's Iris, Slicing the Bread, Into Light, The Rainy Bread,* and two anthologies, *Chopin with Cherries* and *Meditations on Divine Names.* A former Poet Laureate of Sunland-Tujunga, she is the founder of Moonrise Press, and Board Secretary of the Polish American Historical Association. Hundreds of her poems, studies, articles and book chapters appeared in English, Polish, and in translations. She read papers at over 80 international conferences and is a recipient of honors and awards from Polish, Canadian, and American institutions, such as the American Council of Learned Societies, Polish Ministry of Culture, PAHA, McGill University, and the University of Southern California. Two solo exhibitions displayed her photographs of leaves and roses.

Karen Greenbaum-Maya is a retired clinical psychologist, former German major, two-time Pushcart nominee and occasional photographer. Her first full sentence was, "Look at the moon!" Her photos and poems appear in anthologies and in journals such as Sow's Ear Poetry Review, Off the Coast, Blue Lyra, Measure, Otoliths, and, Naugatuck Review. Her poems have received Special Merit and Honorable Mention in Comstock Review's Muriel Craft Bailey Memorial poetry contest. She co-hosts Fourth Sundays, a poetry series in Claremont, California. Kattywompus Press publishes her two chapbooks, Burrowing Song, a collection of prose poems, and Eggs Satori. Aldrich Press publishes her full-length collection, The Book of Knots and their Untying. For links to work on-line, go to: www.cloudslikemountains.blogspot.com/.

Connie Ramsay Bott grew up in Michigan where many of her stories and poems take place. Her work has been published in a number of journals and anthologies, including The Rialto and Frogmore Papers in the UK. Her novel *Girl Without Skin* will be published by Cinnamon Press in autumn of 2017. She conducts creative writing workshops for enthusiastic adults, and has taught courses and summer schools for Warwick University. She has lived in the UK since the 1970's.

Dan Nielsen, Back cover artist. Kirk Douglas was my introduction to Vincent van Gogh. His film, "Lust for Life," premiered in 1956. I saw the TV version sometime in the early 1960s, no doubt in black and white, and was inspired to become an artist. In lieu of formal training, I immersed myself in art history and biographies of famous artists. It became obvious to me that the "vie d'artiste" necessitated a gradual descent into madness fueled by poverty, rejection, and alcohol. So far so good.

Pski's Porch Publishing was formed July 2012, to make books for people who like people who like books.

We hope we have some small successes.
www.pskisporch.com

323 East Avenue
Lockport, NY 14094
www.pskisporch.com

Made in the USA
Lexington, KY
07 June 2017